# GABBY

# GABBY

## CONFESSIONS OF
## A HOCKEY LIFER

**Bruce Boudreau and Tim Leone**

Potomac Books, Inc.
Washington, D.C.

Library of Congress Cataloging-in-Publication Data
Boudreau, Bruce, 1955–
   Gabby : confessions of a hockey lifer / Bruce Boudreau and Tim Leone.
      p. cm.
   Includes bibliographical references and index.
   ISBN 978-1-59797-435-6 (alk. paper)
   1. Boudreau, Bruce, 1955– 2. Hockey coaches—United States—Biography. 3. Hockey players—United States—Biography. 4. Washington Capitals (Hockey team) I. Leone, Tim. II. Title.
   GV848.5.B69A3 2009
   796.962092—dc22
   [B]
                                                                    2009024981

Printed in the United States of America on acid-free paper that meets the American National Standards Institute Z39-48 Standard.

Potomac Books, Inc.
22841 Quicksilver Drive
Dulles, Virginia 20166

First Edition

10 9 8 7 6 5 4

For my mother, Theresa;
my father, Norman;
my wife, Crystal;
my children, Kasey, Ben, Andy, and Brady;
and my brothers, Bryan and Barry.

# CONTENTS

# FOREWORD

**When I think of Bruce Boudreau,** the motto "Never Give Up" comes to mind. Bruce and his family hung tough when weaker families would have packed it in. But Bruce had a dream and never quit, even with disappointment after disappointment.

No player in the American Hockey League (AHL) in the 1980s produced more points than Bruce, but he never got a full-time call to the show. It must have been tough for Bruce to watch players with poorer stats get the call.

It is ironic that when Bruce got into coaching, the same thing happened again. Year after year of championships in the minors—and again no call to the Big Time. Yet he and his family stuck it out.

Finally, a desperate National Hockey League (NHL) team fired its coach and Bruce was put in as an interim head coach. He got his big chance to put all that experience to use and worked his magic for the Washington Capitals. He took a last-place team and turned it into a powerhouse. Bruce has the touch.

It's hard to believe, but he started as a minor-league coach going nowhere, finally got a break and went to the NHL, made the play-offs, and was voted Coach of the Year in the NHL. It's almost like a movie, but it's true. This book takes you through all the slings and arrows and disappointments and failures to the highs of the NHL.

It is more than a sports book; it is a book of life. It is about positive thinking and never giving up. It is about inspiration.

I know you will enjoy it.

Don Cherry
Coach of the Year in the AHL (Rochester Americans, 1973–74)
Coach of the Year in the NHL (Boston Bruins, 1975–76)

# ACKNOWLEDGMENTS

Bruce Boudreau acknowledges and thanks the following people for making this book possible:

Tim Leone, for his passion, drive, and relentless hours of work; all I did was talk. Washington Capitals majority owner Ted Leonsis, Washington Capitals president and owner Dick Patrick, and Washington Capitals vice president and general manager George McPhee, for taking a chance on a minor-league guy they believed in and supporting this book project. Don Cherry, for graciously writing a foreword. Springfield Falcons president and general manager Bruce Landon and Hershey Bears president and general manager Doug Yingst, for continually championing me and helping me get to where I always wanted to be. Washington Capitals assistant general manager and director of legal affairs Don Fishman, for his advice. All the players and assistant coaches—too numerous to mention—whose work and commitment made it possible for me to climb the coaching ladder. All the lifelong friends—too numerous to mention—I've made through the game of hockey.

My mother, Theresa, and my late father, Norman, for the devotion that made me the person I am. My wife, Crystal, and my children, Kasey, Ben, Andy, and Brady, for the sacrifices they made in moving everywhere I had to move. My brother Bryan and my late brother Barry, for all their years of quiet support.

And hockey fans at every stop I've made; they have blessed me with their support and made it so easy for me to love this game.

Tim Leone acknowledges and thanks the following people for making this book possible:

Bruce Boudreau, for the honor of helping him tell his story. Former Potomac Books, Inc., acquisitions editor Kevin Cuddihy, for adopting and championing this book project. Potomac Books, Inc., senior editor Elizabeth Sherburn Demers, production editor Julie Kimmel, marketing and publicity manager Claire Noble, and copyeditor Bud Knecht, for all their thoughtful work on the book. Managing editor Cate Barron, assistant sports editor Jim Carlson, retired sports editor Nick Horvath, executive editor David Newhouse, and sports editor Paul Vigna of *The Patriot-News*, for their support. My friends Mike Vogel, senior writer for WashingtonCapitals.com, and John Walton, Hershey Bears broadcaster, for their invaluable manuscript reviews and encouragement. My friends from the staff of JustSports Photography—Bill Duh, Nancy Attrill, Bruce Tyson, and Paul McFadden—for generously allowing the use of their work. My friends John Keeley and Gary Kriebel from OnFrozenBlog.com for their enthusiasm and generously allowing the use of their photographs. George McPhee, vice president and general manager of the Washington Capitals, for his insight. Nate Ewell, Kurt Kehl, and Paul Rovnak of the Washington Capitals media relations department—the best in any sport in any league—for all their help.

Especially my wife, Amy, for her abiding support and understanding. My daughter, Tamara, for being my biggest cheerleader. My son, Andy, for all the computer time sacrificed to accommodate my writing. My mother, Mary Ann, and my father, Ray, for being my true heroes. My brothers, Steve and John, for their own achievements that have inspired me.

And hockey fans, particularly Hershey Bears and Washington Capitals fans, whose passion allows me to work at my passion.

# INTRODUCTION: ROLE MODEL

**I'm not what anybody pictures** as an NHL head coach. Former Carolina Hurricanes head coach Peter Laviolette has the tall, dark, handsome, well-dressed look. In contrast, I'm the Columbo of coaching. It's like I've got a raincoat and everything.

I'm in my fifties, I'm bald, I struggle with my weight, and I constantly get reminded I'm no fashion icon. But Columbo, stylish or not, knew his stuff and got the job done. Same with me.

I proved that with a long track record of success in the minor leagues, but I was ignored for years and years. A big reason the NHL wasn't interested in me was the fact that I don't have a slick corporate appearance. I don't have a matinee idol face or a muscle beach physique. I don't have the right product in my hair; heck, I don't even have the hair. I'm more Botany 500 than Hugo Boss.

I don't hide from it. It's who I am.

After I led the Hershey Bears to the AHL's Calder Cup in 2005–6, I had a chance to get some exposure in Toronto when Bill Watters, my former agent, invited me to appear on his *Maple Leafs Lunch* show. Par for the course for me, though, I cut my head on a ceiling fan and had to go on TV wearing a big bandage on my melon. I'm sure that didn't help the image.

Bill Watters always has been a big advocate for me. He was curious about why I wasn't getting any NHL attention and made calls to management people he knew. He came back and said, "We've got to get some new suits to

1

make you look better." I found it kind of strange. It was Bill's way of saying my suits weren't flattering and that I was a little sloppy.

I wish I could be trimmer and have a sharper appearance. Believe me, I try. But I've been a diabetic since 1997. Sometimes the medicine I've had to take makes me gain weight.

I'm five foot ten and played at 175 pounds. I've gone as high as 242 pounds, but I've been dropping and would like to get under 200. When you've been an athlete your whole life, you can't stand being overweight.

In the heat of battle, I've had opposing coaches make snide comments about my weight. I try to ignore it or laugh it off, but statements like that hurt. Nobody likes being called fat. That's why I never ridicule heavy people. Everybody wants to be perfect and look good and all that. I truly believe it's the most difficult thing in the world to continue to diet, eat properly, and stay thin. I say that because I haven't been able to do it.

Diabetes hasn't really limited me physically. I'll bet there have been only a half dozen times in my life when my sugar was low and I got woozy and needed something to eat right away. The problem for me is my sugar is too high. I've been fairly good at managing my health, but it can be difficult maintaining a proper life schedule during the season with all the travel and time demands.

There is substance beneath my alleged lack of style. I'm a hockey lifer. I can't live without the game. That's why I stuck with it through decades of minor-league bus rides as a player and a coach. I've gained hard-earned knowledge and wisdom that generate results on the scoreboard.

I'll admit that I was a bad role model as a young player. I lacked dedication and a good work ethic—partly because I was ignorant about what it took, partly because I just wanted to have fun—so I never came close to reaching my NHL potential.

But I'm a good role model as a head coach. My success is a testament to the importance of perseverance. Keep working hard and believe in yourself—don't get too high about the victories or too low about the defeats—and opportunity eventually will arrive. I'm fanatically dedicated. Twenty-four hours a day, seven days a week. Sometimes I think my only conscious thoughts are about hockey: strategy, personnel, scouting, video study. I'm fixated on finding ways to win.

I use myself as an example a lot, try to use my own mistakes as teaching tools. Bruce Boudreau, the carefree twenty-year-old player, is an example of how not to approach professional hockey. Bruce Boudreau, the mature head coach, is a man worthy of emulation.

If you want to psychoanalyze it, you could say my failure as a player fueled my success as a coach. If I'd maxed out as a player, stayed in the NHL for a long time, and made big money, I still would have gone into coaching because hockey is in my blood. The game is my oxygen. But I wouldn't have been as good a coach. If I had fulfilled a potential destiny as an NHL player, maybe I wouldn't have had a destiny as an NHL head coach. Ironic, eh?

I wouldn't have understood people as well as I understand people. I've dealt with players from the Single-A and Double-A levels to the AHL and NHL. Understanding what they're going through is extremely important, and I've experienced everything that a player can confront. I've yet to see a player approach me with a situation that forces me to respond, "Well, that's a new one to me." I've either done it or had it done to me. From being the best to being dumped on.

In 1978–79 I played for the New Brunswick Hawks in the AHL. Eddie Johnston was my head coach. To make a point, he nailed me to the bench for a game against Nova Scotia. Didn't play a shift. And my father, Norman, had taken a train all the way from my hometown of Toronto to Halifax to watch me. Eddie noticed my dad after the game and apologized. He said he wouldn't have done it had he known my dad was there.

So I sympathize and empathize with my players. I've felt what they feel— their triumphs and their frustrations. It makes me pay attention to small details—family visits, personal problems, playing opportunity issues—that help bring out the best in them over the long run.

I push hard to be No. 1. I'm much more intense as a coach than I was as a player. I always wanted to win badly as a player, but my desire was focused solely on playing and not preparation. And preparation is the key that unlocks championships.

Preparation enabled me to make the most of it when the Washington Capitals had the guts to take a chance on a no-name who the rest of the NHL didn't think fit the role of head coach. Maybe I didn't look the part, but I was ready to play the part.

As Peter Falk used to say as Columbo: "Oh, one more thing."

This is an unbelievable dream that has happened to me. The most important thing is to make sure it's not a fluke. The goal isn't just making the play-offs. That's not a satisfactory measure of success. The goal is winning the Stanley Cup.

Every name looks fashionable when it's etched in silver.

# 1

## WAKE-UP CALL

**I get scared when the phone rings** early in the morning or late at night. It's a parent thing.

My gut churned at the sound of a 6:30 a.m. wake-up call on November 22, 2007, which was Thanksgiving in the United States. Uh-oh.

Did something happen to my adult daughter, Kasey, up in Ottawa working for the Senators? Or my college-student sons, Ben and Andy, in Ontario? At least I knew my youngest son, Brady, was safely tucked in his bed in our Harrisburg, Pennsylvania, home.

I breathed a sigh of relief when I heard the voice of Doug Yingst, president and general manager of the AHL's Hershey Bears. I went to bed the night before as Hershey's head coach, pleased with a 2-1 win over the Bridgeport Sound Tigers that put us a game above .500 after a slow start.

Doug told me that George McPhee, vice president and general manager of the Washington Capitals, Hershey's NHL parent club, was poised to call me shortly.

"Bruce, you're going to become head coach of the Washington Capitals," Yingst said.

My excitement woke my wife, Crystal. I motioned her to relax. I told Doug this was awesome news, and I thanked him profusely before hanging up.

Then I got to tell Crystal a dream that so often seemed impossible was a reality: We're going up to the NHL. Finally.

After thirty-two-plus years in the minor leagues: Seventeen years as a player who got some NHL stints but never stuck as a regular and fifteen years as a coach who didn't draw NHL interest until the Caps took a chance early in my sixteenth season.

I was an extra in the classic 1977 hockey film *Slap Shot*. Now I was living a true cinematic Cinderella story. If somebody ever makes my life into a movie, I'd love to have Tom Cruise play me. But I'm realistic enough to admit that Mickey Rooney would be a more appropriate choice.

About ten minutes later, George McPhee called with the official word that I was replacing Glen Hanlon. I felt bad for Glen because I've been on the other end. I know the pain of getting fired.

I gave a thumbs-up sign to Crystal. She jumped up and down on the bed. I wanted to explode with excitement, but I kept myself composed with George to sound professional.

I didn't care that my initial title was interim head coach, not full-fledged head coach. I didn't care whether or not a raise was involved. George told me I'd have total autonomy to play whom I wanted and use the systems I wanted. He said I'd be running practice at 10:30 a.m. that day at the team's headquarters at Kettler Capitals Iceplex in Arlington, Virginia. So much for Thanksgiving dinner. I was headed for a bigger feast.

I hung up, and we ran around the bedroom like Keystone Kops. Get dressed. Pack. I didn't know what to put in the suitcase. We went into Brady's bedroom and told him. His eyes popped open and he jumped up and down on the bed. His innocent nine-year-old's joy made it especially exciting for me.

George swore me to secrecy because he hadn't told Glen Hanlon yet. That was a major challenge. My nickname is Gabby because, well, I like to talk. You know how hard it is not to tell anybody the best news you've ever heard?

I'll be honest. I told Kasey, Ben, and Andy and made them promise to keep it to themselves. Crystal set up the car's GPS—I don't know how to work the darn thing—to direct me from Harrisburg to Arlington. I jumped in my Chevrolet Impala and could barely contain myself.

You might think the ninety-minute-plus drive was a time of reflection. A time to think how proud my late father, Norman, would be to see his son become an NHL coach. A time to think about all the stops I'd made along the way, including Baltimore, which I passed en route to Washington. A time to think about all the detours that could have taken me out of hockey and, indeed, out of life; I was ticketed to fly on United Airlines flight 175 out of Boston, which terrorists crashed into the World Trade Center on September 11, 2001, but my itinerary was changed to September 10 the week before the tragedy.

However, it wasn't like that at all.

I was blank-minded, except for thinking about how I would approach this new challenge. I'd fantasized about being an NHL head coach. Now I didn't know what the heck I was going to do.

My focus was on what I would tell the team and what I would do with practice. I knew I'd have no problem coaching the Caps players I'd had in Hershey. But the respect I had for the Michael Nylanders, Viktor Kozlovs, and Olie Kolzigs—for what they've accomplished and their experience—was enormous. Olie Kolzig, who had been the foundation of the franchise—how was he going to handle this? He was accustomed to Glen Hanlon, who had been an NHL goalie. How were the bench assistants, Dean Evason and Jay Leach, himself a former Hershey head coach, going to react? They were Glen's friends.

On top of that, three quarters of the way down I thought I was lost. If the GPS was wrong, I was going to be late on my first day. Crystal reassured me to trust it and it worked.

As directed, I parked on the seventh floor of the garage at Kettler, which sits atop the Ballston Common Mall. Butterflies stirred in my stomach. I took a couple deep breaths. I had my suitcase and my hockey bag. At last, this was my chance.

●

The first person I saw at Kettler was Brooks Laich, a forward I coached in Hershey. He looked at me and said, "What are you doing here?" It dawned on me that the players didn't know. I didn't know what to say. I just told Brooksie, as innocently as possible, I was asked to come down.

I went into the coaches office, and George McPhee was there. George said he was about to tell the players. He didn't pull me into Glen Hanlon's office, which I thought was a classy move. Glen's office would be closed until he cleared out everything. George went into the locker room and told the players while I sat with Dean Evason, Jay Leach, and video coach Blaine Forsythe. They were extremely magnanimous and said they'd do anything I needed. My head swirled. George returned and took me to meet the players.

To me, this was a critical moment. I could have blown it right away by going in and not knowing what I was doing. The Caps sat at the bottom of the NHL with a 6-14-1 record, which is why Hanlon was released. I wanted this team to believe in itself. I walked around the locker room as I spoke, making sure to look each player in the eye.

"Guys, I know this is a new situation," I said. "It's a new situation for me. But I do know one thing: I know how to coach. We're going to go out there, and we're going to have a forty-five-minute practice right now. Then we're going to get on the bus to play in Philadelphia tomorrow. The one thing I do know is when I was here at training camp, I thought you guys were a pretty good hockey club. You guys are good. You just don't know it yet. We're going to make you know it. Let's get out there and let's have a real good practice. We're going to play the way we're all capable of playing."

I looked over and defenseman Mike Green, who played for me in Hershey, was smiling. I knew Green was happy. And centerman Dave Steckel, another of my Hershey guys, was happy. I went around and talked to everybody individually to say hello. At one point, I forgot what I was saying because I glanced over to superstar winger Alexander Ovechkin and said to myself, "Oh, my God, I'm coaching Alex Ovechkin." I had to regain my train of thought.

I knew I had to get their attention. I told the assistants that it was important to me that the players hear only my voice and that I would run the whole practice.

I hadn't had time to write a practice plan. I initially thought I wasn't going to change much from Hanlon's conservative, defense-oriented systems. Then, I decided, the heck with it. I changed everything to my style, which is a high-pressure game all over the ice.

One time, Ovechkin didn't do something right. I blew the whistle and admonished the team. They weren't at game speed and were sloppy, so I jumped right on them. I took control. The guys started moving after that, and it became a good practice. George McPhee told me later he thought I was going to be fine from the first moment because of that.

I told them, "We're going to learn to attack. We're going to learn to be aggressive. We're going to be an in-your-face team, and we're going to win." My heart pumped fast. It was like an acting thing.

After practice, I met the Washington media. There were a lot of reporters and television cameras. They weren't tough on me, this unknown commodity suddenly arriving on the scene, which I thought was nice. They asked easy questions, and I answered them honestly.

One of the key things about coaching in the NHL is dealing with the media. I thought I handled my first press conference well. They didn't get the standard lines. I revealed that I thought I'd gotten lost on the way down. That's the kind of stuff that coaches don't usually say, but it's the kind of stuff people want to hear. I'm just a regular guy, a lunch-pail guy, who doesn't put on any airs.

●

We boarded the bus to Philadelphia, and I sat at the front. I don't think I talked to anybody the whole trip. At the Four Seasons Hotel, I went to my room, ordered room service, and watched a Philly game tape. It was all so new, from Blaine Forsythe doing the video to a ninety-dollar meal money per diem, about double what I was used to in the AHL.

I was amazed at the amount of the per diem. Then I discovered the room service hamburger cost forty bucks. Forty dollars for a hamburger? Are you kidding me? This was the whole minor-league thing in me.

I watched the Philly game video and prepared exactly as I would for a Hershey game. I woke the next morning, phoned home, and said, "Well, I'm still here." We were taking it one day at a time as a family. It was important to me to do everything the way I wanted it. If this was going to have a bad outcome, it was going to be because I did what I wanted to do.

My debut against the Philadelphia Flyers on November 23, 2007, at Wachovia Center was an afternoon game, so we didn't have a morning skate. In the penalty kill meeting with the team, I didn't change anything because you have to limit your initial changes. In the power play meeting, though,

Jay Leach went through our tapes and I made a change. This was a big part of getting them to think I knew what I was talking about. I wanted Mike Green on the half wall. I wanted Alex Ovechkin in the middle. I wanted Nicklas Backstrom and Michael Nylander down low.

"What's going to happen," I told the team, "is Philadelphia overplays the middle guy. Everybody will overplay Alex. Green can get open. If we can get a pass across there, we're going to have a one-timer that's going to go in."

Lo and behold, the Flyers took a penalty 1:44 into the game. We used my power play setup, and 2:27 into the game we had a goal. Backstrom passed across the ice from the right circle to Green, who scored from the left circle exactly like we'd drawn it up. I think the guys thought, Maybe he's not a hick from Hershey; maybe he does know a little bit about hockey.

What I said worked. If it hadn't worked, it would have been easy for them not to believe and to tune me out from the start.

The crowd was loud. I couldn't remember the last time I was in front of a crowd of twenty thousand. It was thrilling. The speed of the game didn't overwhelm me at all. We rolled four lines. It was important to roll four lines to show everybody they were a part of the team. I was not interested in matching lines. I told the guys within forty-eight hours of taking the job that I didn't plan to match lines the whole season. It had nothing to do with me not being able to do it because it's not hard to do. I simply believe every Caps line should be able to play against every opposition line.

We beat Philadelphia 4-3 in overtime on a goal by Backstrom, who was celebrating his twentieth birthday. One and oh in the NHL. It was a pretty cool thing.

I'm good at making emotional speeches. I don't remember exactly what I told the team before that game, but it came from the heart. I remember telling them that they're good and they'll see they're good when they play the right way. When they won, I told them it proved my point about how much potential they had.

In the past, they were told if they didn't work hard enough they weren't going to win because other teams were better. My whole thing was that other teams weren't better; we were better than them. It's the same philosophy I used when I took the Hershey job in 2005 and inherited a group of Caps prospects who had shaky confidence because they hadn't made the play-offs the previous year when Portland, Maine, was Washington's farm club.

The NHL, unlike the AHL, is not a developmental league. It's a win league. You've got to win. In retrospect, that first victory was huge because we'd need every point we could get.

I would have coached at Wachovia Center that Friday even if I hadn't been called to Washington. Hershey played the Philadelphia Phantoms, the Flyers' farm club, the same day in the same building. After we won, my concern turned to the Bears and my former assistant coach, Bob Woods, who was promoted to interim head coach in Hershey to succeed me. Woody made his AHL head coaching debut that evening on the same bench where I made my NHL head coaching debut.

In a perfect world, I would have been able to stay and talk to the Bears and thank them. They played a major role in propelling me to the NHL because they'd played so well for me the two previous years. We won the AHL's Calder Cup in 2005–6 and returned to the Calder Cup finals in 2006–7 before losing to the Hamilton Bulldogs.

But we had to get going. As our bus pulled out, I saw Hershey's bus pull in. The juxtaposition symbolized a whirlwind forty-eight hours in my life. By the way, Woody and the Bears won 2-1, putting a nice bow on the day for the entire organization.

As head coach in the minors, I selected movies for team bus rides. But I didn't bring one on this trip. We ended up watching *American Pie 3* or something sophomoric like that. I felt really good because I heard a lot of laughter. I sensed the players were beginning to feel good about themselves and regain their confidence. They had to believe that they were good before they could believe they could climb from the basement to the play-offs.

Me? I was interim head coach of the Washington Capitals with one game under my belt. I still could get sent back to Hershey. I had to win to stay in the NHL and avoid the kind of demotion that stung me so many times as a player.

After 2,127 regular-season games as a player and head coach in the minors, I aimed to become an overnight success.

# 2

## MARLBOROS MAN

**Pat Riley, our trainer with the Toronto Marlies juveniles,** hung the Gabby nickname on me in a Junior B training camp. After a summer away from teammates, I was meeting a bunch of new guys and excited to be starting a new season. I just wouldn't shut up. The coach told me to zip it twice in a team meeting.

Pat sat there and said, "Jeez, you're a gabby bleep." Everybody laughed. He kept calling me Gabby for a couple of days. A couple other guys started calling me Gabby and it stuck. I earned it. I talk a lot.

I've had other nicknames that were part and parcel of how I lived early in my life. I was sloppy. For example, another nickname was Dirt. I was like Pigpen in Charlie Brown with a dark cloud around me all the time.

One night when I was playing for the Toronto Maple Leafs at Maple Leaf Gardens, Ian Turnbull wrote Dirt on the top of my big white helmet. I didn't know it was there, like a guy who doesn't know he's got a kick-me sign stuck to his back. Bill Hewitt, son of legendary Leafs broadcaster Foster Hewitt, was up in the booth doing play-by-play with his inimitable rich voice and enunciation: "There's Boudreau with the puck and he's got something on his helmet there. What does that say? Dirt? What the heck is that?" I got the word when I got home because everybody was listening to it on *Hockey Night in Canada*.

Gabby is a friendly, nice nickname. I like it. It's not derogatory. If you're going to be in hockey, you're going to have a nickname. And hockey is the only thing I ever wanted to do.

I was born on January 9, 1955, in Toronto. Every time my dad asked what I wanted to be when I grew up, I said a hockey player. It never varied. I never wanted to work for the fire department or be a policeman, any of the jobs that kids like.

Norman Boudreau, my father, was only five foot two. He was born in Montreal and grew up a Canadiens fan. He was an accountant for Dun & Bradstreet. His office was right across the street from Maple Leaf Gardens. He was a very loyal guy who worked at Dun & Bradstreet for thirty-five years. When his boss took him once a month to the Hot Stove Lounge, which was the famous restaurant in Maple Leaf Gardens, that's all my dad ever wanted. Every now and again he got to see a Leafs game. He was a tremendous hockey fan.

In 1959 George Bell Arena opened near our house near the stockyards in central Toronto. We lived in Little Italy at St. Clair Avenue and Lansdowne Avenue. My dad built a rink in our backyard when I was four, and I played in the George Bell Arena house league at five. Every winter he'd build a rink and play with us. My brothers, Bryan and Barry, were much younger than I. When I was nine and ten years old, it was my friends and me with Dad on the backyard rink.

My father was my inspiration. He drove me everywhere. It didn't matter how far. He was the guy who picked everybody up, and we always had a crappy old car. The first car I remember was a British-made Standard Vanguard. All the cars were used. We never had a new car.

My mother, Theresa, was a bank teller for thirty-something years. We lived with my grandparents, Mary and Herb Boudreau. We lived on the first floor; they lived on the second floor. We didn't have a lot of money. We were on the bottom of the economic food chain. To make extra money—I remember doing this from an early age—we made baby teething soothers. We had an assembly line and made them by the gross. I was the one who had to wet the nipple and stick it in. My thumbs were sore every day.

My dad's parents were killed in a car crash, and Herb and Mary Boudreau adopted him, though I wouldn't know that until I was twenty. They moved from Montreal to Bathurst in New Brunswick, and then my dad moved to Toronto in 1952 to find work. My mom, who was from Bathurst, just followed, and they ended up getting married.

I don't speak French. I'm sketchy on why. We're not sure how old my father was when his biological parents died. We can't find any records of their names or anything. We think they were English from England, but we're not positive.

My dad spoke some broken French. My mom is French and grew up speaking an Acadian dialect. Her maiden name was Roy, like Patrick Roy, the hall-of-fame goalie. But my parents spoke to me in English and I never learned French. Being in Toronto, I learned to hate Montreal right off the bat. We're supposed to hate the Canadiens because of the rivalry with the Maple Leafs.

●

I was an average player as a preteen. I wasn't a top scorer until I was twelve or thirteen. Then I started leading teams in scoring. I got lucky. Everything I did, we won. From the ages of fifteen to twenty, everything I touched turned to gold.

We went undefeated in juveniles. We had the best Junior B team in history, maybe, with the Markham Waxers, the Marlies' Junior B club. My first year in Junior A—it's now called Major Junior—we won the Memorial Cup with the Marlies in 1972–73. My third year in Junior A (1974–75) we won the Memorial Cup a second time.

It was an incredible run. I was a high-scoring centerman who tallied 152 goals and 365 points those three Junior A seasons. My third season, I scored 68 goals and had 97 assists for 165 points, which was a Canadian Hockey League (CHL) record until Wayne Gretzky surpassed it in 1977–78. In those days, there wasn't a professional draft until you turned twenty, so Junior A was pretty darn good hockey.

I excelled at baseball, football, and track and field. Just a natural athlete. A Pittsburgh Pirates scout wanted to sign me one year at a baseball camp. I said, "No, I just came to this camp to have fun, but I'm a hockey player." It was crazy because I could have signed to play Class A ball. They would have signed me for five thousand dollars to go to Florida and play that summer. I wouldn't have missed any hockey, and I still would have been able to play baseball. And I didn't do it. Stupid.

I was bemused by the small-world nature of things when Alexander Ovechkin scored sixty-five goals for the Washington Capitals under me in

2007–8 to break the team's single-season, goal-scoring record of sixty set in 1981–82 by Dennis Maruk. Dennis and I were Junior B teammates, and he beat me by a point for a league scoring championship in 1971–72.

Maruk and I went into the last game trailing the leading scorer by eight points, so we needed nine points to win the scoring title. As fate would have it, we were winning something like 14-1, and Dennis and I each had seven points; we needed one more to tie. With about three minutes to play, I pulled up and waited for a defenseman to catch me and for Dennis to catch me. I passed him the puck, he scored, and we both got a point to tie for the league lead.

With about a minute to go, Dennis had the puck coming down the boards, and it was a two-on-none. He took it to the net without passing to me and scored. Thus, he won the scoring championship. Well, that's Dennis.

The next step was the Junior A Marlies. Toronto kids dreamed about playing for the hometown Marlboros, but they could protect only two of their Junior B players from the Ontario Hockey Association (OHA) draft (it's now the Ontario Hockey League). The night before the draft, they traded me to the London Knights straight up for Mark Howe, Gordie Howe's son, who was playing for the Detroit Junior Red Wings. Mark Howe didn't want to play for London, which had first choice or something. They held the draft and it was ruled that the trade was illegal. They had to do another trade.

In that trade, Dennis Maruk went to London and Mark Howe came to the Marlies. In the course of forty-eight hours, my fate changed: I went from being a London Knight to being a Toronto Marlie and winning two Memorial Cups. Mark Howe and I became good friends. Dennis Maruk had a lot of personal success in London but never won the Memorial Cup.

Defenseman Greg Neeld lost his left eye my first season with the Marlies. Dave Maloney accidentally poked his eye out with his stick in a game against the Kitchener Rangers. Neeld came back with one eye and played. They made a Neeld Shield. They didn't really have face masks at that point. Neeld was the innovator of eye protection. He used a full-face guard and eventually patented it. In today's version it's a visor. The NHL refused to allow Neeld to play with one eye, but the World Hockey Association (WHA) and International Hockey League (IHL) did.

I played with some big names on that 1972–73 Marlies team, which went 47-7-9. Mark and Marty Howe. Wayne Dillon, Peter Marrin, Paulin Bourdeleau, Tom Edur, Bob Dailey, Kevin Devine, Mike Palmateer. I think twenty of us ended up playing pro hockey.

We played at Maple Leaf Gardens. We averaged almost ten thousand people a game. The Marlies in those days got almost as much ink as the Maple Leafs. We were sports section front-page material, a big deal. Our home games were Sunday afternoons when the Leafs usually played on the road. We would get bigger headlines than the Leafs in Monday's papers. Our reporters were the same reporters who covered the Leafs. We had the Frank Orrs and the Jim Proudfoots, who were major names in Canadian sports journalism. It was a great way for a young guy to learn about dealing with the media. We were in such a media market that we'd have four and five reporters in our locker room after every game.

My Marlies head coach was George Armstrong, who's a member of the Hockey Hall of Fame. He was captain of the Maple Leafs for eleven years, the longest tenure for a captain in team history. Armstrong scored the clinching empty-net goal in Game 6 of the 1967 Stanley Cup finals against Montreal, and the Leafs haven't won the cup since. Armstrong was a major influence in my life. He was a little bit like John Wooden in that he never yelled at you. We just had the ultimate respect for him. We all grew up as Leafs fans, and Armstrong was a hero to everybody and a funny guy.

In practice, we would play forty-five minutes of shinny, and for maybe fifteen minutes he'd skate us real hard at the end. From my recollection, there wasn't much structure in his practices. But if we lost a game, we were mad at ourselves because we let our coach down.

I led the play-offs in scoring that season. And that was playing against the likes of Bob Gainey, when we played Peterborough, and Denis Potvin, when we played Ottawa. We won that first Memorial Cup in Montreal at the Forum, but my parents couldn't afford to come and watch.

We beat the Quebec Remparts 5-2 in the first game, and then we lost 3-2 to Lanny McDonald and the Medicine Hat Tigers. We were still alive because it wasn't single elimination. Quebec, led by Andre Savard, had to beat Medicine Hat by a certain amount to get to the final based upon goal differential. The Remparts did just that, and we beat them 9-1 in the championship game. Mark Howe played super, and that's when scouts started to salivate over him turning pro. The next year he went to the WHA as an underage guy to play with his father with the Houston Aeros.

We called George Armstrong "Chief" because he was a full-blooded Indian. Chief was a nervous guy and a smoker who'd sneak a cigarette between periods. In the 9-1 Memorial Cup game against Quebec, he went into a stick room down the hall for a smoke after the first period. He shut the door and locked himself in. We sat waiting to go out, and Chief didn't come. We finally had to go out to play, and he was nowhere to be found. One minute went by, two minutes went by. We changed our own lines because we had no coach. And we scored three goals real quick.

The trainers went looking for Armstrong. They heard him banging in the stick room. Chief came back and saw we had scored three goals. He'd missed five minutes. He joked, "What the hell is this? I'm going back into the stick room."

I loved Chief and would have done anything for him. I was fortunate to have him for three years. The second year I was an assistant captain for him. The third year I was the captain.

In my personality in coaching, you don't see me yelling at players a lot. I talk to them and try to get through to them that way. Chief was like that, and I took that from him. He would pull you aside rather than embarrass you in public. I didn't know it at the time, but it was kind of a model for dealing with the twenty-first-century athlete. I don't think constant yelling works.

We had a lot of great players again on the 1973–74 Marlies. Kevin Devine and I were back. We lost some graduating players, and the Howes and Tom Edur and Wayne Dillon all defected to the WHA. It was quite a different team, a much less experienced team. Talented newcomers like John Tonelli, John Smrke, and John Anderson, who all reached the NHL, came aboard, but they might not have made the powerful 1972–73 team. Mike Kitchen, who made the NHL as a player, head coach, and assistant coach, became a good friend of mine.

Mike was an Ontario farm boy who was strong as an ox. He was an I'll-do-anything-for-you kind of player. You always thought of him as a simple guy, but he evolved to become one of the best assistant coaches in the NHL and deserved more credit for the terrific job he did as head coach of the undermanned St. Louis Blues from 2003–7. Great manners, great respect for everyone, a salt of the earth guy. Mike commands respect because he treats people fairly and he's a nice person. Absolutely one of the best people I've met in hockey. I've never met a man I respected more. You're lucky if you get to call him friend.

We were mediocre in 1973–74 and ended up in seventh place. We were young but showed signs of how good we'd be the next year by winning one round in the play-offs. A lot of us couldn't accept that we were eliminated in the second round. We weren't used to losing and had a hard time dealing with it.

In 1974–75 we were more mature and were the highest scoring team in the OHA. I led the league in scoring. Trevor Johansen was a first-round pick. John Anderson had a great year. Mark Napier went on to win Stanley Cups with Montreal, and John Tonelli went on to win Stanley Cups with the New York Islanders.

Napier was the star in the making. He was the most gifted guy I'd ever seen to that point. At sixteen, he had lived the life of a twenty-two-year-old. Mark was only five foot ten, but he was a ripped 185 pounds with big bone structure. He was cocky and played cocky. They put him on my right wing, and he scored sixty-six goals.

Tonelli was an octopus. He worked so hard that in practice we hated playing against him. He was all over you. You could have predicted he'd do what he'd do. He was a tenacious player. We always thought of him as a farmer's kid who'd blush if you told a bawdy joke, but he got pretty sophisticated in New York.

We won the Memorial Cup without Tonelli. Tonelli and Napier signed pro contracts before the season ended. Napier signed with Toronto in the WHA. Tonelli quit the Marlies when he turned eighteen to remain eligible to play for Houston in the WHA the next season. That sparked a change to an entry draft for eighteen-year-olds. Tonelli also went on to pioneer the Stanley Cup play-off beard tradition.

Without Tonelli, we struggled in the OHA play-offs against Kingston and Sudbury before beating Hamilton to advance to the Memorial Cup in Kitchener. My claim to fame is I set a Memorial Cup record that still stands when I scored five goals in one game against Sherbrooke. But I was minus-one. I think that's where my defensive acumen—or lack of it—came into play.

We beat Sherbrooke 5-4 in overtime of the first game but lost 6-2 to New Westminster in the second. We beat Sherbrooke 10-4 in my five-goal game to get a rematch with New Westminster in the championship game, which we won 7-3. We tossed Chief into the hotel swimming pool during our victory party.

My NHL draft year was 1975. In 1974 I was drafted by the WHA's Minnesota Fighting Saints. I asked my agent at that time, Bill Watters, whether I should go. He thought it would be better for me to stay another year in junior, and I listened to him. I won the Memorial Cup and made a lot of great friends. In the end, though, I don't know if it was better for me or not.

I went on a seventeen-day canoe trip in July 1974 after I was drafted by Minnesota. Our history teacher took a bunch of us on an annual trek. He was from Sudbury, and he'd take us north of Sudbury. Minnesota offered a deal of $250,000 for three years. That was unbelievable money. But there were no cell phones then, no means to contact anybody on a canoe trip. By the time I got back, the Fighting Saints had signed three other centermen and decided they weren't going to sign me that year. So if I hadn't gone on the canoe trip, I probably would have signed with Minnesota and I wouldn't have played my last year of junior.

George Armstrong told me I was ranked thirteenth for the 1975 NHL draft. I was mad because I wanted to be ranked first, and Chief was mad at me because I was ticked that I was thirteenth. I remember going to dinner with Bill Watters and Alan Eagleson, who was Bill's partner and my co-agent. They said the California Golden Seals, who picked third, had me ranked third and that's probably where I would go. Toronto had me ranked seventh and it picked sixth. The Leafs said they were going to pick me if I was available, but they figured I'd be gone. I was pretty ecstatic and pretty confident about my prospects of being a high pick, but it never happened.

In the mid-1970s, streaking was a fad. Everybody on our team streaked everywhere all the time—except me. I was the captain, and I couldn't do that sort of thing. But after we won the Memorial Cup and the season was done, I didn't feel as duty-bound to set a captain's example.

We had a Marlies year-end party about two weeks before the draft. Mike Kitchen, Mark Napier, Craig Crawford, a couple other Marlies, and I all went out at noon drinking. We drank and drank, and at midnight we decided to streak. We were in a bar that was basically a sailor's pub. It had a pair of bathrooms separated by a band set. There might have been ten people in the place, so I agreed to streak with them. It was just a crazy lark.

We went into one bathroom, and I stripped naked and put my underwear over my head. We ran through the bar. Stupid me, I tripped and went headfirst through the band's bass drum. I got up and we ran to the other bathroom. We were getting dressed, laughing our heads off, when we heard a knock on the door. Two plainclothes cops happened to be in the bar checking for underage drinking and saw us streak. Great luck, right?

They pulled us down to the police station and charged us with indecent exposure. We were at the cop shop for a couple of hours before they let us drive home. We made a pact to keep it quiet. At 7:30 the next morning, though, my dad phoned on the way to work. It was all over the radio. The headline in the *Toronto Star* was in red letters: "Marlies Charged with Indecent Exposure." My mom didn't go to work for four days and didn't speak to me for five days. I embarrassed my whole family.

We eventually got the charges dropped. There was a complaint about that and the charges were reinstated, but a judge ultimately dismissed it again. Every now and then I meet somebody who reminds me of that incident. It was such big news.

Mike Kitchen had another year of junior, so it didn't affect him. Mark Napier had signed with the WHA, so it didn't affect him. My draft was in two weeks. I don't know for sure if it cost me in the draft. It's always been in the back of my mind that it did. I went forty-second overall in the third round to Toronto. Not third, not sixth. Forty-second.

That was the most devastating thing in my life up to that point. It was a phone draft. They didn't go to a location and have a draft the way it's done now. They simply phoned everybody.

We had to wait at home, and I paced the floor. When we got the call to say I went in the third round, I bawled my eyes out. My dad was so upset. That's when he revealed to me that he was adopted. I'd never known. He told me something sad that was a lesson about perseverance.

I was happy that the Leafs took me, but I also was disappointed that they'd passed me over twice. They took Don Ashby in the first round and Doug Jarvis in the second. Jarvis was a Peterborough Pete and I was a Marlie. Why would they draft a Peterborough Pete in front of a Marlie? I couldn't understand it. They didn't know Jarvis personally like they knew me. I couldn't come to terms with that.

Toronto offered me a two-way contract where I'd make fourteen thousand dollars in the minor leagues. Minnesota in the WHA offered me thirty thousand dollars a year one way for three years, a huge drop from $250,000 for three they'd offered the year before. Assuming I wasn't going to make the Leafs right away, I decided to go to Minnesota because it was twice the money. We figured down the road I could sign with the Leafs anyway, once I'd established myself as a pro. It ended up not working out too well.

Alan Eagleson eventually got in trouble over defrauding clients like Bobby Orr and lining his pockets while acting as virtual dictator of the NHL Players' Association. Eagleson didn't affect my career except probably in the way he negotiated for me. He'd phone me when he talked to Toronto during contract negotiations in future years. I can imagine a quickie situation between Eagleson and the Toronto front office, like, "OK, let's do Boudreau. Let's give him a twenty-five-hundred-dollar raise and move on. I'll sell that to him." And he did.

When Eagleson and Bill Watters split up, I went with Bill because he was the guy I talked to and he offered me helpful advice as a fatherly figure. I didn't have any money invested with Eagleson because I didn't have much money, so I didn't get hurt by any financial scams.

Now I was headed to the pros. I figured it would be a smooth transition, considering how I'd dominated in juniors.

Yeah, right.

# 3

## SLAP SHOT

In the movie *Slap Shot*, **Paul Newman** is Reg Dunlop, a player-coach trying to hang on in the gritty world of minor-league hockey with a financially troubled club called the Charlestown Chiefs, who played in the rough-and-tumble fictional Federal League. The Charlestown Chiefs were based on the Johnstown Jets of the North American Hockey League (NAHL). Newman's apartment in *Slap Shot* was my real-life apartment as a Jets rookie in Johnstown, Pennsylvania.

Director George Roy Hill came into the Jets dressing room one day and said, "We need a room to shoot a scene, and we need someplace that's run down and probably the worst place you'd ever want to see." Everybody pointed at me. I roomed with Dave Hanson. Our other roommate, Paul Holmgren, had moved out after a short stay. We had a big place. I paid fifty bucks a month, so we weren't living at the Ritz. Dave kept his area neat. My area, not so much. That's where they filmed.

The movie is based on a screenplay by Nancy Dowd inspired by her brother Ned Dowd's experiences as a minor leaguer in Johnstown. Ned Dowd played two seasons for the Jets (1973–75) and was Ogie Ogilthorpe in the film. Pay attention to the background of a couple of game scenes in *Slap Shot* and you'll notice a green-uniformed No. 7 playing against the Chiefs for the Hyannisport Presidents. That's me. The shaggy mop of hair is long gone, but the memories remain.

My roomie Dave Hanson was one of the notorious Hanson brothers, three childlike goons who played bubble hockey off the ice and put foil on their fists to aid their on-ice brawls. All three were actual hockey players, not actors. Dave Hanson played Jack Hanson. Real brothers Jeff Carlson and Steve Carlson respectively played Jeff Hanson and Steve Hanson. Their other real-life brother, Jack Carlson, might have been the toughest of the three, but he was playing in the WHA when the movie was filmed.

Dave Hanson is quite a character. The Jack Hanson role gives him a cartoon image, but Dave is a serious, smart man who was tough as nails and eventually went into hockey management. He was six foot one, 195 pounds, and would flip out in games. When he went nuts, he went nuts. Off the ice, he didn't act like the wild man you saw on the ice. During games, he turned into his alter ego and the crowd chanted "Killer! Killer!" just like in the movie. He was Killer Hanson. His eyes rolled in the back of his head, and you didn't want to fight him.

Dave was the original tough guy on the Jets, and the Carlson brothers arrived and complemented that. The short time we lived together, Dave was like the father in the house because he was the oldest. He'd yip at me about my immaturity. Dave and Paul Holmgren were Minnesota boys and a little closer with each other than they were with the cocky Canadian.

Jeff Carlson was a fun-loving guy. He had mediocre hockey talent, but he would fight anybody. Jeff was the stereotypical tough guy and the life of the party. He was six foot three, 210 pounds, and he'd beat the crap out of people whenever he needed to beat the crap out of people—on the ice and off. He was gregarious and kept everybody loose in the locker room with his jokes and stories.

Steve Carlson was quiet and reserved. Totally the opposite of Jeff. He was a smart guy and became Johnstown's coach during its East Coast Hockey League (ECHL) incarnation. Steve fought when he had to, but he really didn't like it. He wanted to play hockey.

It's my understanding that the Carlsons were a major inspiration for what became the movie. Nancy Dowd saw the Jets as a sad sack club that got braver after the Carlsons arrived. She wrote it up and sent it to George Roy Hill. Hill loved it, and the rest is history.

I watched the dailies once with Paul Newman, George Roy Hill, and

Dave Hanson. It was just the four of us. Paul turned around and said, "I just finished a movie just for the money: *The Life and Times of Judge Roy Bean*. But I believe that this movie is going to be a real hit." I'll never forget that. It obviously was a hit.

Being an extra meant long days of doing nothing. I found out that actors sit around an awful lot on the set. We sat around with our skates on for six and eight hours every day for a week straight, just to get a couple scenes done. Then we went home, and in the summer we had to go to Syracuse, New York, and do the same thing over again. I spent fourteen days in all working on the movie and got paid thirteen hundred dollars.

We spent hours on a scene I was in at the start of the movie. George Roy Hill instructed us that the scene illustrated how Charlestown was getting beaten and not playing well. They shot the front of the net to capture goal-scoring. I was on the green team, and I just skated around the goal like a big ham because I knew that's where the cameras were focused. I never went into the corner and got the puck—probably pretty similar to my actual playing style. Hey, it got me onto the theater screen.

Paul Newman asked me to teach him how to take a slap shot. When somebody that famous asks you to do something, you take it seriously. I was extremely precise about all the techniques involved in a slap shot. After about ten minutes, Paul said, "OK, kid, I've heard enough. I know all I need to know." That ten minutes felt like thirty.

Newman was a down-to-earth man who talked to all the guys. I'd be lying if I said we were on a first-name basis. Hi, Paul. Hi, Bruce. But I met him two or three times, and he was very nice to me. I was deeply saddened when he died in 2008.

I attended the wrap-up party, which was exciting. I got to be good friends for quite a few years with Jerry Hauser, who played Dave "Killer" Carlson, a character based on Dave "Killer" Hanson. Jerry ended up playing in the *Summer of '42* and *The Brady Brides*. I don't remember if I met Michael Ontkean, who played Ned Braden. I see Lindsay Crouse, who played Ned Braden's wife, Lily, every so often on *Law and Order*. I point at the TV screen and go, "That's her! That's her!"

I went to the movie when it opened in Toronto with my girlfriend (now my ex-wife) Mary and watched it with anticipation. "There's me! There's me!" I was on the big screen. *Slap Shot* had a huge buildup in Toronto. It played for years in certain theaters in the city. It was such a cult thing. A hockey movie like it hasn't been made before or since. It's one of the greatest sports movies ever made.

●

Movie aside, we had a real team in Johnstown. I loved playing for the Johnstown Jets. I've loved every town I've gone to.

My 1975–76 season started with Minnesota Fighting Saints training camp in the WHA. To that point, everything in hockey had come so easy for me that I never knew about working out to get in shape. I had no idea. I think I went to camp at 195 pounds when I played junior at 170. I was fat.

The Fighting Saints sent me down to Johnstown right away to send a message, which obviously didn't register early in my pro career. I still partied hard in Johnstown. My statistics were excellent. I had twenty-five goals and thirty-five assists in thirty-four games.

It was my first time away from home, and I was way too dependent on my mom when I was at home. I came back to the apartment one night at about two in the morning, and Paul Holmgren had to get the door because I forgot my keys. Holmer was a mature guy who was serious about the game. He said, "Your priorities are all screwed up." That always stuck with me.

Holmer was somebody I should have learned from. He was a quiet guy from St. Paul, Minnesota. I was a chatty first-round pick from Toronto. I don't know if he resented me or not, but we became friends. I spent Thanksgiving at his house the first year in Minnesota. We both got sent down to Johnstown together.

What a dedicated, hardworking, strong man. Holmgren didn't last in Johnstown too long, just six games, and he got called back up to Minnesota. We didn't live together more than three weeks or a month, but he left an indelible impression on me. Paul's career went on a tremendous upswing, and mine didn't. Paul signed with the Philadelphia Flyers when Minnesota folded that season and became a hard-nosed NHL forward before coaching the Flyers and Hartford Whalers and eventually becoming general manager of the Flyers. He became close with Bobby Clarke in Philadelphia and went from player to management in a hurry.

After starting the season in Johnstown, I got called up to Minnesota and played thirty games for the Fighting Saints. They had a neat arena, the St. Paul Civic Center, that featured glass all the way around the rink instead of traditional white boards. Glen Sonmor was the general manager, and Harry Neale was the head coach.

There were a lot of older guys, and they were a goonie, goonie team. The name Fighting Saints was quite appropriate. They liked the tough guys. Henry Boucha, John McKenzie, Paul Holmgren, Jack Carlson, Jeff Carlson, Bill Butters, Curt Brackenbury, Pat Westrum, Ron Busniuk. They were all tough guys who loved to fight and were good at it.

I scored my first major-league goal on Gerry Cheevers in a game against Cleveland. That night I scored two goals against Cheevers. But we lost 3-2, and I let my man go for the game-winning goal. Harry Neale and Glen Sonmor called me in and ripped me. This was the story of my hockey life from the get-go.

Being an out-of-shape, first-round draft choice, I was picked on pretty good. I wasn't treated well by the veterans. It was a bad experience. In those days it was common practice for older guys to single out first-round draft picks and treat them rough. You went from being top dog to being a piece of garbage. I wasn't used to it and didn't like it.

They put me in the hospital during rookie hazing. They pinned me down on a gurney and tied my legs and arms. They shaved my head and pubic area. Then they put turpentine on the cuts and smeared black tar on my groin and chest. They finished by gluing my armpits and left me lying there bawling like a baby until the trainer came and took me to the hospital. If I didn't love the game so much, I would have quit after that day. It's one of the reasons I've never liked initiations. I've never cut another guy's hair.

When Minnesota folded, I went back to Johnstown to finish the season with the idea of signing with the Toronto Maple Leafs the next season. I could have signed with the Leafs right then and gone to their minor-league team in Oklahoma City instead of dangling in Johnstown. But my agents knew there was a movie being shot in Johnstown. They told me to go there, enjoy being around the filming, and forget the tough times in Minnesota.

The idea of the movie was exciting, and I didn't examine the hockey ramifications. In retrospect, it was ridiculous that I stayed in Johnstown and did *Slap Shot*, even though being in the movie is what everybody always asks me about. I should have signed with the Maple Leafs and gotten some exposure in their organization that season. It would have helped me going into 1976–77. It was another decision that hurt my career.

In addition, the WHA held a dispersal draft after Minnesota folded. I was taken by Indianapolis, where Wayne Gretzky made his pro debut in 1978–79. The only reason I didn't go to Indianapolis, which would have paid my full WHA salary, was Minnesota owed me ten thousand dollars for a signing bonus and Indianapolis wouldn't honor it. Going there also would have been better for my career than returning to Johnstown. Another bad decision among too many.

During my first pro year I was an undisciplined twenty-year-old who was all about having fun. Here's a personal message for young players: Use Bruce Boudreau as an example of what not to do so you don't have to live with the regrets that have haunted me. Paul Holmgren was absolutely right. My priorities were wrong, and I wasn't serious enough about the game. That's strange in light of how serious I am about the game now; my whole life is the game.

My girlfriend, Mary, visited Johnstown to see me play. That provided another way to highlight my lackadaisical attitude. She was in the stands with twelve hundred people, so she was easy to spot. I was on the bench, shouting, "Watch, honey, I'm going to score this shift." Then I'd score. Really stupid, show-off stuff.

As a coach, I'd get mad at a player who did that now. I would really flip out. Despite behaving so unprofessionally, I had almost two points a game with the Jets. The sad fact is I could have had three a game if I had really tried.

I wish I knew then what I know now. It wasn't until I became a minor-league veteran that I realized the importance of working out like a fiend and staying in great shape. It kills me that I basically wrecked my whole playing career my first year in pro hockey. I firmly believe I should have been in the NHL for many years. I ruined it by goofing off, taking everything too easily, and focusing too much on having a good time and too little on my job. It was dreadful.

The game came too easy for me, and it caught up when I turned pro. I was playing with guys who were older and were men. You had to be fit and compete hard, especially because I was a smaller player. I was a snot-nosed rookie with a big ego. That's why vets like Dave Keon didn't like me. I didn't like Keon either.

In Minnesota, Keon and Johnny McKenzie took me aside every day and said, "You're coming to lunch with us." We'd go to lunch—I'm thinking this is a great deal—but they never spoke to me once. They'd leave and make me pay the bill. That went on about four or five days in a row before I told them I wouldn't go with them anymore.

I was dumb back then. I wish to God I could change it all, but I can't. I learned too hard and too late that no matter how talented you think you are, there's no free lunch in pro hockey.

# 4

## ROGER AND ME

I signed with the Toronto Maple Leafs after my pro rookie season and thought I had a good first NHL camp to start 1976–77. I scored the first goal of the first exhibition game and led the camp tournament in scoring.

I figured I had a decent chance to make the Leafs, but I was wrong. A separated shoulder didn't help my cause. I was assigned to Toronto's minor-league affiliate in the CHL, the Dallas Black Hawks. It was there that I got to know Roger Neilson, who was extremely influential in my evolution as a hockey player and coach. Roger had the brightest hockey mind I've ever encountered. The man was brilliant, innovative, visionary.

In Dallas, Neilson was in his inaugural season as a pro coach after a ten-year run as head coach of the Peterborough Petes. Initially, it was tough to get Roger to like me. Peterborough Petes and Toronto Marlies—heated rivals—hated each other.

Roger organized an exhibition game featuring Toronto prospects likely ticketed to play in Dallas against his old Peterborough team. That's where I suffered the shoulder injury. I had to stay behind and rehab in Toronto before heading to Dallas. I played only fifty-eight games in Dallas because of my late start.

Roger wouldn't talk to me for the first three months in Dallas. I tried to get into every conversation, but he ignored me because of my Marlies heritage. When the Marlies won the OHA championship in 1972–73, we eliminated Roger's Peterborough team on a penalty shot with a minute to go.

Petes defenseman Jim Turkiewicz put his hand on the puck in the crease. A penalty shot was called, and Paulin Bordeleau scored. It tied the game, and we only needed a tie to advance. When goalie Mike Palmateer and I skated down to jump on Paulin, we looked at each other and we both were crying.

So it took a while to get Roger to talk to me. Nevertheless, I grew to like and respect him immensely.

When Roger was promoted to Toronto head coach in 1977–78, a lot of Maple Leafs players asked me what he was like. I told them he was great, fabulous, personable, a motivator. When I got the Washington head coaching job, I flashed back to that situation and wondered if the players I had in Hershey were telling the Capitals veterans good things about me.

It took me a while to get going that season, but I heated up and scored something like twenty-four goals in twenty-four games for Dallas at one point. I made my Maple Leafs debut in 1976–77 in a game against the Philadelphia Flyers. Paul Holmgren, my old roommate in Johnstown, gave me an extremely unkind welcome to the league. I had an energy role and was running around a little bit. I hit a guy and was against the boards. Paul flew in and hammered me. Then he dropped his gloves and started punching me. Holmgren got five minutes for fighting and a game misconduct. I got nothing. It ticked me off that I didn't get a chance on the ensuing power play, but I did get an assist in the game.

I was supposed to play my second game against the Buffalo Sabres, but the snow was so bad the game was postponed and they sent me back down to Dallas. I ultimately played fifteen games for Toronto that season, and it should have been at least sixteen.

I was up in Toronto near the end of the season. Dallas was playing Tulsa in the CHL playoffs. Since I was sitting out in Toronto, they asked me if I wanted to rejoin Dallas for a play-off game and then get called right back up. I went down, and we lost to Tulsa and were eliminated from the play-offs. I was supposed to fly back to Toronto the next day.

I asked Roger Neilson if I could switch from a 7:00 a.m. flight to a later flight. I didn't figure I'd play for the Leafs, who had a game that night, and I wanted to hang out with my Dallas teammates. I took a noon flight and arrived late for the game. It so happened that Stan Weir broke his finger in the pregame skate and I would have played. I got lambasted by Leafs management. Dumb mistakes like that probably made me fall out of favor with the Leafs.

In 1977–78 I played more games for Toronto (forty) than I did for Dallas (twenty-two), but it was a frustrating season. I had twenty-nine points in those forty games without playing on the power play. Darryl Sittler got all the power play time. Then Toronto called up Stan Weir (him again), who was having a strong season in the CHL with Tulsa. Weir was on a one-way contract and I was on a two-way, which helped him in the organizational pecking order. They alternated playing us, and it angered me.

In 1978–79 I never really got an NHL chance. I played twenty-six games for Toronto but spent most of the season in the AHL with New Brunswick, which had become Toronto's top minor-league affiliate. I always wanted to be a Leaf so bad that I never complained about my treatment. I never said, "Listen, I'm good enough to play here. I've done what I can do in three years in the minors. Play me or trade me." That's what kids do now.

I played just two games in Toronto in 1979–80. I jumped up to thirty-nine games in 1980–81. The Leafs always called me back because I was the kind of guy that they'd say, "Well, jeez, maybe we can get somebody better. If not, we always have Bruce Boudreau down in the minors."

I had good production in those thirty-nine games (ten goals, fourteen assists). If you combine the forty games in 1977–78 and the thirty-nine games in 1980–81, it adds up to a solid single season (fifty-three points). Those numbers are evidence to me that I could have been a credible NHL player. Bill O'Flaherty, whom I later worked with when he was director of player personnel for the Los Angeles Kings and I coached their AHL affiliate in Manchester, New Hampshire, told me my problem was that I was too slow and too small. "And, Bruce," he'd say, "that's not a good combination."

I had a reputation as an offensive player, but I learned to play pretty well defensively. In Toronto, Roger Neilson put me in defensive roles. It's one of the reasons I'm now so familiar with defensive hockey. Roger told me, "If you can't play defense, you can't play in the NHL."

I really had to study the whole concept because I didn't believe him at first. But it made sense. I covered the likes of Bobby Smith and Neil Broten; I'd shadow them all over the ice. In the last regular-season game in 1980–81, we went into Quebec and we needed a win to make the play-offs. My job was to cover high-scoring Peter Stastny. Stastny got nothing, and we beat the Nordiques. I knew I could play defense, but I didn't necessarily like it because I thought I was pretty good offensively.

Roger Neilson was a fundamental figure in my life. I get most of my coaching personality from my junior coach, George "Chief" Armstrong, and Roger Neilson. Like I said before, I learned how to treat players by watching how Chief treated us. Roger was the statistical, organized oracle. He took everything into account. You couldn't fool him at anything.

We did video when video wasn't cool. Roger invented video study for hockey. We watched it and watched it. He would stop it, and he knew when to stop it. I learned so much about how to play the game from Roger.

If you know me, you know I can't retain anything outside of hockey. Academics. Honey-do lists. I think it's a man thing. My wife, Crystal, can tell me thirty times a day to do something, and I forget it all the time because maybe I'm really not listening to her. But I retain everything related to hockey. When you're interested, you're going to retain information. Roger had an approach that was interesting, and I retained everything he said. Being with him made me an awful lot smarter about hockey.

Toronto fired Roger during the 1978–79 season, but we kept in touch. When I started my hockey school in St. Catharines, Ontario, I went to Trinity College in Toronto to study his camp. I spent a day with him to see how he did it. I followed that plan, and I still use that model for my camp more than two decades later.

Late in my playing career, I went to the Chicago Blackhawks because of Neilson. He was their co-head coach, and he recommended they sign me for 1985–86. I played my last NHL game that season.

This is the kind of organized guy Neilson was. When he had cancer, Roger wrote all his friends a good-bye letter before he died in 2003 at age sixty-nine. He wrote me one. It arrived in Manchester, and I couldn't read it. I had Crystal read it because I wouldn't have made it through reading it myself. I didn't really want to know what was in it. She might have told me some bits and pieces, but mainly I put my head in the sand and played ostrich. Roger Neilson meant so much to me, and I couldn't face the finality of his death.

●

Playing for the Maple Leafs is a fairy tale come true for a Toronto kid. From 1976–83, I played 134 regular-season games and nine play-off games for the Leafs. Though I never stuck for a full season, I treasure the memories.

If you were a popular Toronto Maple Leaf in the 1970s, you had the world by the tail. You didn't want to play in any other city. Nobody blamed the players for the bad Toronto teams. Everybody blamed owner Harold Ballard. No matter how bad we were, Ballard took the heat.

I knew Ballard didn't know me well because he always confused me with Pat Boutette. He'd see me and say, 'Hey, Boutette, Boutette.' I'd say, "No, it's Boudreau." He'd say, "Oh, yeah, yeah, Boudreau." Rumor had it that Ballard never forgave me for signing with Minnesota in the WHA after I was drafted by the Leafs.

When we were good, like in 1977–78 when we upset the New York Islanders in the Stanley Cup play-offs, the city was incredible. It was a Hollywood-type thing. You were invited to all the events.

Toronto is a tougher place today. Now everybody blames the players when the Leafs aren't good. They're quick to cut. There's a ton of media criticism. Back in the 1970s the Toronto Blue Jays were in their infancy and the Leafs were still on a pedestal.

When people ask me who was the greatest player I ever played with, I always mention two names: Darryl Sittler and Borje Salming.

Darryl Sittler was the team captain and never took the easy way out. I'll always admire him. He worked for everything and demanded the same from his teammates.

One time I had twenty-five points in twenty-one games and had either come off the ice early after practice or gone on late before practice. Darryl grabbed me by the throat and said, "Listen, you have got to stay on and work harder. That's why you're not up here full-time. I'm the best player on this team, and I work the hardest. If I'm still on the ice, you should still be on the ice." I became a better player for it.

Darryl was the big guy in Toronto, and you knew it. I stayed at his house sometimes. Darryl, Jack Valiquette, Lanny McDonald, Tiger Williams, and I all lived in the same area, so I hung out with them. I wasn't as high on the status pecking order as Darryl, Lanny, and Tiger. In that group, I sort of had the Joey Bishop role in the Rat Pack.

Borje Salming would fit into today's game so well. What a defenseman. He could block shots and control the game. I just wish he would have taken a little bit more of a leadership role. Borje was everybody's friend, but he didn't talk enough. When he talked, people listened. Borje was a classic quiet Swede and the first Swedish superstar in the NHL. Probably every Swedish player will be measured against Borje forever. I'd say he's the father of hockey in Sweden.

I roomed with Borje one night on the road, and we both slept in and missed the team flight. It was totally Borje's fault, but I shouldered the blame. Borje still played the next game. I sat for a while.

I also have tremendous respect for Lanny McDonald and Dave "Tiger" Williams.

Lanny is one of those guys you wish you could have been, a model for how everybody should act. He led the perfect life. He was a star, but he remained incredibly well-grounded and had a tremendous work ethic. An unbelievable family man. A gracious man who had no enemies.

Lanny, Jack Valiquette, and I played cards together every game day, from the team meal until 5:00 p.m. Lanny always said he needed only twenty minutes of rest to get his body ready for a game. Like clockwork at 5:00, he'd leave the card game, take his twenty-minute nap, and play a great game. Lanny and Darryl Sittler were the best of friends, but Darryl never played cards with us.

Tiger Williams. What a piece of work. What a funny guy. Tiger was the best self-made hockey player in history. He was only five foot eleven and 190 pounds, and he holds the record for the most all-time NHL penalty minutes (3,966).

I was still a Marlie when I saw Tiger the first time in training camp with the Leafs. We'd watch their camp workouts and try to learn stuff. Tiger didn't cut his hair all summer, growing it out into a big afro. Everybody else skated around in a casual warm-up before the first camp practice. Tiger, on the other hand, skated as hard as he could to the goal line and launched himself into the glass. He bounced off, fell down, shook out the cobwebs, and proceeded to do it again at the other end. It scared and intimidated the other players. That's the essence of Tiger Williams. It was the smartest thing I'd ever seen.

One summer Tiger was invited to be on ABC's *Superstars* show. On the show athletes from a variety of sports competed in a decathlon-type competition for prize money. Tiger asked me to be his trainer, which was highly ironic given my casual approach to training at the time. Tiger was an outstanding runner, and he lifted weights. When he ran, I'd sit there with a stopwatch. He never beat the time he wanted to beat, but he'd do it again and again. He worked so hard.

At one session, Tiger ran four and a half miles backward and beat Jack Valiquette and me while we ran forward. He was that fit. Tiger commanded respect, and he was a loose cannon at the same time.

One year when Tiger came into training camp, his hair was all messed up and he had scars and scrapes all over his legs and a face like he'd been run over by a truck. I asked what happened.

"I've got to tell you a story, Gabby," Tiger said. "I was on our flatbed truck. We needed some plywood for the farm, so we went down to the local lumberyard. My buddies and I piled up fifty sheets on the back of the flatbed, but we forgot to bring rope to tie it down. I told the guys, 'No problem. You guys take off, and I'll hold onto the wood.' We were doing about sixty down the road, and all of a sudden the plywood started flying and I was flying on a magic carpet. I started bouncing on the road."

Tiger Williams was afraid of nothing. We were together with our wives at a dinner party at his house. He had an extensive gun collection. By the end of the evening, he started talking about his guns and said he owned an elephant gun that was the most powerful gun known to man. Tiger was easy to egg on, so I questioned his claim about the gun and he said he would prove it.

Leafs teammate Jerry Butler lived two doors down from Tiger. Tiger got the elephant gun, took me outside, and told me to watch. Then he shot the brick chimney on Jerry's house. Took half of it out. It just exploded. We ran back into the house, and Jerry phoned two minutes later.

"I know it was you, Tiger," Jerry said.

I know it happened because I was there. But I still can't believe it happened.

When I was in Springfield in the AHL in 1987–88, Tiger played his final NHL season with my buddy John Anderson on the Hartford Whalers. The three of us had a wonderful reunion dinner at Tiger's house. I wanted to be like Tiger because he was so hardworking and dedicated. If I'd understood the ingredients he used to make himself a success, I would have played in the NHL a long time. Tiger couldn't skate. He wasn't very skilled. Yet he had three twenty-goal seasons, plus a thirty-five-goal season with Vancouver in 1980–81. He did whatever it took.

In the Maple Leafs–Islanders series in 1978, Tiger took it upon himself to run Billy Smith. He knew in order for us to win, he had to run the goalie. And running Billy Smith, who wielded a vicious stick, was taking your life into your hands. Tiger fought Dave Schultz and all comers. His face was complete leather. I deeply admired him, and it's no surprise to me that he's a smart businessman today.

Basil McRae was another tough guy I played with in Toronto and also in St. Catharines in the AHL. Big Baz was a smart tough guy who became a terrific businessman and is now a part owner of the Ontario Hockey League's London Knights. He's another guy I wish I'd listened to more.

Jack Valiquette and I were close friends in Toronto. We were famous for not being in shape. One time we decided to do the Scarsdale diet in an attempt to get more fit. We made it through breakfast fine. But our resolve quickly dissolved, and by 10:30 a.m. we were dining at a burger joint. Another time, we got memberships at a swank fitness institute. Our workouts consisted of taking a sauna and drinking Diet Coke.

I grew up with goalie Mike Palmateer. We played together in midget, Junior B, Junior A, Dallas in the Central Hockey League, and Toronto. Mike was a winner. He had success everywhere until he got traded to Washington in 1980.

Mike and I golfed all the time. Mike would play horribly and then win all the money on the eighteenth hole. He was a big name in Toronto, right up there with Borje Salming and Darryl Sittler. I admired him for never forgetting his roots. His childhood friends remained his friends. He didn't change. Mike followed the beat of his own drummer. All goalies are goofy, but he wasn't goalie goofy.

Rick Vaive never got the respect he was due in Toronto and it's unfortunate. Rick had three straight fifty-goal seasons and is the only person in Leafs history to do that. Rick never treated you like he was above you, and we hung out frequently in the summertime.

I created a team in Toronto's metro ball hockey league, which was in its infancy then. I got Rick to join the team, but then I had to ask him to quit because of his temper. My brother Bryan and Mike Palmateer's brother Jeff were on the team. We had some pro players and some junior players, and we usually won.

The problem was all these eighteen-year-old Italians we played against thought this was their Stanley Cup. They ran us and yapped at us. Their parents yelled. Rick got run and yapped at from the stands. Next thing you know, he jumped into their bench and started a big brawl.

After the game, I said, "Rick, I don't think you should be playing ball hockey anymore. You're way too high profile a guy to get into a bench brawl."

He said, "Yeah, Gabby, I think you're right. I lose it a little bit too much."

I also played with my nonbiological twin, Randy Carlyle, in Toronto and Dallas. A lot of people thought we were brothers then, and we could pass for brothers now. Roger Neilson misunderstood Randy. Randy was a great defenseman, but he was limited to secondary roles with the Leafs.

When Borje Salming was injured in the play-offs in 1977–78, Randy stepped up and did a tremendous job. Before he could develop into a full-time Maple Leaf, they traded him to Pittsburgh that year and he won the Norris Trophy in 1980–81. The Leafs traded him too soon. Randy is one of the most underrated players ever. Not too many people win the Norris Trophy. I don't think he's gotten his due as a great player.

I was happy when Randy won the Stanley Cup as Anaheim's head coach in 2006–7. I enjoy seeing old friends do well. When he was an AHL head coach in Manitoba, I wanted to beat him really bad when our teams played. It's the same when my teams play John Anderson's teams. Old friends are also your greatest rivals.

Looking at Randy now, I think he's doing something to his hair. He was balder five years ago, and now his hair looks like it's coming back. I wonder if he's into Rogaine. I don't want him to grow a full head of hair because then he'll blow me away.

# 5

## BURGER MEISTER

**My Toronto Maple Leafs ties ended in 1984.** I got a contract termination notice from the team that year. I had no idea what was happening. I didn't know anything about the fine print of qualifying contracts and stuff like that. I did re-sign with the Leafs as a free agent with the intent of being in the organization for 1984–85.

However, I had played with a guy named Slava Duris in 1981–82 in Cincinnati in the CHL, and he had since started playing for a team in Germany. I made thirty thousand dollars a year at this point. My then-wife, Mary, always said, "Why don't you go to Europe? They make a lot more money there." I never wanted to go, but Slava Duris phoned and asked if I was interested in joining his team in Iserlohn.

Iserlohn offered me a contract for a hundred thousand marks, which was roughly fifty thousand tax-free Canadian dollars. That's a big difference: I probably took home eighteen thousand dollars after Canadian taxes. I phoned Toronto's general manager, Gerry McNamara, and asked him if I could get let out of my contract to go to Europe. He magnanimously allowed it and told me I had been a good soldier for the Leafs.

I got a passport and went to Germany. I was so into hockey that I wasn't interested in any of the cultural stuff. I couldn't have cared less. One time Mary said, "Why don't we drive to Paris? It's just six hours away and we have four days off." But I wasn't interested in going to Paris. It might have been pretty ignorant, but that was my reaction.

Bavaria is a beautiful part of Germany. I was asleep while on a team train trip through there and they tried to wake me to look at the countryside. I didn't give a darn about the countryside and kept snoozing. It was all about hockey.

Mary and I had a little two-bedroom apartment. While Slava Duris lived in luxury, I was the typical Canadian kid willing to take whatever they gave me. My daughter, Kasey, had been born before we went. My son Ben was born in Germany, and I had a hand in his delivery.

They had a midwife system in a hospital setting. We went to the hospital, and they called the doctor. The midwife did all the prepping. The doctor got stuck in traffic, and Ben was having a hard time coming out. I held his head while the midwife gave Mary an apesiotomy, a procedure in which an incision is made to widen the opening. I almost fainted.

We messed up by not getting Ben dual Canadian-German citizenship. We didn't file the required papers. If we had done it, at twenty-one he could have gone over there and played hockey as a German, which is what he later wanted to do.

About the only German I learned was how to read the train schedules and how to order two hamburgers, fries, and a Coke at McDonald's. That's pretty much the only thing I've retained. The language gap taught me how difficult it is for European players when they come to North America. That's probably the best thing I learned over there, being the guy in the minority on speaking a language. That's given me empathy for the European players I've coached.

There were only two other English-speaking guys on that Iserlohn team. We used to drive forty minutes every day to the Dortman train station or the Cologne train station to get a *USA Today*. Luckily, there was a U.S. Army base in Iserlohn where we rented VHS tapes. We'd watch five or six movies a day because there wasn't any English TV. I did watch *Magnum P.I.* in German to try to pick up some of the language. We also played Scrabble a lot. That was the routine: hockey, movies, Scrabble, McDonald's.

I had a pretty good year—produced forty-seven points in twenty-nine games—but that wasn't enough hockey for me. Back then, a player could come back to the AHL as late as the middle of February. The Baltimore Skipjacks, affiliated with the Pittsburgh Penguins, wanted to sign me for the rest of the season. I signed a one-year NHL contract with Pittsburgh with an option for another at thirty thousand dollars.

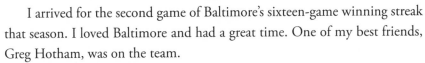

I arrived for the second game of Baltimore's sixteen-game winning streak that season. I loved Baltimore and had a great time. One of my best friends, Greg Hotham, was on the team.

Greg was the straight man and I was the funny guy. He was so quiet that after a year of playing with him you might not know he existed. We lived together in Cincinnati. He was just a treat to be around. We went to the CHL All-Star Game in Salt Lake City in 1981–82, and we had the same agent, Bill Watters. Bill phoned us and said we were both going to be traded by Toronto. We were excited because a trade meant the chance to play in the NHL again. Greg was traded to Pittsburgh, and nothing happened with me, which was par for the course. I was really disappointed.

We had a strong AHL team in Baltimore that included Tom Roulston, Tim Tookey, Marty McSorley, and Jon Casey. McSorley, whom I also later played with in Nova Scotia in the AHL, was nicknamed "Magic" for his ability to think he was good. Marty would get the puck and try to wheel and deal, and the guys would derisively call him "Magic."

Marty would proclaim how good he was and we'd all chuckle at him, but he worked hard enough to make it and he made it big in the NHL. He was as big and strong as they come. I give him full credit for saying he was going to do something and then actually doing it. We laughed at him, but he got the last laugh because he was willing to pay the price. Marty made it and most of us didn't.

We eliminated Rochester and Binghamton to reach the Calder Cup finals, where we were favored to beat a Sherbrooke club that was sub-.500 in the regular season. But Sherbrooke had a young goalie named Patrick Roy getting his first taste of pro hockey. He was just nineteen and had joined the team after his junior season with Granby in the Quebec Major Junior Hockey League ended. We lost in six games in Roy's first exhibition of clutch pro play-off performance.

Baltimore's coach, Gene Ubriaco, who'd later coach Mario Lemieux in Pittsburgh, had a good influence on me. I still use some drills I learned from him. He was a smart guy. A little wild behind the bench, though.

That summer I declined the option to stick with Pittsburgh, and the Chicago Blackhawks (via Roger Neilson) offered me a contract. Chicago shared an AHL affiliation in Nova Scotia with the Edmonton Oilers. I signed a two-year deal with the Blackhawks to play and also be their liaison in Nova Scotia because Edmonton supplied the coaching staff. I was assigned to report back to Chicago on how its prospects were playing.

I played seven games for the Blackhawks that season. One of the reasons I was called up was because Denis Savard was hurt. Denis was a really nice guy. He came off the ice during a game in St. Louis because his skate was undone. I jumped out to take his place for a face-off, and they hovered around a little bit. That gave Denis time to get his laces tied, and they pulled me off the ice. That might have been my only partial shift of the whole game. Denis apologized after the game. He said he had his head down. If he'd known I was out there, he said, he would have let me take the full shift. It made me feel good that he thought that. Other than that I don't remember much about Denis. I hung out with Jim Ralph, Rick Paterson, and Bob Murray.

I played my last NHL game with Chicago in Chicago Stadium. I got one shift. The game before that I got one shift. The game before that at Vancouver, I got one shift and one goal—and that shift was only eight seconds long. I jumped onto the ice on a line change, and Al Secord took the puck behind the net. The Canucks were getting a penalty. I crossed in front of the net, Secord passed, and I scored. That was my last NHL goal, my last NHL point.

I never thought that last NHL game would be my last NHL game. The rest of my playing career was spent in the AHL and the IHL.

The final NHL totals for the Toronto Marlies hotshot who once thought he should go first in the draft: 141 games, 28 goals, 42 assists.

●

I played in a dozen cities in North America as a minor leaguer. Johnstown, Dallas, New Brunswick, Cincinnati, St. Catharines, Baltimore, Nova Scotia, Springfield, Newmarket, Phoenix, Fort Wayne, Adirondack. Call me a Rand McNally on skates. Throw in Germany and maybe I qualify as a World Atlas too.

In Dallas, where I played from 1976 to 1978, Roger Neilson scheduled practices at 9:00 a.m. Dallas is a fun town when you're in your early twenties. Given the late hours we kept, we obviously didn't want to practice that early. Our older guys asked Roger to start practices later so we could get more sleep.

He agreed. See, Roger wanted to practice early, watch his video, and play golf in the afternoon. Roger liked intense two-hour practices. If anybody griped, his answer shut them up: It's only two hours; everybody else works eight hours a day.

We played in the fairgrounds by the Cotton Bowl and averaged about 3,500 spectators a game. Fort Worth was our biggest rival. Because of a shoulder injury and Toronto recalls, I only played eighty total games in Dallas over two seasons and recorded ninety-three points.

Mary and I got married in 1978 and went to New Brunswick starting in 1978–79. I played for the Moncton-based New Brunswick Hawks in the AHL from 1978 to 1981. Moncton is a French-English town, so there was a lot of French-language stuff I didn't understand. The people treated us great.

The second year in Moncton, Mary and I lived with Jimmy Jones and Mark Kirton. We were Toronto's three depth centermen. Anytime somebody was called up, there was a big fight in our house. Two guys hated it, one guy liked it.

The Chicago Blackhawks also were affiliated with New Brunswick. Darryl Sutter, Rick Paterson, Ron Wilson, and goalie Murray Bannerman were among the Chicago guys on the team. Sutter, Paterson, Wilson, Toronto prospect Joel Quenneville, and I all became NHL head coaches.

Rick Paterson is the salt of the earth—one of my best friends. He made it for seven years in Chicago as a penalty killer. He just worked his rear end off and got along with everybody.

I never imagined Darryl Sutter would become the major hockey figure he did. Darryl was always a little grumpy. He was a pure goal scorer. He wasn't a physical player, but he competed really hard. To see him transform into a really tough coach, though—I didn't see that coming. Darryl was a competitive, determined bugger who hated to lose, and he has done so well for himself. I know Chicago management loved him.

Joel Quenneville was always smart in the way he played and the way he talked. Joel was one of the boys, but he was the one of the boys who had common sense. If somebody had plans to do something stupid, he was the one who cautioned against it. When Joel went to St. John's in the AHL as a player–assistant coach, you could see he was being groomed under Marc

Crawford and was going to someday be a head coach. Ron Wilson, who coached Washington to the 1998 Stanley Cup finals, has a personality that can be off-putting if you don't know him. But I know him, like him, and understand where he's coming from. He was as skilled as can be and also cerebral, analytical, and sarcastic. I got along well with him because I was one of the better players, but he was hard on guys who weren't up to snuff in talent. You knew that if he wanted to coach he had the ability to do it.

Ron didn't know if he wanted to play defense or forward. He could stickhandle like a magician and make plays with the best of them. But on defense he wasn't physical enough, so they moved him to forward. Great power play guy.

The smartest thing Ron did, when he realized he wasn't going to make it in the NHL, was go to Switzerland and become the most dominant player in Europe in the 1980s. He made good money. A guy like me was stubborn and wanted to play in North America.

In a foreshadowing of my chocolate-flavored future, New Brunswick lost to the Hershey Bears in the 1979–80 Calder Cup finals. In the regular season, Hershey was a sub-.500 team that we beat six times in a row. We were a strong, confident team that should have won the Calder Cup. We were a much better team than Hershey, but sometimes that doesn't matter. The Bears won two games in double overtime and claimed the series in six games.

In 1980–81, defenseman Jack O'Callahan and goalie Bob Janecyk from the 1980 U.S. Olympic team were New Brunswick teammates. I didn't get to know either one of them as well as I should have.

It's funny how the 1980 Olympics are bigger now than they were in 1980, at least to me. I didn't realize how big a miracle it was until years later when it finally dawned on me that these college kids played against a bunch of fabulous Russians who played at the highest level in the world.

Janecyk, Jim Craig's backup on the Olympic team, was a nice, quiet guy. He didn't play much in New Brunswick because he was behind Murray Bannerman, who would become the No. 1 goalie in Chicago. Jack O'Callahan was a fun-loving guy who smiled a lot. He was a pretty good right-handed defenseman. He got beat one-on-one a little bit but was solid.

In Cincinnati in the CHL in 1981–82, my then-wife, Mary, went home during the season because she wanted to give birth to our daughter, Kasey, in Canada. I had my first hundred-point season as a pro for the Cincinnati Tigers. Forty-two goals, sixty-one assists, 103 points. I had a chance to win the league scoring title, but I was happy when the Maple Leafs called me up. I needed ten games to qualify for my NHL pension, and it was classy of them to bring me up for a dozen games. I didn't play well, and that was really my last kick at the can with Toronto.

I didn't play any regular-season games for Toronto in 1982–83. My four play-off games that season were my last in a Toronto uniform. I lost the 1981–82 CHL scoring championship to Bobby Francis, but I got my NHL pension. That amounts to the grand total of $212 a month for the rest of my life.

The Leafs changed their farm team from Cincinnati to St. Catharines in 1982–83. It's fifty miles from Toronto, so we bought our first house in St. Catharines and I started my summer hockey school in 1981. All my kids call St. Catharines home. In two seasons with the St. Catharines Saints (1982–84), I totaled 231 points. In 1982–83 I had career highs in goals (50) and points (122), but Ross Yates beat me for the AHL scoring championship.

After spending 1984–85 in Germany and Baltimore, I played for Nova Scotia in the AHL from 1985 to 1987. It got to be frustrating as a Chicago Blackhawks–contracted player and club liaison in a dual affiliation with Edmonton. Larry Kish, the Edmonton-employed head coach, would play only the Oilers players.

Esa Tikkanen was there for fifteen games. He used snus, a muddy kind of chewing tobacco, and he'd take a syringe and shoot the stuff up in his top cheek. I couldn't believe it the first time I saw it. He'd tell Larry Kish what his on-ice assignments would be, and he'd put himself on the power play. Esa thought he was in total control. He was a high-maintenance guy, but he was a disturber who could play. I think he was down from Edmonton because Glen Sather was punishing him for doing something stupid.

Ron Low was Kish's assistant and also played six games in goal. Larry Kish didn't give Ron a lot to do, which was maybe a mistake because Ron ended up being an NHL head coach. I rode the stationary bike with him an awful lot the two years I was in Nova Scotia. Ron told me how hard he had to work for it, and he'd stay on that bike for hours at a time.

As a goalie, Ron gave me a tip that stuck with me. He hated a drill where the goalie stood stationary in the net while players took warm-up shots. Because of that, I have my goalies move from side to side in warm-up drills instead of standing still.

We didn't make the playoffs in 1985–86. In 1986–87 we had Murray Eaves, Alfie Turcotte, Don Biggs, and me. In AHL history, you tell me where a team had four better offensive players. Biggs, Eaves, and I all produced multiple hundred-point seasons in the AHL. And Turcotte was a first-round pick. It was an underachieving team. We should have won a Calder Cup. Instead, we finished fourth and were eliminated in the first round of the play-offs.

# 6

# MELROSE PLACE

**I turned thirty-two in 1987** and was more than a decade into my career. I still thought I could play in the NHL, but I became more interested in making good money in the minors. A one-way minor-league contract, if you're willing to accept it, tends to pay more than the minor-league end of a two-way NHL contract.

Originally I agreed to re-sign for 1987–88 on a two-way with Chicago, which was pulling out of its dysfunctional dual affiliation in Nova Scotia and putting its prospects in Saginaw, Michigan, in the IHL. But I reneged on that agreement to sign an AHL-only deal with Springfield. Springfield's offer was for $40,000 American in base salary and Chicago's offer was for $35,000 Canadian at the minor-league end of the two-way.

Springfield general manager Bruce Landon, who has become one of my closest friends, relentlessly pursued me. Bruce lobbied me hard on the golf course one day. I kept saying no because I already had agreed to the deal with Chicago. Well, Landon had a persuasive round. I had to tell the Blackhawks I changed my mind and was signing a two-year deal with Springfield for 1987–89.

With Springfield, I could make $46,000 each season if I achieved all my scoring bonuses. If you put a bonus in front of me, it was a terrific carrot. I would kill to reach a bonus, and I got all my bonuses in Springfield.

I won the AHL scoring championship for the Springfield Indians in 1987–88 (116 points). Springfield was affiliated with the New York Islanders, but I was on that AHL-only deal. That meant I got passed over when the Islanders called up guys, even though I was by far the team's leading scorer. I was really bothered when they called up Todd McLellan, who finished that season with seventy-two fewer points than I had. McLellan later coached Houston to an AHL championship in 2002–3, three years before I did the same thing in Hershey, and eventually became head coach of the San Jose Sharks.

In 1988–89 in Springfield, Mary decided she couldn't move anymore and she stayed in St. Catharines. That was the beginning of the end for the marriage. Stuart Burnie and I lived in an apartment, and Mary visited with the kids every couple of weeks. Mary knew at that point she wasn't going to be able to continue as a hockey wife. Hockey wives have tough lives. We'd moved twenty-something times in ten years. She wanted the house and the white picket fence.

That's one of the reasons that, for the the first time in my career, I asked to get traded. Springfield was down in the standings. I led the team in scoring, but the head coach, Jimmy Roberts, wanted to play all the kids. Thus, I asked to get traded to the AHL's Newmarket Saints. Newmarket is close to St. Catharines, which allowed me to be closer to my family.

It didn't go as well as I wanted the rest of 1988–89 in Newmarket. I had twenty-three points in twenty games, but we lost in the first round of the play-offs. I didn't have an agent, and it got hectic trying to find a team for 1989–90 as a thirty-four-year-old.

I signed with Saginaw in the IHL for thirty thousand dollars as a player–assistant coach. It turned into a mess when I arrived in August. Saginaw had no players signed and no NHL affiliate. It was going to be a horrible team. Then the club folded. It was the end of August and suddenly I didn't have a hockey job. I was beside myself. I thought I was involuntarily retired.

Mary wanted me to quit. Her sister wrote up a résumé for me, and I applied to be the director of city operations for St. Catharines. A pretty big title. There were 250 applicants, but my résumé made me look like I was the prime minister of something. I was one of the final three candidates.

A guy named Jim Brady, who was a Junior A lacrosse coach in St. Catharines, did the hiring. Brady was a sports-oriented guy, which probably helped me reach the final three and get an interview. But it was the first job

interview of my life. I had no idea what I was talking about. I was the stupidest
guy. Brady must have shaken his head after I left. I didn't get a call back. Had
I gotten that job, hockey would have been done. The way life turns.

It was now around September 10, and I was really sweating. Adam Keller,
general manager of the IHL's Phoenix Roadrunners, asked me to play for
him. They offered $25,000. I'd dropped about $20,000 in salary from the
previous season; that's definitely going in the wrong direction. I had a wife
and three kids and a measly $25,000 offer, but I had to take it.

To pocket extra money, I didn't join the Pro Hockey Players' Association.
Each team has to pay the PHPA, the union for minor-league players, for each
member player. So Phoenix gave me the money it would have had to pay if
I'd joined. I brought a pair of extra skates and grabbed an extra $250 because
the Roadrunners didn't have to buy me skates. We used Air Canada miles to
travel between Phoenix and St. Catharines. I got a crappy little apartment.
The Boudreaus were a low-budget operation.

Mary agreed to come to Arizona, and our daughter, Kasey, started first
grade in Phoenix. I had a good 1989–90 season, leading the club in scoring
with forty-one goals and sixty-eight assists. Phoenix is a fabulous city. Jim
McGeough was my left winger. I'd flip pucks up, and he'd outrace everybody.
He'd get three chances a game, he'd score one, and I'd get the assist. Our team
was lousy, though. We won just twenty-seven of eighty-two games.

Garry Unger was the head coach. As nice a guy as you're going to find, but
maybe the worst coach you'll ever see in sports. He would sit on the boards—
it was really funny—and go through a book looking for new practice drills.
There was no concept of organization. Unger would come to practice five
minutes before it started, riding his motor bike right into the dressing room.
Garry had an outstanding NHL playing career, but at that point he had no
clue as a coach.

Wayne Gretzky's younger brother Keith, a career minor leaguer, was on
the team. I didn't get the sense that he really wanted to be a hockey player.
Keith has become a heck of a scout, but I never had the impression he wanted
to stay in the game. He was skilled, but he was physically slight and didn't
really like the rough stuff, as none of us did. He didn't have Wayne's drive,
and I can't imagine how tough it was playing in the shadow of his brother.

Mary went home during the season. I drove straight to St. Catharines after the season ended and surprised her. Her first reaction: "What are you doing here?" I pretty well knew it was up. When I signed a deal with Fort Wayne in the IHL for 1990–91, she filed for divorce to end a thirteen-year marriage. I'd meet my second wife, Crystal, in Fort Wayne. Fortunately for me, she understands the whole vagabond hockey life.

●

The end of my marriage was heartbreaking, but a rewarding 1990–91 season with the Fort Wayne Komets in the IHL helped offset some of the pain. I reunited with my best friend, John Anderson, my old teammate from our Toronto Marlies days.

John started a year behind me with the Marlies. He never drank. He never partied. He was pretty religious. I was pretty well the opposite. Sometimes you look around a room, though, and sense you're going to like a guy. That's the way it was with John and me. When we played in Dallas in the CHL together, I assisted on his first pro goal and sort of showed him the ropes. When John and I got called up to Toronto, I assisted on his first NHL goal.

We were road roommates in Toronto, and we always remained friends. We drifted apart a little bit when John went to the Hartford Whalers and I was in the minors. In Fort Wayne, we became really tight again and have been close ever since.

John became an extremely successful head coach with the Chicago Wolves, first in the IHL and then in the AHL when the Wolves were one of six franchises absorbed by the AHL in 2001 after the IHL folded. Anderson's Wolves won two Turner Cups and two Calder Cups.

Having John around is sort of like having a childhood friend I grew up with. We've helped each other along the way, whether it be marital problems or hockey situations. We've been there for each other, and I'm sure we'll always be there for each other.

After a thirteen-year NHL career with Toronto, Quebec, and Hartford, John Anderson played in Italy in 1989–90. He was fed up with playing, but I talked him into playing for Fort Wayne in 1990–91. I told him I knew better than anybody that down deep he still loved hockey. "Hey," I said, "if it's the last year for both of us, we'll have a lot of fun together." Plus, with my life in divorce turmoil, I needed him. John got a $28,000 contract, higher than my $27,000 deal, but I had the bigger apartment.

I knew none of the Komets except for John. Lonnie Loach played on a line with John and me. Best line I ever played on. Lonnie, John, and I were as tight as you could be, and it was the most enjoyable season I ever had as a player. Loach won the IHL scoring championship. Usually, if I dug my teeth in, there was nobody on a team who would beat me in scoring. I tried hard to get ahead of Lonnie, who could skate like the wind. He had a fabulous year and finished with 131 points to my 120.

The Komets were a lot like the 2007–8 Washington Capitals. We were an independent team that wasn't supposed to accomplish much. But we went to the Turner Cup finals and lost to Peoria, a strong team that won nineteen in a row during the regular season. We took Peoria to six games before losing.

Loach, Anderson, and I were one-two-three in league scoring when John suffered a charley horse injury. He was sidelined until we trailed the Peoria series 3-0, and then he made a miracle comeback. John hadn't skated in six weeks, but he took the morning skate before Game 4 and told head coach Al Sims he wanted to play.

We won at home to stay alive. John scored three goals in the first thirty minutes before his leg gave out again. He also played without a helmet against my advice. I bet that storybook performance is the No. 1 thing Fort Wayne fans remember in their hockey history.

We bused to Peoria after Game 4. It was clear John wasn't going to be able to play Game 5. I joked that it would be neat if I could match his hat trick in Game 5 and keep us going. Sure enough, I scored three goals in the third period, and we won. The magic ran out in Game 6, and Peoria took the series 4-2. John moved to New Haven in the AHL the next season.

I spent the 1991–92 season in Fort Wayne before ending my playing career with Adirondack in the AHL. I led the Komets in play-off scoring, but we were eliminated in the first round by Kalamazoo. At that time, AHL rules allowed IHL players to join AHL teams when their season ended.

Barry Melrose, Adirondack's head coach, wanted high-scoring Colin Chin to join his team from Fort Wayne for the Calder Cup play-offs. Chin didn't want to go. My friend Melrose, who had been a teammate in Cincinnati, St. Catharines, and Toronto, asked me to come instead.

I didn't join the Red Wings until the second round of the Calder Cup play-offs. In my first Adirondack game, I played with Kelly Hurd and Lonnie Loach, two former Fort Wayne teammates. I scored a goal on my first shift, and we swept Springfield. There was a twelve-day break between that series and Adirondack's next series against Rochester. I waited ten days. By that time, the Detroit Red Wings, Adirondack's parent team, ended their season and assigned Mike Sillinger and Keith Primeau to the AHL.

Bryan Murray, who like me has coached the Hershey Bears and Washington Capitals, was Detroit's general manager. Melrose wanted to play me, but Murray said he didn't want a thirty-seven-year-old playing instead of his younger prospects.

I said, "Barry, I'm not going to play. If you need me, I'll come back."

I missed my kids, so I went home to St. Catharines. I left with Barry's blessing. I kept in touch and sent telegrams of good luck, but I didn't play in the Rochester series or the Calder Cup finals against St. John's.

Adirondack won the Calder Cup. I didn't get a ring. However, those four postseason games I played—one goal, one assist—got my name on the Calder Cup as a player. I rank eleventh in all-time AHL points (799) and eleventh in all-time assists (483), and was honored with the league's Fred T. Hunt Memorial Award for sportsmanship, determination, and dedication to hockey in 1987–88. Yet that brief Adirondack stint is how my name got carved on the league's silver grail. Go figure.

I keep a picture of Barry Melrose in my house. Every time I see Barry, we have a good time. I got him to come to the ECHL All-Star Game when I coached in Mississippi. When I coached in Manchester, I got Barry, the poster boy for mullet hairdos, to appear at our popular mullet night promotions.

When Barry was traded from Winnipeg to Toronto in 1980–81, I got called up from New Brunswick the same day. Barry was introduced to his new Maple Leafs teammates, but we didn't say hi to each other. I don't know why. We got into a fight at his first Leafs practice. It might have been the only practice fight of my whole career. It was more Barry fighting me and everybody breaking it up. There were no real punches thrown. We apologized after and found out that we liked each other.

We were in Cincinnati and St. Catharines together while Barry was back and forth with Toronto. He played that mugging, I'll-do-anything-for-you style. He was a country bumpkin from Saskatchewan. He was big and strong, and that was the era for big and strong. Barry would fight anybody; he wouldn't win any fights, but he'd fight anybody.

When I bought my first house in St. Catharines, my first wife, Mary, couldn't be there after the closing. Barry and I bought a bottle of champagne, went to the house, sat on the carpet, and christened the house.

Barry is one of those good friends you rarely see, but when you run across each other you get right back to where you were. He's evolved. He's a big name. Because he coached the Los Angeles Kings, he deals in a different culture than I do. I never knew what I would see when Barry was on ESPN. He had so many different looks. Some nights with that goatee he looked like Colonel Sanders. And he's the one guy in the world who shouldn't talk about my suits because he wore the same dang suit every week.

Despite closing in on age thirty-eight, I felt confident about landing a contract for 1992–93. It turned out, though, that I played my last game for Barry Melrose.

# 7

## COACH BOUDREAU

**From the minute I knew I wasn't going to be** a regular in the NHL, my goal was to become a coach. I wasn't comfortable with the idea of doing anything outside hockey. Frankly, I never believed I was capable of doing anything outside hockey.

The *Toronto Sun* did an article about my coaching ambition when I played in Newmarket. From 1979–80 onward, I was either the captain or player–assistant coach on all of my teams. I groomed myself for coaching the last eight years I played. I was player–assistant coach in Cincinnati. I was head coach Doug Carpenter's player–assistant coach for two years in St. Catharines. I was a player–assistant coach both seasons in Fort Wayne. As a liaison for Chicago for two years in Nova Scotia, I wasn't technically an assistant coach, but I was the Blackhawks' representative on the team.

That said, I looked toward the 1992–93 season confident that I'd still be playing. Call it delusional, but during the previous season in Fort Wayne it was still in the back of my mind that an NHL club might call me up. I produced 313 points my final three seasons as a player, and I thought it would never end. My goal was to play as long as Gordie Howe. I thought I could play until I was fifty. I wanted to do things nobody had done before. If I couldn't do it at the NHL level, I planned to do something noteworthy at the minor-league level.

I had begun going to the NHL draft the year before, just to see and be seen. I went to the draft again in Montreal in 1992 with my friend John Anderson. I was upset that I hadn't been re-signed by Fort Wayne. I worried that the Komets wouldn't re-sign me, despite the fact I'd had eighty-four points in 1991–92. I didn't have any interviews set for coaching jobs in Montreal. Our objective was just to go and mingle. I ended up meeting Larry Gordon, owner of the IHL's Cleveland Lumberjacks.

Gordon relocated his IHL franchise from Muskegon, Michigan, to Cleveland in 1992. But he was putting a Colonial Hockey League team in Muskegon to fill the void, and he wanted to know if I'd coach there. He initially asked me to serve as player–assistant coach, but I wasn't interested.

Gordon came back the next day and offered me $32,000 to be head coach. Since I had made $27,000 the year before, this was a huge raise. One of the Muskegon co-owners owned a travel agency, so the contract also included an end-of-season trip of my choice to the Bahamas, Florida, or Hawaii. And a company car. Well, I retired as a player and agreed to become head coach of the expansion Muskegon Fury.

The afternoon I took the job, I visited my friend Barry Melrose, who was starting his first season as head coach of the Los Angeles Kings, in his Montreal hotel room. Barry gave me good advice on the differences between playing and coaching and offered to help me anytime he could. I still use some Melrose drills. One thing I've taken from Barry is the idea of emotion. He's an emotional coach and knows the right words to say. He really works on players' emotions. I do that to a certain extent too.

When Fort Wayne management made a big splash about my new job, I realized they'd had no plans to re-sign me. By retiring, I let them off the hook. They didn't have to go through the bad press of cutting loose one of their most popular players.

●

Boy, your first year coaching, when you come from being a player, you don't have a clue. I thought I knew hockey. We sit there as players and say we can coach because we know hockey. In reality, there's much more to being a coach than you think: recruiting players, getting affiliates, longer work hours. I had no idea what I was doing.

I quickly learned that minor-league marketing was almost like pro wrestling marketing. Building hype against another city puts people in the seats. I raided this guy Paul Kelly from the Brantford Smoke, a Colonial

League club located in Wayne Gretzky's hometown. The general manager of the Brantford team called me every name in the book, so I responded by calling him every name in the book and challenging his team. When we went to Brantford, we sold out; when Brantford came to Muskegon, we sold out. Hey, I realized, people eat up this kind of stuff.

Getting players to come to Muskegon was tough. The lying you almost have to do in recruiting is sort of comical. But I got the Los Angeles Kings as one of our affiliates. We also had the Pittsburgh Penguins as an affiliate through the Cleveland Lumberjacks connection, and the Fort Wayne Komets as an affiliate through my old ties to the club.

As Muskegon's head coach, I was invited to Cleveland's training camp. This was my introduction to Scotty Bowman, who was coming off the 1991–92 Stanley Cup as head coach of the Penguins with Mario Lemieux. I was allowed to sit in on meetings about their players. There I was, with Barry Smith, Scotty Bowman, and the Cleveland coach, Rick Paterson. I sat there in awe of Bowman.

When Scotty talked, he didn't make obvious points about whether a player was a terrific skater or had a great shot or stuff like that. He always had insightful comments. "I really liked the way he didn't turn away in the corners. I liked his positioning because he never left the front of the net." It left me thinking, Wow, this is why he's a hockey genius. I absorbed those things. I look for characteristics like that when I assess players because of Bowman.

When Scotty later became head coach of the Detroit Red Wings, I phoned once and told him I was having a hard time matching lines on the road. I asked him how he did it. The first bit of advice he gave me was to change lines every whistle because home teams don't like changing lines every whistle. He also told me to go out slow on line changes and face-offs all the time; slowing down the game helps take the home crowd out of the game. I still try to do that, though rules changes adopted since then make it a bit harder.

As a first-year head coach, I learned I wasn't a player anymore. I went out a couple times with the players, but they treat you differently when you're the coach. You're not one of the boys anymore. I backed off and stopped doing that. As much as you want the players to play for you and like you, it's a different feeling altogether.

We went 28-27-5 in the regular season in Muskegon in 1992–93 and lost in the first round of the play-offs. Marc Saumier was an excellent player for that level, which was akin to Single-A in baseball. Brett Seguin was a first-year player for LA and had a good minor-league career.

I recruited Doug Shedden, who had played in the NHL for many years. Doug was a teammate in Newmarket. He called me fifteen games into the season and told me he wanted to play. I invited him and let him live with me. Since I had a company car, I gave him my extra car. I bent over backward to get him because I knew he'd be one of our better players.

Halfway through the season, Shedden got a call from Wichita to coach in the Central Hockey League. I told him to do it. Then he made me angry by trying to recruit some of my players to go to Wichita. That was pretty dastardly. To give him the benefit of the doubt, I decided maybe he was ignorant of protocol because he was new at coaching too. But I stayed mad at him for years, and it eventually fueled a great East Coast Hockey League rivalry when I was in Mississippi and he was in Louisiana.

It's my belief that in the minors you have to have an identifiable player who becomes your marquee player for marketing purposes. In Muskegon, I targeted goaltender Chris Clifford for that role. He played in Muskegon and Saginaw in the IHL for years and was a popular guy in the town. But Clifford played horribly. Couldn't stop a beach ball. So much for that experiment.

I had another bad experience when I was dumb enough to let the team drink on a long bus trip from Muskegon to Thunder Bay. That's a fourteen-hour ride. The drinking started when we left at 8:00 a.m. After about seven hours, the players were smashed. It was extremely embarrassing. I stewed about the behavior and did everything I could not to say a word. I'd allowed it, right?

We were a game under .500 with two games left in the regular season, but we won the last two to finish over .500. We lost our first two first-round play-off games at Thunder Bay, and we lost Game 3 at home to go down 0-3. I don't know where it came from, but I got really passionate about not getting swept. We won Game 4 and Game 5. I focused on the ability to persevere in my pregame speech for Game 5, and it hit a nerve and motivated the players. I didn't know I had that kind of speaking ability until I started coaching. I was always a fairly passionate player, but I was never a vociferous locker-room guy. After that speech, the players jumped up and shouted, "Yeah!" I had said something that touched their nerves, and they couldn't wait to get on the ice. They showed mental toughness by winning 5-0 because the reward was to go on that long trip back to Thunder Bay still facing long odds.

We returned to Thunder Bay—no drinking on this bus ride—and won Game 6 in overtime 7-6 to force Game 7. We lost 5-4 in Game 7, but I was really proud of the group. I had learned as a coach how to inspire people to be greater together as a team than they were as individuals.

I chose Hawaii for my end-of-season trip and watched Barry Melrose coach Wayne Gretzky and the Los Angeles Kings in the Stanley Cup finals against Montreal from a tropical perch. But before that I went back to Fort Wayne to help as an assistant. Claude Noel, Dayton's head coach in the ECHL, also came aboard, and we helped Al Sims, my old head coach. In 2006 Claude and I faced off in the Calder Cup finals when he was Milwaukee's head coach—Noel won the Calder Cup in 2004 with Milwaukee—and I was Hershey's head coach. Noel also was on that Hershey team that beat our New Brunswick team in the 1980 Calder Cup finals.

Fort Wayne won the Turner Cup, and Al Sims got a job as an assistant coach with the NHL's Anaheim Mighty Ducks. I got an interview for his job and owner–general manager David Franke hired me. I was delighted to be able to make such a quick coaching jump to the IHL, a Triple-A league like the AHL. I now made $45,000 a year. With a car and bonuses, it was the most I'd made in my life. I thought I was rich.

Al Sims was a popular coach in Fort Wayne. I had the tough task of following somebody who had won a championship. The standards were high for the Fort Wayne Komets under the David and Michael Franke ownership. In North American pro hockey, only the NHL's Original Six teams and the AHL's Hershey Bears have played longer under the same name in the same city than the Fort Wayne Komets.

We had an excellent first season in 1993–94. We went 41-29-0 in the

regular season and advanced to the Turner Cup finals before losing to Atlanta
in six games. We would have beaten Atlanta, but we lost three players,
including thirty-plus-goal scorers Colin Chin and Mitch Messier, to injuries
in Game 5. I was named IHL Coach of the Year. David Franke told me I'd
earned my coaching stripes. Then he fired me in 1994–95, a season in which
labor-management strife led to a shortened NHL season.

We were an independent team with no NHL affiliation, so we got none
of the younger NHL players who were sent to their minor-league affiliates to
play because of the lockout. The Komets simply were outmanned in talent
and started the season 0-6 after going 0-5 in the preseason.

I got booed at home at the Allen County War Memorial Coliseum.
That hasn't happened in any town before or since because I've been a pretty
popular coach wherever I've gone. Ownership didn't know how to handle it.
The Frankes fired me when we were 15-21. They asked my old teammate,
Colin Chin, to take over. Chin was the team captain but was out for the
season with a knee injury. Colin felt uncomfortable about it, but I told him
to take the job.

Chin was the best captain I ever saw. Granted, I was usually the captain.
Colin was a tremendous leader. He paid the price. He blocked shots and
could score. And he kept the team together. He's one of those guys like Dave
Steckel or Boyd Gordon who nobody notices, but when they're on your team
you appreciate them so much. Chin was the most popular guy in Fort Wayne.

The firing did and didn't take me by surprise. I'm always a worrywart.
If I lose three games in a row, I think I'm going to get fired. But they pulled
the trigger after I held a two-hour practice and did a lot of teaching. Thus,
I was surprised to see Michael and David Franke sitting in my office when
I finished. I was really hurt when they said they were letting me go, though
now we're good friends again. I went home and cried all day.

I was fired on January 10, 1995, the day before the NHL lockout ended.
I did a lot of scouting all over the place on my own dime to be visible, show
people you're out there, get the sympathy vote for being fired. I stayed out of
Fort Wayne because I was embarrassed. I thought I was a failure.

Then I got an assistant coach–assistant general manager job with Jean
Perron with the San Francisco Spiders in the IHL. Perron won the Stanley

Cup in 1985–86 as head coach of the Montreal Canadiens with rookie goalie Patrick Roy, who backstopped his team to the NHL title the year after he and Sherbrooke beat our Baltimore club in the Calder Cup finals. After a twenty-minute meeting, Perron said to me, "I've heard great things about you. I'm offering you a deal." Two years at $65,000 per year. Tremendous money.

Crystal and I got married in Fort Wayne that summer. Immediately after the wedding, we drove thirty-six straight hours to San Francisco. We got there right before the IHL dispersal draft. Perron showed me the list of players he had signed. I asked, "Do you want me to be honest? Or do you want me to be the good soldier? These guys all stink." He let me do a lot of the drafting since I was familiar with IHL personnel.

Perron told me he wanted to coach for only one more year because he wanted to become an NHL general manager. I figured maybe that would leave an opening for me to ultimately step up to head coach in San Francisco. It was a nice situation and a nice place to be—except for the fact that I got fired three games into the season. Yeah, 1995 was a trying year in my life. Fired in Fort Wayne and fired in San Francisco. I thought I'd never work in hockey again.

I'm still baffled by the whole Jean Perron episode. We thought we were going to be pretty good in 1995–96. The first game gave a good indication that we weren't. Los Angeles beat us 5-1 before a sellout crowd at the Cow Palace. The team spent a hundred thousand dollars on fireworks and entertainment for a season-opening extravaganza, and we got smoked.

We lost the next game to Minnesota in overtime. Our third game was in Utah. We led in the third period before they tied it with about forty seconds left. I asked Jean if he wanted to call a timeout. Perron called a timeout, but all the players came over to me for guidance. I told them to ask Jean. I knew this wasn't good for Jean's pride or my situation. That I had made a slight adjustment in our trap at second intermission, when Jean wasn't in the room, also added to the confusion and tension.

We traveled home to San Francisco after losing, and Perron phoned me at 7:30 the next morning. He told me he didn't want me to come to the rink anymore. I was stunned.

"You don't like the trap, and you're coaching against me," he said. "We can't have that."

"Whoa," I replied, "what are you talking about?"

"Don't come to the rink," he repeated. "You'll get your full pay. For the next two years, you stay at home."

I was dumbfounded. I phoned the owner and the general manager; they didn't know I'd been fired. Jean made the decision arbitrarily. The president and the owner tried to get me back on the team to no avail. Washington Capitals great Rod Langway replaced me, becoming player–assistant coach. Langway was thirty-eight and past his prime as a defenseman, but Perron thought he could still play and signed him. From the day he got him, I think Jean wanted him as the assistant coach over me.

Two weeks after getting relieved of my duties, I asked to scout, and Perron said that was OK. I went all over the country and made detailed reports. Jean called me in about a month later, and I saw all my folders sitting right where I had put them. He hadn't looked at them.

In December they cut off my salary despite promising to fulfill my contract. The Spiders, who folded after the season, were losing millions and trying to save money. One of the ways was to not pay me. I phoned the league and got a lawyer. I wasn't allowed to talk to the players, and I couldn't look for another job if I wanted to stay and fight for the money owed me. I was caught in a bizarre spiderweb. It was like being under house arrest. I tried to negotiate a buyout, and they offered ten thousand dollars, which I turned down. At least they said I could go home.

Crystal and I packed up a big U-Haul truck. I thought I was done with hockey. We started driving across the country with no place to live. We didn't know where we were going to stop. We decided on St. Catharines because of my kids and my hockey school.

The seventeen-foot U-Haul was packed full, and they weren't going to let us over the border into Canada with all this stuff. I told them I was Canadian and bought the possessions in Canada. They were supposed to do a full inspection, but the border-crossing lady at Niagara Falls took one look inside the jammed truck and said, "Forget it, I'm not going through all that." She let us across.

Merry Christmas. I had no money coming in. We were living off retirement accounts and registration money from my hockey school. Phoenix in the IHL offered me a job as an assistant coach, but it only wanted to pay me meal money and for half a hotel room. Ridiculous. I couldn't take that. I wondered where my life was headed.

In March I got a call from Steve Bartlett, my agent at the time. He told me there might be an ECHL expansion team in Mississippi and the owner was interested in talking to me. I drove to Roanoke, Virginia, to watch an ECHL game and interview for the Mississippi Sea Wolves head-coaching job. They offered it for $60,000, and, of course, I accepted.

●

Hockey became a quick hit in Biloxi, Mississippi. The ECHL is Double-A hockey. The crowds were tremendous. I loved the people, and they treated me great. Plus, I was grateful I had a job for the 1996–97 season.

Remember, I learned from my days in Muskegon how to market. I asked which state was Mississippi's top enemy and was told it was Louisiana. Doug Shedden, who had angered me when he tried to steal my Muskegon players, was head coach of Louisiana's ECHL franchise. I bad-mouthed Sheds and said we hated the people of Louisiana. And we sold out every game against them.

After the season started, I was invited to a Mike Ditka celebrity golf tournament at an Arnold Palmer golf course in the Gulfport area. Tom Landry was there. Johnny Unitas and Mike Bossy were there. A lot of famous Chicago Bears too. And me. I was a bit starstruck. Johnny Unitas was a big hero of mine, and here I was rubbing elbows with him.

A puzzled Ditka said, "Who's Bruce Boudreau? He's one of our celebrities?" I felt pretty small because he had no idea who I was. Then I had to sheepishly go up and shake Ditka's hand.

At that tournament, I golfed with a guy who was a Sea Wolves season ticket holder. He knew nothing about hockey. He told me, "You know, I like that good old sport. It's a lot like football. A lot of fighting stuff. You know, I really like that good old black boy you have, Roger Maxwell. You know why? He goes out there and he beats up all those little white boys. And if he gets beat up, who cares? He's a black boy."

That was my introduction to the South. I was a wide-eyed Canadian boy. When somebody says something like that to you and says it matter-of-factly, as if it's just a way of life, it stays with you. That was a wild and awful statement for a man to make, especially to a stranger. It was something I wasn't accustomed to. He was just a big, old-time, overweight southern boy. That was the only overtly racist thing told to me personally in Mississippi. I didn't see or hear that from anybody else. The Mississippi friends I hung around with didn't have that attitude.

That first season, fans didn't have a clue what they were watching, but they took right to hockey. Mississippi Coast Coliseum is a terrific building right on the Gulf of Mexico. The players were fan friendly, and we had a marketing presence all over the city.

During the first shift of the first game, Kevin Evans, who amassed 505 penalty minutes in 1996–97, knocked a guy out at the twenty-nine-second mark. That did it; that sold hockey to southern Mississippi. The second time we played Louisiana we had a huge crowd thanks to all the trash-talk buildup. I told Roger Maxwell, who chipped in with 276 penalty minutes that season, that when he fought he needed to fight to hurt. Roger had a habit of just toying with guys and gently putting them down.

Maxie picked on Louisiana's toughest guy and hammered him. Busted up his face. That guy had to go to our locker room, which is where all the players were treated when they got hurt. On Maxie's next shift, Doug Shedden sent out his next toughest guy. Maxie broke that guy's jaw, and he joined his teammate for treatment.

At first intermission, we went into our locker room and heard all this moaning from these guys in pain. Oh-oh, ouch-ouch, oh-oh. Roger turned to me and asked, "Was I tough enough?" It still makes me laugh.

The Sea Wolves went 34-26-10 in 1996–97 and lost in the first round of the play-offs. In 1997–98 we went 34-27-9 but missed the play-offs by one point even though we won our last nine games. I worried that I was going to get fired. The day after the season ended, though, I was offered a two-year extension.

Ownership's faith in me was rewarded when we won the Kelly Cup in 1998–99. We made two big acquisitions that off-season. We brought back Troy Mann after trading him away in 1997–98. Troy's the first guy I signed in Mississippi. He was an average ECHL player, but I consider him an up-and-comer as a coach and I've tried to help groom him. I told him to get out of hockey for years because he's a smart guy with a degree from the University of Toronto. But he stayed in the game and made $14,000 and $15,000 at the start of his coaching career when he could have made much more in the private sector. Troy advanced to ECHL head coach, and he was hired as assistant coach of the Hershey Bears in 2009.

We also brought in ECHL veteran Bob Woods because Mann said he would make a terrific player–assistant coach. And we had a thirty-five-year-old Russian named Mikhail Kravets. Kravets played the way you're supposed to play. He didn't care how old he was. He blocked shots, he fought, he did anything. The Czech Vaclav Nedomansky also was a tremendous scorer.

After we started 2-5, we re-acquired Kevin Hilton from the Western Pro Hockey League. We went twenty-five games without a loss after he arrived. The last piece to the puzzle was getting Chris Schmidt healthy. He was injured all year but played six games, enough to qualify him to participate in the play-offs. Schmidt was a six foot three perfect defensive forward. And goalie Travis Scott backstopped it all.

We went 41-22-7 in the regular season, finished second to Louisiana in the Southwest Division, and were underdogs in every play-off series except one. We beat higher-seeded Florida three straight in the first round in a best-of-five series. We beat higher-seeded South Carolina three in a row in a second-round best-of-five. After that, we played the Pee Dee Pride, which was by far the best team in the league in the regular season. We beat the Pride in five games in a best-of-seven and survived a triple overtime where Travis Scott faced seventy-one shots. Scott puked in his mask but refused to come out.

Nobody gave Scott, who was undrafted, an opportunity as an NHL prospect. Scouts didn't like his form, so teams wouldn't take a chance on him. If this happened to all goalies with unconventional form, Dominik Hasek wouldn't have played in the NHL. All Travis did was stop the puck. He might make a save with the back of his head, but he made the save. To me, goaltending is about keeping the puck out of the net, and that's what he did. Travis had guts of steel. He eventually went to Russia and became Russia's best goalie for a year or two. I think he made more than a million dollars a year. More power to him. He deserved it.

We played Richmond, the only lower-seeded club we faced in the postseason, in the Kelly Cup finals. And we fell behind 3-1 in the series. We won Game 5 and went back to Richmond for Game 6. I saw the champagne ordered for their Kelly Cup celebration in front of their dressing room and used that in the pregame speech.

"They've got the champagne ready," I told the team. "They're not thinking of playing. They're thinking of the celebration."

We routed them 7-3 in Game 6 and brought it home for Game 7. I didn't think Game 7 would be tough. I thought we'd win easily. It ended up that we were down two goals after the second period. Kelly Hurd scored one of the nicest goals I've ever seen to draw us within one, but we were still down a goal with about four minutes remaining. In that kind of situation, I like to put a defenseman into a forward role, and Bob Woods scored with about two minutes left to tie it up. I've still got the picture of Woody celebrating that goal. It's a fabulous image of complete joy on a guy's face.

Talk about drama. Game 7 of the championship series went to overtime. At about the ten-minute mark, Richmond got a two-on-none breakaway with its two best players, Forest Gore and Ryan Craft. Starting from their blue line. I said to myself, "It's been a good year." They zoomed down and Craft passed the puck to Gore. Gore shot at the open net. Travis Scott dived across, and the puck hit the heel of his glove and rolled wide. I couldn't believe we were alive.

In the second overtime, Richmond got a breakaway on the first shift on clean ice. Again, I figured we were done. But Travis made a five-hole save. In the process, he fell backward and knocked himself out on a post. After five minutes of recovery time, he stayed in the game.

In the third overtime, Richmond got called for a penalty around the ten-minute mark. On our power play, Kevin Hilton shot the puck, Chris Schmidt deflected it into the Richmond net, and the Mississippi Sea Wolves were Kelly Cup champions. It was around 12:30 a.m. and the place went nuts. There were more than eight thousand people in attendance. Sold out to the rafters. I ran into the on-ice celebration pile. That was the debut of my patented two-inch vertical victory leap, later showcased in happy moments with Hershey and Washington.

It was a special season. It's hard to tell people up North it was a special season because they kind of look down their noses at the ECHL. No matter what championship you win, it's something you fought long and hard for for many months. It's a great memory.

We had a victory parade and the route was jammed. Crystal and I rode in a convertible, and people came out of stores to salute us. One merchant offered us an oak chair. Another guy threw a bean bag chair in the car. We were just handed stuff. It was a wonderful way to ride into the sunset, so to speak, in Mississippi.

# 8

## MONSTER CHANGE

**After we won the Kelly Cup in Mississippi,** I went to the 1999 NHL draft in Boston. Bruce Landon, my old Springfield friend, told me that Los Angeles Kings general manager Dave Taylor wanted to interview me for the new American Hockey League head coaching job in Lowell, Massachusetts. The Kings were going to be the lead affiliate in Lowell, with the New York Islanders also supplying players.

I had a horrible interview with the Kings front office people: Dave Taylor, assistant GM Kevin Gilmore, and player personnel director Bill O'Flaherty. But I think they liked my personality. Plus, in Mississippi I sent a report after every game to Dave Taylor on the three or four Kings prospects who played for me. Because of that, I think Taylor thought I was organized, and I was offered the head coaching job of the Lowell Lock Monsters.

The Kings sent the offer by fax: $75,000. It took me two weeks to make a decision. Though it was a step up from Double-A to Triple-A, it meant a pay cut because Mississippi had offered me an $85,000 contract. Dave Taylor finally asked, "Are you going to sign with us? Or do we go somewhere else?"

I decided if I wanted to advance up the coaching ladder, which would hopefully someday lead to the NHL, I had to take the Lowell job. I held a press conference in Mississippi and cried about leaving. I had a beautiful car in Mississippi, a top-of-the-line Oldsmobile, and I drove around like a king. When I arrived in Lowell, Tom Rowe, the Lock Monsters president and general manager, gave me a broken-down Dodge Stratus. In retrospect, though, I can't believe I considered turning down the job. The AHL is one step removed from the NHL.

We had some good players in Lowell, where we went 33-36-7-4 in 1999–2000. Rich Brennan was a good defenseman, a perennial AHL all-star, and a Calder Cup winner. It was Jason Krog's rookie year, and he'd go on to have a career similar to mine (fringe NHL roster player, dominant minor-league player). Craig Charron was a good guy, a classy veteran, but I never got to meet his uncle, Jim Craig, goaltending hero of the 1980 U.S. Olympic hockey team. I made Dave MacIsaac captain because he'd won a Calder Cup with the Philadelphia Phantoms in 1997–98, but he was a bad choice for the job. Martin Laitre gave me headaches. I had goalie Roberto Luongo as a pro rookie. I'd say he's done well for himself. We swept St. John's 3-0 in the first round of the play-offs, but then we got swept by Providence 4-0 in the second round.

In 2000–2001, the joint affiliation with the New York Islanders blew up. The Isles were supposed to send three defensemen and five forwards, and the Kings were in charge of providing the rest of the roster. But the Islanders sent down too many defensemen, which made it hard to be fair in providing playing time. We had eleven defensemen, and you dress six for games. Guys had to sit out.

One day Tom Rowe called me when I was driving home and told me to get back to Paul E. Tsongas Arena. The Islanders had suddenly yanked all their players out of Lowell and moved them to New England Division rival Springfield. It was a total blindside. We had no warning that the Islanders and general manager Mike Milbury were so unhappy.

Kings management was irate at Milbury. We lost six major guys from Lowell's roster and had to supplement with ECHL call-ups the rest of the season. We went 35-35-5-5 and made the play-offs. We would have had a strong team if the Islanders hadn't bolted.

One game we were so short on personnel that we used a bartender named Tom Ashe on defense against Hartford. Ashe took off work early to play for us. The first time we played Springfield after the Islanders moved their players, Tom Rowe put one-thousand dollars cash on the board to beat them. It was an emotional game, and we won. Our Kings guys were motivated to beat the Islanders' allegedly better players, who were allegedly slighted in Lowell because they weren't playing above our allegedly worse LA players. Our players took it as a personal affront. It was heated every time we played Springfield, which finished in last place in the division that season.

In addition to the Islanders mess, we had a brief mini-circus when we had a three-goalie situation. Veteran Steve Passmore made it difficult. Passmore drew a start after sitting for four or five games and suffered, I recall, a tough overtime loss and went into a rage. He shattered his stick on a locker-room wall. He charged into my office screaming and complaining about how the lack of playing time hurt his sharpness. I phoned LA management and told them they needed to get rid of the guy. Kings general manager Dave Taylor sent Passmore to Chicago in the IHL the next day.

I wasn't a goalie, so they can be puzzling to me. You've got to communicate verbally with them a lot and get to know them. It takes time. One of the reasons I never pulled Cristobal Huet in Washington's Stanley Cup play-off series against Philadelphia in 2007–8 was because I had pulled him in the play-offs when I had him in Manchester in the AHL. He might have forgotten all about it, but I didn't want to take a chance because he might have remembered. Had I pulled him in, say, Game 3 against Philadelphia, it might have put him in the mind-set that, Well, here he goes again; he's pulling me and loses faith in me fast.

You want goalies to be as ready as they can be. When I have meetings with them, I ask them what kind of practice shots they like. I ask them how many shots they like. I also get feedback from the goalie coach.

You've got to communicate with and assess every player on your team. It's my job to find the Achilles' heel on each player and use that against them, work it to the advantage of the entire team. If you have to yell at someone to motivate him, you have to yell at him. There are other guys that you have to pat on the back and instill confidence in to get them playing their best. Other guys you might have to challenge so that they say, "I'm going to show you." There are other guys you've got to fine.

You put those individual pieces together—touching the appropriate buttons on each player—into an overall concept that pushes the team to believe it can win every time it steps on the ice. No matter who the opponent is. No matter who you have or don't have in the lineup. Lack of personnel is a cheap excuse. The team that plays the smartest and works the hardest usually wins.

●

Lowell's Tsongas Arena is a beautiful building. It's got 6,400 seats and nice facilities. If I had to build a minor-league rink, I would use the Lowell rink as a model. But the team had lousy attendance, except when we played the Providence Bruins. Bruins fans came from the Boston area to watch their club's prospects.

One bonus to coaching a club in New England: convenient travel. Most of your opponents are just a short bus trip away. Not that I mind bus rides. I find them enjoyable, which is a good thing. I can't begin to calculate the number of bus miles I've traveled in my life.

The key to riding a bus is having good pillows and bringing a blanket. Get a blanket, pillows, and a good movie. One of my favorite blankets was a baseball-motif quilt that I'd borrow from my son Brady. There's no democracy when it comes to movies; the coach has to select them. You don't want young players picking the movies because then you usually end up with something that features loud noise and stupidity. I'm a film buff and think I have pretty good taste. Consider me Roger Ebert with a whistle.

Once you've got the three basics lined up—good pillow, good blanket, good movie—you have your wife make a nice little snack. That's it. You're all set to go. After that, it doesn't matter how long the trip is—as long as you remember to bring your dress pants.

One season in Hershey, I forgot my dress pants when we made a trip to Bridgeport. Bob Woods, my assistant coach, suggested we both wear team warmups on the bench during the game so we'd look alike. It was a generous idea from Woody, who had remembered to bring all of his clothes. But we opted for a Plan B. I summoned our broadcaster, John Walton, for a meeting I told him he wouldn't like. Walton is extremely passionate, one of the best play-by-play guys around, including those in the NHL. I asked John if I could wear his dress pants, and he kindly loaned them and wore team warmup pants in the radio booth. Woody laughed so hard he nearly cried when we made the exchange. I'll admit to some difficulty breathing and barking orders during that game; it had been a while since I'd worn pants with a sub-40-inch waist.

In the 2000–2001 play-offs, we lost in four games in a best-of-five, first-round series to Worcester. Worcester had the AHL's top points total during the regular season. We outplayed the IceCats in the first game and lost 4-3 in overtime. Like an idiot, I put Marcel Cousineau in goal over Travis Scott, my Mississippi goalie, for Game 2 because we'd lost Game 1 with Travis in net. We decisively outshot Worcester and lost 4-3 again. If I'd kept Travis in, we'd have won that game and tied the series. We won Game 3 before getting eliminated.

I was proud of the team, but I remained embarrassed about the Islanders episode. As an AHL head coach, you don't want to make an NHL affiliate unhappy. I took it personally. Mike Milbury phoned me maybe twice during the whole saga, and I don't remember the conversations.

Milbury criticized me a little bit on television during the 2007–8 Stanley Cup play-offs when Washington fell behind Philadelphia 3-1 in our first-round series. Milbury called us the "Crapitals," ragged on Alexander Ovechkin, and said he didn't know what the hell the coach was doing. Then we won two games in a row to tie the series. At least Bob McKenzie defended me every time Milbury trashed me. I don't know if Milbury's negative commentary stemmed from bad Lowell memories or what.

●

During 2000–2001, plans already were in place for the Kings to start an AHL expansion team in Manchester, New Hampshire, for 2001–2. Tom Rowe got mad at me because in December I attended a press conference in Manchester where the Kings announced their move. He thought that was disloyal to Lowell, but I was a Kings employee.

I had to negotiate a new contract to continue as LA's AHL head coach in Manchester, and I didn't have an agent. I was concerned about my ability to represent myself. I figured I'd ambitiously angle for a three-year deal that paid $85,000 the first year and $95,000 the final two years. The Kings, who were very generous to me financially, faxed an initial offer sheet of a three-year deal for $90,000, $100,000, and $110,000. I chuckled to myself, played it coy, and accepted the contract in about two seconds.

General managers love me because I'm an easy mark when it comes to contracts. It's never been about the money; it's always been about the job. It's like a marriage. I would be lost without the game; the game wouldn't be lost without me.

I don't know of too many guys who think about hockey more than I do. I'm sure there are some. I'm sure the Roger Neilson–types who don't have wives are twenty-four hours a day with it with no life. All I do is think about the game. That is why my first marriage failed. This is why my second wife, Crystal, is so great. She knows it can be an all-consuming business.

I met Crystal my first season as a player in Fort Wayne in 1990–91. I was almost thirty-six years old and reeling from the breakup of my first marriage. I saw her leaving a Komets game in December, and we sort of bumped into each other. I said hello, and I asked how old she was. If she were twenty, I never would have gone out with her. But she was twenty-one—just barely. Her twenty-first birthday was ten days before. I didn't ask her out at that time, but she attended a team party held by the Komets booster club in February. Crystal agreed to go out with me. I don't know if she knew what she was getting into. She's a country girl from Lagrange, Indiana.

Crystal was a gymnast. For our first date, I watched her serve as a judge at a high school gymnastics meet. I sat in the stands with all these teenagers, thinking, What am I doing? I owned a white Chevy Impala at the time. It broke down while I was driving Crystal home. It honestly was a mechanical failure, not one of those classic first-date male ploys. I was a total gentleman. I hadn't dated in seventeen years—thirteen years married and four years going out with Mary before that. I proceeded quite slowly.

I was by myself and needed a babysitter. I drove seven hours to St. Catharines every second Thursday night to pick up my three kids and bring them to Fort Wayne for the weekend. We had an afternoon game every Sunday, and I drove them home Sunday night. Monday was an off-day, and I would stay overnight Sunday in St. Catharines and then drive back to Fort Wayne.

When I had the kids on weekends, Crystal helped look after them and took them to all the games. I thought, Wow, what a woman. That's quite a burden to put on a twenty-one-year-old. I asked her to marry me my second season in Fort Wayne. We got married in the summer of 1995 in Fort Wayne.

Crystal's been a rock through all the moves, all the twists and turns of my career. We bought a house in Mississippi, figuring we'd be settled there for a while. Had to sell that one. We bought a house in Manchester, New Hampshire. Had to sell that one. We bought a house in Harrisburg, Pennsylvania. Had to put that one on the market too.

Though the homes come and go, our son, Brady, and I have a permanent foundation: Crystal Boudreau.

# ⑨

# ROYAL PAIN

**Starting an AHL expansion franchise in Manchester,** New Hampshire, in 2001–2 was exciting. But that challenge was tempered by a tragic dose of perspective on September 11, 2001.

I was supposed to be on United Airlines flight 175 out of Boston, which flew into the World Trade Center in New York. Los Angeles Kings pro scouting director Ace Bailey and scout Mark Bavis were on the flight and were killed. Ace and I became fast friends when I coached in Lowell. There wasn't a more lovable guy in the world than Garnet "Ace" Bailey, who was like a big brother to me. Ace, who was Wayne Gretzky's roommate during the Great One's first season in Edmonton, possessed a geniality and charisma that made him a beloved figure throughout pro hockey.

The original itinerary called for me to be on the Tuesday flight from Boston to Los Angeles for the start of Kings training camp. But Kings head coach Andy Murray decided he wanted Bobby Jay, my Manchester assistant coach, and me there a day earlier. Thank God Andy's a stickler for details, and thank God Kings general manager Dave Taylor listened to coaches when they wanted something. The week before, John Wolf, Taylor's assistant, told me he changed my flight because Murray had scheduled a precamp meeting and dinner with all the coaches in the organization. I would fly to LA on Monday, September 10, instead of Tuesday, September 11. I wasn't peeved about the switch. I was happy that Andy wanted me there early. I didn't know he had saved my life.

The weekend before September 11, Kings player personnel director Bill O'Flaherty's daughter got married in Lake Placid, New York. Ace Bailey picked me up in Manchester, and we drove to Lake Placid. We had to take a car ferry across Lake Champlain from Vermont to New York, and Ace chatted with fellow passengers and offered them beer. Typical, gregarious Ace. He knew everybody in hockey.

We were hungry when we arrived in Lake Placid. The lights were out when we checked into our hotel room, but we started ravenously searching for food before we turned them on. Ace pointed out a big bowl in the shadows and suggested I dig in. I started eating what I thought were peanuts. They tasted stale. Ace tried them (or at least pretended to try them) and agreed they were stale. He encouraged me to keep eating, noting they weren't half bad given our hunger. When we turned on the lights, I discovered I'd been eating potpourri. Yum-yum. At the wedding reception, Ace made sure to tell everybody that foolish Bruce dined on potpourri, never mentioning that it originally was his idea. I was always Mutt to his Jeff.

We returned home Sunday morning. I suggested to Ace that he get his Tuesday flight changed to Monday and travel to LA with me. Ace checked with John Wolf. A flight change would cost $750. Ace didn't want to hit the Kings with that expense and opted to stick with the Tuesday flight. He dropped me off, and I shook his hand, gave him a man hug, and told him I'd see him Tuesday.

I flew to Los Angeles on Monday with Bobby Jay, and on Tuesday morning, September 11, at around 6:00 a.m. Pacific time, my wife, Crystal, phoned and told me to turn on the TV. I did and saw all the stuff happening with the terrorist attacks. I went to Bobby Jay's room. He's from Boston. We went to the rink to continue watching and word started to drift out that one of the planes involved was United flight 175—the flight taken by Ace Bailey and Mark Bavis.

My family knew that I was scheduled to travel to Los Angeles from Boston for training camp. A lot of people feared that I was on flight 175. My kids started bawling and ran out of school, but they phoned Crystal and learned that I was OK. Crystal said she got twenty-five calls and had to keep reassuring people that I was safe. It gives me goosebumps to this day to think about all this stuff and how it went down.

After a while, Dave Taylor called me outside and said he had just talked to Kathy Bailey, Ace's wife. Ace indeed was on the flight. My friend Ace Bailey was dead. I broke down crying. Taylor told me privately because he knew we were close. I had a hard time dealing with it. Ace was a mountain of a man who protected you in any situation.

Dave Taylor held a meeting with the players, who'd also arrived on Monday, and broke down talking about Ace and Mark. Their deaths made everything about that whole season sort of secondary. When I lost Ace, I lost the guy who defended me to Los Angeles management if things went wrong in the AHL. It was a major loss for me as an employee; it was a devastating loss for me as a friend.

Kathy Bailey said Ace almost missed the flight. He overslept, and she drove him, and he just barely made it onto the plane. Of course, I don't know the true story because I wasn't on the plane, but I guarantee that Ace would not have gone down without a fight. It wouldn't surprise me to learn that he was dead before the plane hit the World Trade Center; I know his character. He wouldn't have stayed in his seat and let the terrorists operate without resistance.

There was a memorial service in Boston, where Ace lived. There also was a charity event Crystal and I attended in Boston. We had a babysitter for our son, Brady. She phoned us halfway through and told us our house had exploded. Brady left the faucet running in the upstairs bathroom sink. The babysitter, not realizing the sink was running, went downstairs once Brady fell asleep. Water overflowed and seeped into the kitchen ceiling light sockets—and boom. Lights exploded to the tune of about four thousand dollars in damages. That girl didn't babysit for us anymore.

The Manchester Monarchs hold an annual golf tournament. After Ace died, Monarchs president Jeff Eisenberg transformed it into the Ace Bailey Golf Classic. A fitting and classy move by Jeff.

●

There was a love-hate relationship in Manchester. The fans loved me and I loved them; some people in management hated me. I did a lot of public speaking and was visible and good at selling myself to the people. I'm what you call a colorful figure. But Hubie McDonough, the Monarchs' director of hockey operations and a Manchester native, didn't like me from the day we met.

I think it had to do with the fact that I'm such an average Joe and don't dress neatly. Hubie's office was beside mine, and I think he hated the fact that I'd have Jerry Springer on and be laughing my head off while I did my work. Hubie's more upper-crusty and has that corporate polish.

Before it ended in ugly fashion, I had a tremendous four-year run in Manchester. The Monarchs had great success on the ice, at least in the regular season. Off the ice, it was often a soap opera. Maybe we all should have battled it out on a *Jerry Springer* episode.

The Monarchs had to play their first thirteen games on the road in 2001–2 while construction on the new Verizon Wireless Arena, a beautiful state-of-the-art building, was completed. We started slow and fell into last place in the AHL's North Division, but we finished at 38-28-11-3 and took second place.

We had good players: Eric Healey, Joe Corvo, Ted Donato, Jaroslav Bednar, Brad Chartrand, Adam Mair. We did get so depleted by injuries and callups at one point, though, that I had assistant coach Bobby Jay play four games and Hubie McDonough play five games because I was so sick of calling up guys.

We lost 3-2 in a best-of-five, first-round play-off series against a strong Hartford team. It was a good season, and we were extremely happy with the club's reception in New Hampshire. We averaged more than eight thousand a game in attendance. Our attendance increased every year, and the Monarchs became one of the AHL's most successful franchises. We just couldn't get past the first round of the play-offs. I don't know what it was. We were snakebitten.

In 2002–3 we went 40-23-11-6 and again finished second in the North Division. Sean Avery played a prominent role in sinking us in the first round of the play-offs against a forty-win Bridgeport team that placed second in the East Division. Following the NHL season, the Kings, who didn't qualify for the Stanley Cup play-offs, sent us seven players: Steve Kelly, Tomas Zizka, Joe Corvo, Jason Holland, Jerred Smithson, Cristobal Huet, and Sean Avery. On paper it gave us a tremendous play-off roster, but in reality it threw off everything.

I didn't know Sean Avery. Since he had played in Grand Rapids in the AHL when he was with the Detroit Red Wings organization, I phoned Grand Rapids general manager Bob McNamara and Red Wings goaltending coach Jim Bedard to get some background information. Bedard told me that after Detroit general manager Ken Holland traded Avery to the Kings, he got a standing ovation in the Grand Rapids locker room because the players were so happy to get rid of him.

Now Avery was my problem. He didn't want to play in the AHL play-offs. I guess he thought it was slumming. We got a rental car to make life easier for him. When Bridgeport eliminated us, Avery left the next morning without attending the traditional season-ending meetings and abandoned the car someplace without telling anybody. They couldn't find the car for two weeks, and management hit him for the rental cost because of that.

After the morning skate before the first play-off game, Kings assistant general manager Kevin Gilmore gave me grief about the shoddy way Avery had practiced. Gilmore asked me what Avery was doing on the ice.

"I don't know," I replied. "You want to talk to him? I'm not getting through to this guy."

All the focus of Game 1 against Bridgeport was directed on Sean Avery and his antics instead of on doing a good job. Avery went into a corner on his first shift, and the puck went back the other way. Everybody on the bench looked down at Avery to see what he might do. Nobody cared about the game. That epitomized the effect Avery had on the team.

Avery had two goals and an assist as we got swept in three games by Bridgeport. We all know he's a good player. He can score. He can play the game. He just didn't care whether we won or lost, and he hurt team chemistry.

Almost to a man in our end-of-season meetings, the players told me they hated Sean Avery and that they were going to try to kick the crap out of him at 2003–4 training camp. I believe it every time I hear a negative story about Avery.

Avery wasn't the only player the Kings reassigned who didn't play well. The whole bunch struggled. Mentally, they were still in LA. Joe Corvo came into my office when he came down and told me the last game he played in LA gave him fifty for the season, which automatically turned his contract into a one-way deal for 2003–4. His mind clearly wasn't on the Calder Cup play-offs.

Since that experience, I've been skeptical about the value of getting a late-season talent infusion from your NHL parent team. You get high-caliber players, but it always takes them time to adjust to coming to the minors. In the short term, it can hurt a team more than help. And in the play-offs, the short term can be lethal.

●

Heading into the 2003–4 season in Manchester, I got a two-year contract extension: $120,000 the first year, $130,000 the second. From my historical five-figure-salary perspective, I felt rich beyond rich.

Before that third season in Manchester, Bobby Jay left to become director of hockey operations for San Antonio in the AHL. I needed a new assistant coach. Along with head coach Robbie Ftorek, Jim Hughes had been fired as an assistant coach by the Boston Bruins. Hughes lived in New Hampshire and wanted the job, but I didn't know him from Adam. During the job interview, I told Jim I needed a loyal assistant. Jim stressed that he was an extremely loyal guy.

That sold Hughes for me. I gave the Kings my stamp of approval, and he got the position. Little did I know he'd end up being the guy who'd replace me.

Adding Hughes as my assistant was a good move and a bad move all in one. Jim absolutely has a bright hockey mind. However, I never met an assistant coach who wanted the head coach's job so bad.

This meant I had two guys working against me: Hubie McDonough and Jim Hughes. My final two seasons in Manchester were extremely difficult, but I made it through because Monarchs president Jeff Eisenberg was a tremendous friend who gave me a shoulder to cry on. I also had the players on my side; I've always had good relationships with players. And I had Dane Jackson, our strength and conditioning coach, as an ally.

Dane was my captain the first two Manchester seasons and became an assistant coach in 2003–4 after retiring as a player. You sit there and think he can't be this nice all the time, but he was. I would have been a complete basket case without him. Dane went on to become an assistant coach at the University of North Dakota, his alma mater, and he's going to be a head coach at some level some day because of his work ethic and desire. He's the kind of guy you're proud to be associated with.

After two years of tension, in 2003–4 Hubie McDonough and I had our first major face-to-face blowup when we traveled to Utah in December. We needed to add a player, and Hubie, insisting that he have a role in personnel since it was part of his job description, asked to handle the situation. There was a possibility we'd get a player reassigned by the Kings, but we still were a man short when we arrived in Utah. I conducted practice, walked into the locker room, and discovered a forward indeed had been reassigned from the Kings, necessitating a change in my line combinations. I was angry because nobody told me about it before or during practice. Hubie introduced the guy, but I wasn't very cordial and visibly showed my disgust. That upset Hubie, who took me outside and started screaming that I needed to let him do his job.

I told McDonough I wanted to continue the conversation later. I was still stewing about the incident at pregame warmups, and we lost 6-0. I received a morale-boosting call from Bill O'Flaherty, who told me "only your friends call when you lose," but I still didn't sleep that night. I met Hubie the next morning and asked what his problem was. Hubie ripped into me. He told me I was the worst leader, the worst coach, the worst practice coach, the worst of everything that he'd ever seen in pro hockey.

I was struck mute while Hubie lambasted me. Then I found out that Kings assistant general manager Kevin Gilmore, another guy with corporate polish whom I sensed disdained my rumpled style, was coming to the second game of back-to-back games in Utah. I figured I was getting fired. I phoned home and told Crystal I expected to be unemployed after that night's game. Before the game, I approached winger Steve Kelly.

"Steve, more than ever, I need you to play a big game for me," I said.

Kelly passed the word to the players, and we won, even though we were short-handed five times in the third period. Nobody said a word to me following the game, but I'm sure they had planned to gas me if we lost.

From that point on, I avoided talking to McDonough. Meanwhile, Hubie and Jim Hughes got real tight. It was a trying situation that kept deteriorating.

In addition to the hockey turmoil, my father, Norman, died in November

2003 at age seventy-three. It was a devastating blow. There are so many things that you remember about your dad. My son Ben and I were on vacation in Mississippi one time when Ben learned he had to return to Canada because he was going to be able to play in a Don Cherry–run camp. I drove twenty-four straight hours to get him there.

People asked me, "Why did you do that?" My answer: Because my dad did it for me. Whenever I asked my dad why he had done all those things for me, he'd say that's what dads do. They take their kids everywhere and do whatever they can to help them. I'd sit there, grateful to have such a giving father, and thank him.

You don't realize what a profound commitment was made to you as a child and how much your parents did for you until you're an adult and a parent yourself. Rushing to your ball game after work. Rushing home to get you to practice after work. My dad made sacrifices driving all over the place for my brothers and me.

I knew when I had success—making the Toronto Maple Leafs or whatever it was—and how happy it made him. He was overjoyed. My dad's memory drives me and at the same time makes me sad. He wanted me to succeed and loved me so much that he would do anything for me. It bothers me deeply that he's not here to reap the benefits, that he didn't get to see me coach the Washington Capitals and win the Jack Adams Award as 2007–8 NHL Coach of the Year. How proud he'd have been.

Cancer claimed him. When they told him he had it—I was in the room— the doctor said he had anywhere from six weeks to six months to live. My dad's heart was bad, so they couldn't operate. Dad was gone four weeks later.

It's amazing how these things go. He was in a hospital bed and he couldn't talk, but he refused to die until I showed up. Once I showed up, it was like it was OK for him to leave because all three of his sons were there. He said his good-byes to everybody. The memory of the moment still chokes me up. Norman Boudreau stood five foot two, but he was a giant to me.

Jim Hughes ran the Monarchs while I was at my dad's funeral. I returned to Manchester on a Thursday after leaving the previous Saturday. Hughes welcomed me back. Then I went to practice and noticed he'd changed all my systems.

We were basically a .500 club until February because I wanted them to play my way, and Jim tried to pull them another way. We went 40-28-7-5 and finished second in the Atlantic Division. Our first-round play-off matchup against third-place Worcester turned into a fiasco. We lost in six games, another quick exit. I should have taken my problems with Hughes to Dave Taylor and Bill O'Flaherty. I thought I could handle the situation myself. I couldn't.

●

The 2004–5 season, my last in Manchester, began splendidly despite all the office intrigue. It was the NHL lockout season, and we had a lot of the Kings' top young players down. I got them to do exactly what I wanted in training camp, and we won our first seven games. We lost the eighth game in Worcester and then won thirteen in a row for an amazing 20-1-0-0 start.

Two losses followed, one in overtime. I was a little disappointed, but we were 20-2-1-0. Kevin Gilmore phoned me, said he'd watched the second loss, which was to Hartford, and told me it was a disgrace. Twenty wins in twenty-three games and negative feedback? Unbelievable. It was two hours before a game, and I hung up on Gilmore. That was the first time I had ever hung up on management.

We hovered four or five games over .500 the next forty games. It's like leading a game 5-0 after the first period. You're not going to win 15-0. The AHL regular season is eighty games long. You can't maintain a seventy-win pace.

Since we tailed off, it gave them another chance to get all over me. There were times Jim Hughes screamed in practice, trying to take over the team from me. It seemed obvious to me that Hubie McDonough and Kevin Gilmore had Jim's ear and encouraged him. Dane Jackson was in my corner, but they were trying to fire him too. The management team continued to malfunction. I still made the mistake of not telling Dave Taylor or Bill O'Flaherty.

Around the sixtieth game, all hell broke loose. We maintained first place in the Atlantic Division, but Rochester had passed us for the best record in the league. Kevin Gilmore visited Manchester from Los Angeles to interview the players. Centerman Mike Cammalleri phoned me right after he met with Gilmore.

"They're trying to hang you," Cammalleri told me. "All us players banded together and told them we're playing for you. But he's asking questions to find out how bad you are as a coach."

I'm proud of what Cammalleri has accomplished. He scored forty-six goals in 2004–5 in Manchester and went on to be a thirty-goal scorer for the Kings. I identified with Mike because we're both small. I knew right off the bat he'd be a terrific player. He's extremely intelligent, and I realized the thing to do was let him play.

The players knew what I was about and considered the situation a mess. Gilmore followed the player meetings with a meeting with the coaches. He told us we were doing a bad job and that we might not be back in 2005–6. But he offered a one-year contract extension, which brightened my spirits some. I knew I was going to get gonged at the end of the season, but at least I'd have a one-year extension that would give me a cushion while I found my next job.

We finished 51-21-4-4, took first place in the Atlantic Division, and tied with Rochester for the most wins in the AHL. Rochester (112) edged us by two points for the regular-season championship, but we were the top play-off seed in the Eastern Conference. We opened the postseason against fourth-place Providence—and lost in six games. A fourth straight first-round elimination.

Our goaltending killed us. We had a 1-0 lead in the third period of Game 6, and Mathieu Garon surrendered an awful goal on a shot by Brad Boyes from just inside the blue line. Providence won 3-1 to close out the series. Our guys were devastated and cried in the locker room. A season that began with a rocket start ended with a teary splashdown.

I figured I'd lost my job, but I didn't know for sure. My future wasn't mentioned at the postseason meetings. I kept wondering when I'd officially get the contract extension. Finally, on June 10, Kevin Gilmore flew into Manchester. He brought the contract extension and scheduled a meeting. At this point, since so much time had passed, I guessed I'd keep my job. I expected to get a lecture and be told that I had to change everything. I planned to tell Gilmore I didn't want Jim Hughes retained as assistant coach, but I knew they wouldn't have let me boot him.

Hughes was in my office right before the meeting. He acted all nicey-

nicey. Gilmore walked in, and Hughes excused himself to go to the trainer's room. In retrospect, it seems clear to me that Hughes knew exactly what was going to happen when I met with Gilmore and Hubie McDonough.

Gilmore gave the the promised contract extension. Then he told me they were going in a different direction and they no longer wanted me as head coach.

On the one hand, I got the extension; on the other hand, I got fired. Gilmore said Mr. Anschutz wanted Manchester to start winning. Kings owner Philip Anschutz had never been to a game in Manchester, and his name had never been brought up before. But they pinned it on Mr. Anschutz. I heartily agree that our first-round play-off futility was a negative, but I contend that averaging forty-two victories a season is winning. I know Hubie and Kevin were the ones who got me fired. I know Dave Taylor and Bill O'Flaherty still wanted me, and despite what happened in Manchester I retain a world of respect for those two men.

I'm still mad at myself for shaking Hubie McDonough's hand and thanking him for the opportunity in Manchester before exiting that meeting. Hubie didn't deserve the respect of a handshake. I inquired about my staff and was told everybody was fired, including Jim Hughes. But Hughes was invited to reapply for the head-coaching job. I knew that was a joke, and the punchline arrived when Hughes was "rehired" to replace me.

I was crushed by the firing. We had to leave so many friends we'd made in Manchester. I love the city, and I love New Hampshire. Monarchs fans and I had a mutual love affair. Manchester hosted the 2005 AHL All-Star Classic, and I got to coach the PlanetUSA team because we had the league's best record at the season's midpoint. The Verizon Wireless Arena crowd gave me a huge ovation, louder than any player got. I had my own newspaper column once a week. I had a radio show doing movie reviews every Monday. I was the public face of the franchise. I knew Jim Hughes couldn't fill that role.

This was like a divorce where you tell your wife, "Yeah, I'm going to get somebody more beautiful than you, and I'm going to get her tomorrow because I can." I immediately phoned my friend Bruce Landon, general manager of the AHL's Springfield Falcons, to inquire about job leads. I knew Portland and Hershey had open AHL jobs.

I was interested in the Portland Pirates because Rick Paterson and Bob Murray, two men I respect, would be involved with the club, which was starting a new affiliation with Anaheim. Plus, I enjoy living in the Northeast. I was interested in the Hershey Bears because I thought they'd be good in 2005–6. Washington was moving its AHL affiliation from Portland to Hershey. I had seen plenty of the Capitals' prospects in Portland because we played them so many times in the Atlantic Division with Manchester. The talent base impressed me. I believed they had underachieved and were capable of being an excellent team.

The day I was fired in Manchester, I thought it was the worst thing that had ever happened to me professionally. It turned out to be the best thing that ever happened to me.

# 10

## SWEET SEASON

I always enjoyed playing games in Hershey, Pennsylvania. The Hershey Bears are the most tradition-rich franchise in the AHL. They're the league's version of the Montreal Canadiens or the New York Yankees.

Before 2005–6 Hershey had won eight Calder Cups since joining the AHL in 1938–39. Historic Hersheypark Arena, which the Bears left following the 2001–2 season, was one of the best arenas ever built for watching hockey, ranking right up there with Maple Leaf Gardens, Chicago Stadium, and the Montreal Forum. I was there the last time Hershey clinched a Calder Cup on home ice in 1980 as a member of the losing New Brunswick Hawks.

Being head coach of the Hershey Bears is one of the most prestigious jobs in hockey. I'd argue it's the most prestigious coaching job outside of the NHL. Since 2002–3, the Bears have played at 10,500-seat Giant Center, an NHL-caliber facility. I love the fact that hockey-crazy Hershey is a small town—a small town made famous by Milton S. Hershey's chocolate company.

After two straight non-play-off seasons, the Bears had ended a nine-year affiliation with the Colorado Avalanche that produced a Calder Cup under head coach Bob Hartley in 1996–97. The Washington Capitals, Hershey's affiliate when they won that 1980 Calder Cup, were coming back, and they needed an AHL head coach. Tim Army, Washington's AHL coach in Portland the three previous seasons, had left for the head-coaching job at Providence College, his alma mater. As a newly unemployed head coach, I was keenly interested in pursuing the open head-coaching job in Hershey.

At my behest, my friend Bruce Landon, president and general manager of the Springfield Falcons, contacted Bears president and general manager Doug Yingst. Landon and Yingst are longtime friends and colleagues from the AHL's Board of Governors. Yingst told Landon the Bears wanted somebody with a Hershey background.

I phoned Doug, and he told me to send a résumé. He said if they didn't come up with anybody they liked before the NHL entry draft in June, I'd get put on the candidate list. Well, they didn't find anybody, and they brought me to Hershey for an interview in July while the Caps were holding their summer developmental camp for prospects at Giant Center.

In my mind, Bruce Landon sold Doug Yingst on me enough to get the interview. Caps general manager George McPhee didn't know me at all. I felt I hit a home run with the interview because I was so familiar with Washington's players. In Manchester, we had played Portland twenty times the previous two seasons and won nineteen times. They asked me about players, and I delivered detailed scouting reports. I told them I loved their young prospects like Tomas Fleischmann, Jakub Klepis, and Brooks Laich. No other candidate who interviewed for the job could have known Washington's prospects as well as I did. As soon as I left, from what I gathered, they said that's our guy.

Meeting George McPhee for the first time was fun. I went out for a beer that night with Doug. George phoned me the next day and told me to keep it quiet, but the Caps wanted to hire me. George was working on Alexander Ovechkin's entry-level contract and keeping tabs on prospects camp at the same time he was dealing with me, so he was extremely busy. The Portland Pirates, switching from Washington to an affiliation with the Anaheim Ducks, were interested in me too. Bob Murray, senior vice president of hockey operations for Anaheim, whom I knew from our days with the Chicago Blackhawks, had phoned me on vacation in Mississippi and asked if I'd be interested in the Portland job. He said he didn't need to interview me. He knew I was good enough. I told George that Portland was interested, and George asked me not to answer the phone for twenty-four hours. I agreed.

About twenty-eight hours later, George McPhee formally offered me the Hershey head-coaching job. They flew me back to Hershey for an introductory press conference. The rest—it's a love story.

*I'm forever indebted to my parents, who did everything for me. That's my mother, Theresa,
in the middle and my late father, Norman, on the right.*
Courtesy of the Boudreau family collection.

*Getting honored for my 1,000th professional point while playing for the AHL's Springfield Indians
in 1987–88. I rank eleventh all-time in AHL points (799) and was inducted into the league's
Hall of Fame in 2009. The guy on the right is unidentified.*
Courtesy of the Boudreau family collection.

*I played my last game for Barry Melrose with the Adirondack Red Wings in the 1991–92 AHL play-offs. I played just four games for Melrose, notching a goal and an assist, but that short stint got my name on the Calder Cup as a player.* Courtesy of the Boudreau family collection.

*On the day of my marriage to my wife, Crystal, in 1995. From left to right are Stu Burnie, son Andy, Greg Hotham, me, Paul Evans, son Ben, and John Anderson. My best friend John Anderson was my best man. John and I paid a lot of dues as minor-league coaches, but we both eventually made it to the NHL as head coaches.* Courtesy of the Boudreau family collection.

*Celebrating the 1998–99 Kelly Cup championship with the Mississippi Sea Wolves after a dramatic Game 7 victory in the finals. A lot of hockey people look down their noses at the ECHL, but it's special any time you win a championship.* Courtesy of the Boudreau family collection.

*Here's Team Boudreau. Starting with me clockwise from the left are son Ben, son Andy, daughter Kasey, son Brady, and wife Crystal. They've all sacrificed a lot for me to pursue a career in hockey.*

Courtesy of the Boudreau family collection.

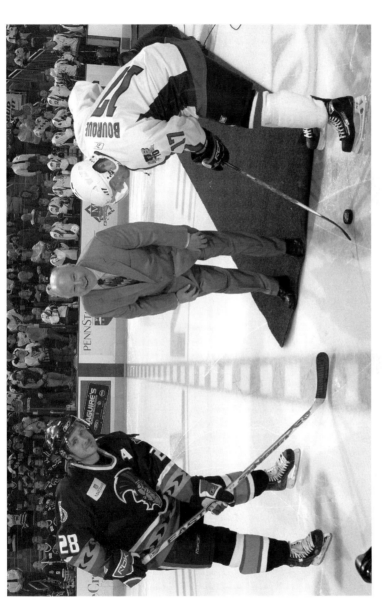

*After I was promoted to head coach of the Washington Capitals, I returned for a ceremonial puck drop before a 2007–8 Hershey Bears game at Giant Center. Lawrence Nycholat (left), who played for the Binghamton Senators that night, is one of the premier defensemen in the minor leagues and helped the development of our young players tremendously when I had him in Hershey. Caps draft pick Chris Bourque (right) is the son of Hockey Hall-of-Famer Ray Bourque. Courtesy of JustSports Photography.*

*We held a victory rally at Giant Center in Hershey, Pennsylvania, after beating the Milwaukee Admirals in six games to win the 2005–6 Calder Cup. Hershey Bears captain Boyd Kane (center) and assistant coach Bob Woods (right) hold the cup while I look on.*
Courtesy of JustSports Photography.

*I'm holding a press conference during the 2005–6 Calder Cup finals in which my Hershey Bears played the Milwaukee Admirals. That's the hideous lucky tie I wore to help the cause.*
Courtesy of JustSports Photography.

*Here is my two-inch vertical victory leap after Eric Fehr's overtime goal for Hershey won Game 7 of the 2005–6 Eastern Conference finals against the Portland Pirates. I had to tuck my shirt back in before shaking Portland head coach Kevin Dineen's hand.* Courtesy of JustSports Photography.

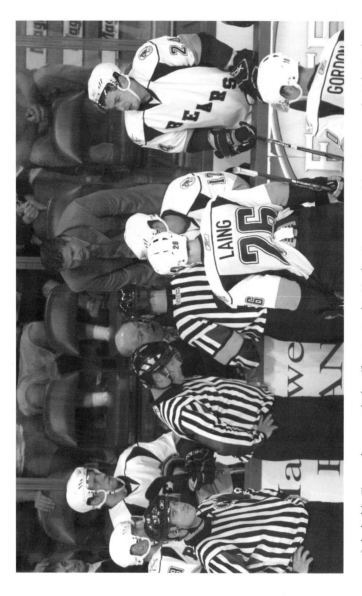

*It looks like I'm not happy with the officiating in this Hershey Bears game. My assistant coach, Bob Woods, leaning in, seems entertained by the conversation. No. 24 (far right) is instigator Louis Robitaille. Louis kept me—and the refs—busy with his antics.* Courtesy of JustSports Photography.

*I'm calling in the Hershey troops for a strategy session in the 2005–6 play-offs. No. 5 is Mike Green. I love being his coach, and he's going to win the Norris Trophy someday.* Courtesy of JustSports Photography.

*I coached the AHL's Manchester Monarchs from 2001 to 2005. It was often a soap opera off the ice. We had tremendous success on the ice during the regular season, but we could never get past the first round of the Calder Cup play-off. Courtesy of JustSports Photography.*

*It was an honor for me to have the opportunity to coach the great Sergei Fedorov.*
Courtesy of OnFrozenBlog.com.

*I'm going over some chalkboard stuff during a Washington practice. That's Nicklas Backstrom on the left and Alexander Ovechkin on the right. Courtesy of OnFrozenBlog.com.*

*Fans have been wonderful to me at all my hockey stops. Here I'm signing autographs after a practice at Kettler Capitals Iceplex in Arlington, Virginia.* Courtesy of OnFrozenBlog.com.

Alexander Ovechkin is the greatest hockey player on the planet. And, lucky me, I get to coach him.
Courtesy of OnFrozenBlog.com.

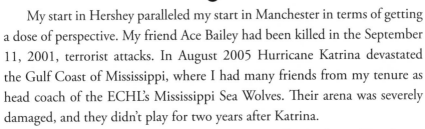

My start in Hershey paralleled my start in Manchester in terms of getting a dose of perspective. My friend Ace Bailey had been killed in the September 11, 2001, terrorist attacks. In August 2005 Hurricane Katrina devastated the Gulf Coast of Mississippi, where I had many friends from my tenure as head coach of the ECHL's Mississippi Sea Wolves. Their arena was severely damaged, and they didn't play for two years after Katrina.

A lot of my Mississippi friends were pretty well wiped out. Here I was, excited about a new job, and a lot of my friends were left with nothing. When I visited, the extent of the damage was staggering. TV didn't come close to telling the story. You couldn't imagine it unless you saw it in person.

My new Hershey assistant coach came from Mississippi. I hired Bob Woods, who played for me on our Kelly Cup team and had gone on to serve as Sea Wolves head coach. It was a natural choice. Bob had ties to me and to Hershey, where he played on the Bears' 1996–97 Calder Cup club.

It was hard for Bob to leave Mississippi. I told him that if he wanted to progress in coaching, he had to step up to the AHL. He took a pay cut like I did when I came to the AHL in Lowell. A lot of people in hockey don't understand the dilemma, but I do. When you live down there, you come to love the place and the people, and you want to stay forever. Katrina hit a week after Woody accepted the Hershey job. Bob's house suffered only minor damage, and he was able to sell it right away because there was such a housing shortage.

I knew the Bears wanted an assistant with Hershey connections. Mitch Lamoureux, a former Baltimore teammate whose number is retired in Hershey, was a guy they wanted me to interview. But I focused on Woody and was fortunate to get him. Loyalty was a big priority after Manchester. Bob is the most loyal guy in the world.

Woody is a rock. He's everything that I'm not, which is why we've always gotten along so well. He was the quiet guy and the responsible guy. I'd come out with the ideas, and he'd remember the ideas. As player–assistant coach in Mississippi, he was a smart guy whom I could run ideas past, and he'd comment on them intelligently. Bob supported me in Hershey and was a great listener. We worked together well as a team. He is a good husband and father, an extremely reliable person. I don't think he's ever done anything he's ever had to be sorry about.

On the eve of the opening of Hershey's training camp, I walked into the team hotel and the first person I saw was Graham Mink. I recognized him from Portland, and he recognized me from Manchester. I told him he was a tremendous power forward and that he'd score forty goals in 2005–6. The encounter gave me a good vibe.

That was one of many sales jobs. When you go to a new team and a new town, you have to prove yourself all over again. My big thing was coming in really organized. I had to show them that I knew what I was doing. Manchester's success against Portland gave me some built-in credibility.

At our first pre-camp team meeting, I told the players they better be ready to win the Calder Cup. My slogan for the season, which I placed on the cover of the training camp manual and on T-shirts, was "Raising the Bar." They had underachieved in Portland. I wanted to make sure from the get-go that they understood we were going to accept nothing but winning.

Doug Yingst and Bears trainer Dan "Beaker" Stuck later told me they walked away from that meeting feeling that we were, in fact, going to win the cup. I had injected an expectation of winning, which was a change from the atmosphere in Hershey the previous two seasons.

Doug has become a mentor for me. I still talk to him almost daily. We think pretty much the same way. He's passionate about winning and Hershey. Winning consumes him. Doug knows his stuff and is a guy some NHL team should pluck as a general manager prospect.

Beaker is simply the all-time best trainer I've encountered in my thirty-plus years in pro hockey. I've never seen him in a bad mood. His job, other than the regular job of helping treat players, is to make players feel good. He has a gift for doing that. No matter how emotionally down players get, Beaker finds a way to make them feel good. What a tremendous asset to Hershey. Beaker goes out of his way to do anything for anybody. I have never heard anybody say a bad word about him.

The players I inherited in Hershey played a defensive-oriented system in Portland under Tim Army. Army apparently thought they were offensively limited. Granted, he had Tomas Fleischmann at nineteen and Jakub Klepis at nineteen and all these other young guys. Army was mechanical and conservative in his approach and didn't allow them to be themselves. I did a one-eighty in style. I turned them loose, and it was a breath of fresh air for them.

I knew Jared Aulin and Dave Steckel—both had played for me in Manchester. Washington signed Steckel away from the Los Angeles Kings, who had drafted him in the first round out of Ohio State in 2001. Brian MacLellan, Washington's assistant general manager, had asked me what I thought of Steckel. I told him I liked him and thought he could blossom into a good NHL player. The Kings wanted to re-sign him, but they gambled by not offering him a contract before the draft and allowed him to become an unrestricted free agent. By doing that, the Kings got a compensatory draft pick and figured they could still re-sign Steckel because they assumed he wouldn't be a target for another team. Wrong. I was like a little boy in the school yard going "nah-nah-nah" after Washington signed him.

I didn't know how good the 2005–6 Bears were going to be when the season started. We had promising first-year players like Eric Fehr and Mike Green, both first-round draft picks. Veteran minor-league defenseman Lawrence Nycholat was an unbelievable addition. Veteran defenseman Mark Wotton and goalie Frederic Cassivi were also important signings.

Boyd Kane, who had captained the Philadelphia Phantoms to the Calder Cup the previous season, was another key signing. Originally, I didn't think it was a good signing because I'd never been a Kane fan, but I made him team captain and he was a hard-nosed player and an outstanding penalty killer. It was a pleasantly tough field of candidates; I easily could have picked Nycholat or Wotton as captain. In fact, I named Nycholat captain in 2006–7. During 2005–6 Wotton was really an unofficial captain. When I wanted to do something, I ran it by "Wotty" before I ran it by anybody.

Major in-season trades brought us Colin Forbes and Kris Beech. We acquired Beech from the Milwaukee Admirals based on the recommendation of Chicago Wolves head coach John Anderson, who said he was the best centerman they played against all season. Kris plays well in the AHL, and I don't know why his skills never translated into playing well in the NHL.

We lost our season opener 3-2 on the road against the in-state rival Wilkes-Barre/Scranton Penguins. The Baby Penguins got off to a tremendous start like my Manchester Monarchs had the previous season. The Norfolk Admirals also were a strong team in the East Division.

We also lost our second game—our home opener—to Wilkes-Barre/Scranton in a shootout. But our third game, our first win, gave me a quick sense that we could be quite good. We visited the Rochester Americans and beat them 5-3. At that point, the Amerks had Jason Pominville and Derek Roy, who'd both go on to play prominent roles with the Buffalo Sabres, and were a strong team.

We were consistent. We never lost more than two in a row in regulation during the regular season, and I take pride in that. It's important not to have too many lows, to always get back on the horse after a loss. We had a stretch of twenty-one games with only one regulation loss.

The players began to believe they were good. It's important to have a team that likes winning, and they realized they liked it. We had outstanding leaders in Wotton, Kane, Mink, Nycholat, Forbes, and Cassivi. You can't get minor-league veterans better than those guys. They helped me keep reinforcing a winning attitude.

I returned to Manchester in November and obviously wanted to win. We were horrible and lost 6-5 in overtime. We beat Manchester 2-0 when the Monarchs visited Giant Center in February. Our instigator, Louis Robitaille, in his inimitable way, got into a pushing match at the bench. Monarchs head coach Jim Hughes said something to him, and Louis turned around and replied, "Well, at least I'm not backstabbing you so you lose your job." It went right to the heart of the matter and really upset Jim.

I was thinking, Louis, how could you say that? Deep down inside, though, I was sort of happy that he had. Frankly, I shouldn't be vengeful like him because that firing opened the door to better days for me. In the larger scheme of things, despite occasional low moments that are part and parcel of hockey life, I'm an extremely fortunate man.

We also played Portland four times in the regular season. Our former Pirates were motivated for those games, which turned out to be a preview of the play-offs. There also was irony in the fact that before affiliating with Washington Hershey had considered affiliating with Anaheim, which ultimately placed its prospects in Portland. And, had I not gotten the Hershey coaching job, there was a chance I might have been coaching in Portland. It all made for intense games even though we weren't division rivals. The Bears and Pirates developed a quick dislike for each other.

The Pirates, who won the Atlantic Division and produced the best record in the Eastern Conference, came to Hershey for two games in January, and we beat them twice. We visited Portland in March, losing the first game 3-2 in overtime and winning the second 4-1. That second game at Portland showed we could play with anybody anywhere.

Going back to Portland was an eye-opener for Louis Robitaille. He had been a fan favorite there as a Pirate and got booed as a Bear. A lot of times, booing is a sign of respect for a great player. For Louis, maybe they just didn't like him anymore. He's one of those guys fans love when he's on their team and hate when he's on the other.

We kept chasing the Penguins in the East Division and got close a few times. Any time you play your best in a stretch to gain on a team ahead of you, it usually ends up being not quite good enough. Eventually you're going to tail off, and the team you're chasing is going to snap out of the funk that allowed you to gain ground.

We finished the regular season 44-21-5-10 and placed second to division champion Wilkes-Barre/Scranton.

●

When we had our whole team together, we were as good as any AHL team's been in quite a while. We were so big and strong up front that nobody could control us in the play-offs. We had centermen like six-foot-two Brooks Laich, who came down from Washington for the play-offs, six-foot-two Kris Beech, and six-foot-five Dave Steckel. It's rare to have a collection of big centermen like that in the AHL. Joey Tenute was one of our leading scorers, and in the postseason he was relegated to the fourth line because we were so deep.

To win in the play-offs, everything has to come together—and it did. We had guys who were perfect for each position and each situation. Everything fit.

In the first round, we played third-place Norfolk, which had won the regular-season series against us. Owing to building-availability issues, we faced an odd series schedule where we hosted Game 1 and played the next two at Norfolk even though we had home-ice advantage. That put a lot of pressure on us to win Game 1. And that was on top of the pressure I already felt after all the first-round frustration in Manchester. A first-round defeat by Norfolk might have put a final nail in my coffin, reputation-wise, as a play-off coach and wrecked any NHL aspirations.

We won 3-2 in Game 1 on Boyd Gordon's goal at 6:11 of the third period. It eased a lot of stress because we'd led 2-0, and the Admirals came back to tie it 2-2, getting the equalizer forty-one seconds into the third period.

In Game 2 Mink had a hat trick, and we won 5-2. Minker is a really good AHL player. He's had his injury woes, but he's a guy you want on your team. Worst practice player in history, though. It had nothing to do with staying out late; he's just not a good morning person. I'll always have a soft spot for him.

In Game 3 we trailed 2-0, and Louis Robitaille changed momentum by goading Norfolk tough guy Shawn Thornton to take a major penalty and a double-game misconduct. Beech scored on the ensuing power play to cut the deficit to 2-1, the first of four straight Hershey goals. Laich's goal at 16:52 of the third gave us a 4-2 lead, but he incurred an inadvertent high-sticking major off the face-off following the goal. The Admirals scored twice on the five-minute power play to send it to overtime. But Brooksie's redemption goal at 1:52 of double overtime won it 5-4 for a 3-0 series lead.

We won 5-1 in Game 4 at home to sweep. Sigh of relief. I'd made it through the first round. That set up a showdown against Wilkes-Barre/ Scranton, which had a seven-game series in the first round against Bridgeport. The Penguins advanced but didn't look good. They finished ten points ahead of us, but we were confident and we swept them too.

That season Robitaille was extremely effective at antagonizing foes. He was new to the division, and opposition players weren't wise to his tricks. Against Wilkes-Barre/Scranton, he continued to get under the skin of Dennis Bonvie, the AHL's all-time penalty minutes king, and Penguins pest Daniel Carcillo. They took penalties that helped us win games.

Despite his reputation, Louis has acumen when it comes to hockey. His problem is he plays to the crowd too much. I'm convinced he doesn't think he has much ability. In junior hockey, he survived by being the most popular player. He originally went to Quad City in the United Hockey League when he turned pro. He got called up to Portland and stayed there because he became a popular player. His thought process is that he makes teams by being popular, not by being good.

Louis sits on the bench and looks at the crowd. He does things to play to the crowd rather than to play the game. The crowd still would like him if he cut out the sideshow because his style is fun. He drove me nuts with his antics. I constantly told him to shut up because of his yapping at the opposing bench.

We held on to win Game 1 at Wilkes-Barre/Scranton 5-4 after taking a 4-0 lead. The Penguins scored two short-handed goals late in the second period and eventually closed within 4-3 before Eric Fehr gave us breathing room midway through the third.

Frederic Cassivi pitched a 5-0 shutout in Game 2 as we swept the games at Wachovia Arena and continued the domination with a 4-1 victory in Game 3 at Giant Center. We won 1-0 in Game 4 on a Laich goal. I had a talk with Brooks and Colin Forbes before Game 3. Brooks wondered why he wasn't being more productive. I flat-out told him he wasn't playing well. It was another example of an NHL player struggling upon return to the AHL. After that, Brooks scored on a regular basis.

Though the Wilkes-Barre/Scranton series lasted just four games, we were physically beaten up after being relatively free of serious injuries all season. We lost Graham Mink to a sports hernia in the regular season, otherwise he would have scored those forty goals. Mink was back in time for the play-offs. Against the Penguins, we took two big hits on the blue line. Lawrence Nycholat and Mark Wotton—two of our top defensemen—suffered shoulder injuries. Defensive depth had been a serious concern all season, and play-off attrition hit us hard in a spot where we could least afford it.

Wotton made a believer out of me. The first time I saw him practice, I said, "What the heck did they sign here?" He can't shoot. He can't skate. But he gets the job done and grows on you. Wotty's a solid family guy, and mark my words, he's going to be a good coach.

Portland awaited in the Eastern Conference finals. Because of the blue-line injuries, we brought in Tyler Sloan from the ECHL. Junior addition Jeff Schultz, a first-round Washington draft choice, stepped up in a pressure situation. And Jakub Cutta, who struggled with a mysterious body trunk injury during the regular season, was an unsung hero during the whole postseason run. We improbably won the first two games at Cumberland County Civic Center, getting another shutout from Cassivi in a 5-0 series-opening win and following with a 2-1 Game 2 triumph on Mink's goal 1:52 into overtime.

The Game 2 win made us 10-0 in the play-offs. At that point, we thought we were going to sweep Portland too. But we blew a two-goal lead at home in Game 3 and lost 6-5 in double overtime.

Cassivi got his third play-off shutout in a 4-0 Game 4 victory that sent us back to Portland, leading 3-1.

In Game 5 we led 2-0 entering the third period but wasted a chance to close out the Pirates, who scored three times in the final twenty minutes to win 3-2. The Pirates won 5-3 in Game 6 to force a seventh game at Giant Center. Lawrence Nycholat, who had missed the first three games of the series with his shoulder injury, went off in the locker room. He told the team, "That's it. We're not losing again." Nycholat, like Mark Wotton, was a quiet leader, and when he erupted like that, it had an impact.

I'd have Lawrence on my team any time. He commands a high AHL salary, but he's the kind of guy who is worth whatever you pay him in the minors because he's an excellent player who adds the intangible bonus of being an outstanding mentor for your young prospects. Nychy made Mike Green and Jeff Schultz better players. They developed and quickly became contributors to the Caps because of the time they spent around Nychy. Nycholat made Mike Green a player that first year. Nychy might have made one-way money and didn't play much in the NHL, but it was a cost-effective signing because of how much it helped Mike Green.

There was a six-day gap between Game 6 and Game 7. During that break, we kept an eye on Anaheim's progress in the Stanley Cup play-offs. We wished my old Toronto teammate Randy Carlyle and the Ducks success because we wanted them to keep playing. If they were eliminated, highly touted players Dustin Penner, Ryan Getzlaf, and Corey Perry were slated to be reassigned to Portland. Well, Anaheim was eliminated, and the talented trio—all three are now NHL stars—arrived in time for Game 7.

Before Game 1, Portland's head coach, Kevin Dineen, requested that we keep our practices closed to each other. I said no problem. But the day before

Game 7, I spotted Kevin and his assistants in the stands at Hersheypark Arena, where we occasionally practiced. I had changed practice to 10:00 a.m. from a scheduled 11:00 a.m. start to make double sure Dineen wouldn't be around. Granted, I didn't specifically tell Dineen to stay away, but I assumed he would based on our previous agreement.

I started working on the power play and was mad at the players. We were all cranky because we'd wasted two chances to close out Portland. Bob Woods noticed Dineen in the stands. I took a deep sigh, blew the whistle, and loudly pointed out Dineen in unprintable language. I'm not usually like that. I don't think it was consciously premeditated to get the guys going, but maybe it subconsciously was. Dineen stood and replied in unprintable language that included an insult about my weight. It turned into an F-bomb festival that continued under the stands after practice. The confrontation added to the excitement for Game 7.

Game 7 was a classic, though I don't think we should have let the series go seven. It was one of the most exciting games you'll ever see and capped one of the greatest series in the history of a storied franchise that's played in the AHL for more than seventy years. There was so much hatred between the teams. The players hated each other. The coaches hated each other. Bob Woods and Portland centerman Zenon Konopka, jawing nose-to-nose, almost had a fight between the benches before Game 2 in Portland.

In Game 7 Portland took a 2-0 lead, but we showed the resilience we'd demonstrated all season by coming back. The game was tied 3-3 at first intermission. Dustin Penner scored his second goal, a short-hander, at 13:26 of the second, to give Portland a 4-3 lead, an edge that held until late in the third.

Frederic Cassivi made a huge third-period save to keep it from going to 5-3. Boyd Kane had a monstrous physical shift midway through the period that gave us a jolt. We were all over them the last ten minutes but just couldn't score.

Portland's goalie, Jani Hurme, was unfairly maligned during the series. He was terrific in the last three games and made forty-two saves in Game 7, including a fabulous late save on Tomas Fleischmann that I momentarily feared was our last gasp. But Graham Mink converted the rebound from that save to tie it with 2:09 left. The crowd of more than eight thousand went nuts, and we went into overtime.

No matter what we tell you, coaches are nervous in these situations. A coach doesn't want to be the one who makes the mistake that costs the game. I never know whether to be conservative and outlast the other team—wait for them to make a mistake—or whether to just go for it. It's a tough call. Roger Neilson always wanted to outwait foes because he thought his teams were better conditioned.

In overtime Ryan Getzlaf missed a golden chance to end the series. Dustin Penner was into the game. Corey Perry was into it. Getzlaf, though—I could tell he wasn't sharp. He had an open net and hit the side of the net. He puts that shot in ninety-nine out of one hundred times.

Next thing you know, Eric Fehr scored from the top of the right circle at 9:07 of overtime to send us to the Calder Cup finals. Eric played eleven games in Washington and got reassigned to Hershey for the play-offs. He could have played not to look bad, but he played to win. That's who you want on your team. However, Eric had struggled in the Portland series and was scratched in Games 4 and 5. He was on the fourth line in Game 7, but for some reason he was out with second liners Brooks Laich and Colin Forbes when he scored. Eric's usually a humble, respectful young man, but he was bold enough coming out of juniors to boast that he's a player who scores big goals. That big goal certainly proved him right and created bedlam in the building.

I jumped up and down on the bench, then ran onto the ice and leaped on the player pile like a drunken fan. Then I realized, Wait, I'm the coach and I shouldn't be doing this. I had to tuck my shirt back in before I shook Kevin Dineen's hand.

The Calder Cup finals against the Milwaukee Admirals were almost anticlimatic. I didn't know much about Milwaukee. On paper, the Admirals looked formidable. They won the West Division championship in the regular season. After a seven-game series against Iowa in the first round of the play-offs, they swept Houston in the West Division finals and swept Grand Rapids in the Western Conference finals to reach the Calder Cup finals.

I knew Milwaukee had an excellent head coach in former Bear Claude Noel and dangerous scorers in Darren Haydar and Simon Gamache.

Defenseman Shea Weber was an impressive prospect, and their goalie, Pekka Rinne, had been dominant in the postseason.

Milwaukee made us look bad for the first forty minutes while beating us 2-1 in Game 1 at Bradley Center. It took most of Game 1 to mentally put the Portland series behind us and begin playing up to our capabilities, and it meant we trailed in a series for the first time the entire postseason. In the third period we showed we could play against a team we worried was a juggernaut. Lawrence Nycholat scored late, and we had some chances to tie in the final four minutes.

My buddy, Chicago Wolves head coach John Anderson, who was quite familiar with Milwaukee from the West Division, had given me a thorough scouting report and reassured me we could win the series even though we were considered underdogs. Tomas Fleischmann, with two goals and two assists, was magic in a 6-3 Game 2 triumph that gave us home-ice advantage and, in our minds, exposed Rinne as a big netminder who wasn't all that agile. His size meant a lot of pucks hit him, but he was vulnerable if you made him move.

That said, Rinne shut us out 2-0 in Game 3 in the first Calder Cup finals game ever played at Giant Center. We mustered twenty-one mostly inconsequential shots in our worst game of the play-offs.

We were horrid in front of a sellout crowd of 10,840. I think it was because after winning Game 2, we figured we were going to sweep the rest of the series and clinch it on home ice.

We refocused and had strong wins in Game 4 (7-2) and Game 5 (6-4) to head back to Milwaukee with a 3-2 series lead. After the Game 3 stinker, we outscored Milwaukee 18-7 in the final three games of the series and finished the play-offs with a staggering plus-thirty-seven goal differential.

Before Game 6 I recounted Richmond's chance to take us out in Game 6 of the Kelly Cup finals when I was with Mississippi in the ECHL. I remembered the champagne stacked outside Richmond's locker room that its players never got to drink. I cautioned our team against the same complacency.

We took a 4-0 lead in the first 21:45 of Game 6. Despite the four-goal bulge, we were extremely nervous and almost comically scared at times. At one point, Graham Mink turned around to me on the bench and said, "Don't give me the puck. I can't touch it. I can't feel anything." He was so genuinely swayed by the emotion of winning.

The clock slowly, inexorably ticked down toward a 5-1 triumph. Near the end, trainer Dan "Beaker" Stuck sneaked my son Brady onto the bench for the final moments, which made for a wonderful experience for both of us.

During the cup run, Frederic Cassivi and Tomas Fleischmann really stood out. Fleischmann, who had thirty-two points in twenty games, was amazing. Freddy, named AHL play-off MVP, was zoned in. Quite frankly, though, I would have voted for Fleischmann for MVP. You could have picked Flash and Freddy 1-A and 1-B. Flash was too good. He was dynamic every time he touched the puck. I've never seen a player do at the AHL level what he did in those play-offs. Stickhandle. Make plays. Drive the net. Play tough. Sometimes Flash was so dazzling that I got caught up in watching him and forgot to coach.

But I don't want to take anything away from Freddy, who went 16-5 in the play-offs after going 34-19-6 in the regular season and playing in a staggering sixty-one games. If you don't have goaltending, you're not going to win in the play-offs. Freddy was a rock and made great saves when we needed great saves. Any time a goalie wins you a championship, you have a soft spot for him. Freddy's a great teacher for young goalies. He's quiet, low maintenance, and has an even personality that is a steadying influence on a team. When I'd yank him in the regular season, I'd go, "Freddy, what's up? I'm sorry I had to pull you." He'd say, "Oh, don't worry." Everything rolled off his shoulders. Freddy's similar to Olie Kolzig. Olie was the team leader in the dressing room in Washington, and Freddy was a team leader in Hershey.

AHL lines don't get better than left winger Fleischmann, centerman Kris Beech, and right winger Graham Mink. They had a dangerously complementary dynamic. Mink was strong in the corners and in front of the net. Beech could stand tall in the slot and dish. Flash could make a play or score from anywhere.

As a rookie the previous season in Portland, Flash had only nineteen points. His progression to a thirty-goal regular season and his subsequent explosion in the play-offs epitomized what I had stressed back at the start of training camp: These guys were good and just had to prove it to themselves. They did, and we drank from the Calder Cup.

I slept on the team plane on the way home from Milwaukee while the players partied up a storm. I had one beer and snoozed with a smile on my face. Winning was the prize. I didn't need any other reward or celebration. To be the last man standing was a tremendous feeling.

Washington general manager George McPhee was an insightful counselor for me. The Caps weren't in the Stanley Cup play-offs, and he followed us during our whole play-off drive. George kept telling me to enjoy the ride because stuff like this doesn't happen too often. Because of all the concerns that go into coaching, though, I can't honestly say I knew how to enjoy the ride. But to live in that moment, where my team and I strived for excellence and achieved it, was an unforgettable experience.

The reception we received when we arrived back in Pennsylvania at 4:30 a.m. was amazing. Fans greeted us at Harrisburg International Airport and Giant Center to congratulate us on winning the ninth Calder Cup in franchise history. That evening we had a raucous celebration at Giant Center with almost eight thousand people in attendance.

We brought all the wives and girlfriends into the locker room before it started and showed them our pump-up video. The pump-up video, produced by Bears staffer Lamont Buford, better known as "Puckhead" to Hershey fans, was important to us in the play-offs. I began playing it at the start of the postseason, using highlights of our regular season to inspire us to even bigger things. After every round, we increased it by seven or eight minutes with the highlights of our series wins. It was forty minutes long by the end. Watching it one last time together was emotional.

Two nights after the public team celebration, country music star Tim McGraw held a concert at Giant Center and invited us on stage. Fortunately for everybody in attendance, I didn't have to sing, but it felt like we were living out the lyrics of McGraw's hit song, "Live Like You Were Dying."

During the play-offs I began wearing a lucky tie. It was a hideous thing with an abstract green color scheme that resembled vomit. You might be tempted to pour sawdust on it, but there was magic in that silk. And, yes, it was silk—not polyester. I'd worn the tie sporadically with some superstitious success. I wore it for Game 2 against Milwaukee, but I didn't put it on for Game 3 and we lost. Thus, I had to wear it every game after that. For Games 5 and 6, the players made sure in the morning skates that I'd be wearing it regardless of how sullied and stained it became.

Somehow Bears general manager Doug Yingst purloined the tie during the frenzy of our celebration at Bradley Center in Milwaukee. I thought I'd lost it. Three days later Doug presented the tie to me in a frame.

I promised my friend Billy Laberge, owner of Billy's Sports Bar & Grill in Manchester, New Hampshire, that I'd bring the Calder Cup for a visit if one of my teams ever won it. Billy jokingly nicknamed me "One-and-Done" because of our first-round woes in Manchester. One-and-done no more, I delivered the cup as promised when it was my turn to have it during the summer. I got positive feedback from a lot of people. However, a lot of people thought I was sticking it in the face of the Manchester people. That wasn't the intent.

The Hershey Bears clinched the Calder Cup on June 15, 2006, a year and five days after my Manchester firing.

To that point, it was the greatest year of my life.

# 11

## GOOD-BYE KISSES

**American Thanksgiving in 2007**—the day I was promoted to the Washington Capitals—was a tremendous day for me. Canadian Thanksgiving in 2006 was horrible. On that day, October 9, I found out my youngest brother, Barry, was killed the previous day while hitchhiking.

We had suffered so much personal tragedy in recent years. My father and my wife Crystal's mother had both died. Now this. Was it ever going to stop? There are so many bad things that mix in with the good. It means you're getting older, I guess.

I was in Doug Yingst's office at Giant Center talking with Doug and trainer Dan "Beaker" Stuck. I excused myself to go to the restroom, when my brother Bryan, the middle brother of us three, called my cell phone. He said, "I've got to tell you something." It was in a tone that you instinctively know means terrible news. My heart went in my throat. My initial thought was that my mom had passed away.

"Barry's dead," Bryan said.

"No, don't tell me that," I pleaded.

"He got hit by a car on the 400."

I returned to Doug's office like a zombie and looked at him and Beaker. I said, "My brother's dead." Next thing I know, I fell to the floor. Doug and Beak helped me up and gave me big hugs. Doug drove me home. I got in the car and drove straight to Toronto.

On Canadian Thanksgiving a lot of Toronto people go to their summer cottages. It's the last real chance to go before winter takes hold. Ironically, I'd had a lot of friends call complaining about a huge traffic jam on Highway 400, a key north-south route linking Toronto to central and northern Ontario, that delayed their trips. Well, the traffic jam was because of Barry.

Barry got into a little fight with my mother and wasn't going to Bryan's for Thanksgiving dinner. Mom went to Bryan's alone. I think Barry felt guilty and decided to hitchhike up to join them. He got left off on one side in Barrie, about forty miles north of Toronto, and had to cross the 400. Instead of walking a hundred yards and taking the sky walk, he tried to cross an eight-lane highway. He made it past the first two lanes, the way I heard it, and got hung up at the third lane. A car was coming too fast and he stopped. Barry got caught in the path of fast traffic with nowhere to go. A maroon Oldsmobile Alero hit him doing sixty. Highway 400 was closed from 4:00 p.m. to 9:00 p.m. because of it.

I was so worried about my mom. Since my dad died, Barry had lived at home and was her companion. Mom was more upset with Barry's death than my dad's. Barry had been the one who kept her going because my mom and dad had been so inseparable for all those years. Mom is hanging in there, though.

Theresa Boudreau is the quiet one in our family. Usually, the women in the family are the strongest, and that's the case in our household. She's all of four foot eleven, ninety pounds, but you don't want to cross her. She was the glue. It always seems like it's the father who gets the credit for carting kids around, but it's the mother who stays at home and does all the work to keep the family going. She told my dad to go to practices and drive everybody everywhere, but she's the one who ran the ship.

My mom's not demonstrative in a rah-rah fashion, but she's a bundle of nerves. I offered to buy her the "NHL Center Ice" package so she could watch Washington Capitals games, but she didn't want it because it makes her too nervous. She watches the sports ticker, and if we're losing, she turns it off. She's had it tough with my dad and my brother dying. We talk on the phone about twice a week, and now that Dad and Barry are gone our conversations are longer.

Mom still lives by herself in a big house in Toronto. That concerns me, but she wants to stay independent. She's driving herself around again. She's had a license, but my dad always drove everywhere. Now she drives short distances. She still shovels snow in her driveway and cuts the lawn. I hope I'm as spry as she is when I'm in my mid-seventies.

At five foot ten, I was small for hockey. But we're baffled that I got so big, relatively speaking, with a four-foot-eleven mother and a five-foot-two father. It's unbelievable. Barry was about five foot four, and Bryan is about five foot five. And I became a monster. All the gene pools for height must have combined and added a few inches. You can go back generations, and there's nobody big in our family.

●

In 2006–7, we lost a lot of players off Hershey's 2005–6 championship team to free agency: Graham Mink, Boyd Kane, Mark Wotton, Kris Beech. I talked to all of them. They wanted to stay in Hershey, but they also wanted a chance to play in the NHL. Other teams promised them that opportunity, and they signed elsewhere. Can't blame them. That's life in the AHL, where there's high season-to-season roster turnover.

We added Alexandre Giroux, who was a premier goal scorer in the league. When the Bears signed Matt Hendricks, I figured he'd be buried on the depth chart and was a wasted signing. I didn't have a clue about that kid, and he'd show me he was a player. I knew free-agent addition Quintin Laing from the Norfolk Admirals, and I knew he was going to replace Kane in a checking-line leadership role.

One thing we didn't have was a No. 1 centerman or the depth we'd enjoyed at the position during the Calder Cup season. We started with Joey Tenute, Dave Steckel, and Petr Taticek. Then Taticek left to return to the Czech Republic after playing one game. The position remained a trouble spot all season.

We opened 2006–7 with a goal of making history. We wanted to win consecutive Calder Cups. We wanted to make a claim to being one of the best teams in AHL history. Complacency can be a problem the season following a championship, but the returning guys liked the taste of victory and were ready to pay the price again. Holdover guys like Lawrence Nycholat made sure the new guys had a championship hunger. It was a chance to step up for

Tenute, Eric Fehr, Chris Bourque, and Jakub Klepis. They all had supporting roles during the cup run but now had to play major roles.

Bourque, son of hall-of-famer Ray Bourque, has a tremendous work ethic on the ice. His whole life has been about playing hockey. He's driven to succeed, and he works his rear end off to accomplish that and overcome his size handicap (he's five foot eight, 180 pounds). Bourque's one of those guys you want to see succeed.

We had a tremendous start to the season and kept the consistency and momentum going from 2005–6. We took off from the gate and won ten of our first twelve games, though one of the losses was a shootout defeat to Bridgeport on the night our Calder Cup banner was raised at Giant Center. The top three teams in the league, in my opinion, were all in the East Division: Wilkes-Barre/Scranton, Norfolk, and Hershey. We couldn't shake those clubs despite our start. Any one of the three teams, which all finished with more than one hundred points, probably would have had 124 points in another division. The Bears kept pushing to the point that other teams became worn down. Plus, we knew how to win from the previous season.

We won the division and posted the best record in the league. Hershey set single-season club records for wins (fifty-one), points (114), and road wins (twenty-five). Combined with the 101 points in 2005–6, it marked the first time Hershey produced consecutive one-hundred-point seasons in its long and storied history.

In January I got to coach the Canadian team at the AHL All-Star Classic in Toronto because I was head coach of the defending Calder Cup champions. We lost 7-6 to PlanetUSA at Ricoh Coliseum. Despite the loss, it was a treat to return home for such a festive event and see family and friends. Our Hershey team charter bus broke down in New York on the way back home. That trip presaged another painful bus ride home from Ontario in June.

In the first round of the play-offs against Albany, neither Bears goalie Frederic Cassivi nor River Rats goalie Tyler Weiman were sharp. Freddy struggled relative to the season before. He broke his collarbone and also spent a long recall stint in Washington. His numbers remained solid, though, and we were a good defensive team despite my tag as an offensive coach.

Tom Rowe, who was with me in Lowell, coached Albany. I respect Tom a lot. We've had some great battles, but we've always stayed friends. We won that series in five games after losing Game 2 at home in overtime on a goal by former Bear Shane Willis.

That set up a play-off rematch with Wilkes-Barre/Scranton in the East Division finals. I never felt as threatened by the Penguins as I did by Albany, which played hard-fought, physical games against us in the regular season. We expected to beat Wilkes-Barre/Scranton because we'd done it the year before. We took them out in five games, winning three games in overtime. Alex Giroux's Game 5 overtime goal gave us a wild 7-6 victory to close out the series.

And who do we draw in the Eastern Conference finals? Yep, the Manchester Monarchs. I played down the soap opera aspect of the matchup. We expected a tough sled and were surprised that the Monarchs didn't make adjustments during what turned out to be an easy series. They were small and played the same way all four games. The lack of competitiveness stood in stark contrast to the heated 2006 conference finals against Portland. It wasn't even close. We outscored Manchester 18-5 in a four-game sweep.

My biggest thrill in beating Manchester had nothing to do with the politics of when I coached there. It was watching my team on the bench hugging each other as conference champions. This team followed up 2005–6 to win something in its own right. It's extremely rare for a team to advance to the Calder Cup finals two straight years. It showed me how much we wanted to win. Manchester was our seventh straight series win over the course of two years. That tied the AHL record for consecutive play-off series won.

Ultimately, the easy series against Manchester hurt us. It didn't prepare us for the Hamilton Bulldogs, who we played in the Calder Cup finals. Hamilton finished in third place in the North Division. The consensus was that we'd win, despite the fact that the Bulldogs had eliminated hundred-plus-point teams Manitoba and Chicago to win the Western Conference title.

Hamilton reminded me a bit of our 2005–6 club, and I should have anticipated how strong the Bulldogs would be. I saw on tape what they did to every other team. Maybe I let up. Maybe we took it a little too easily. I don't know.

The Bulldogs were a determined team that never had home ice in any series. Yet they won Game 1 in every series, including a 4-0 victory over us at Giant Center in the opening contest of the finals. In goal they had first-round Montreal draft pick Carey Price, who had forty-six saves in Game 1. Nineteen-year-old Price joined Hamilton after his junior season with Tri-City in the Western Hockey League ended and played with cool precision amid play-off pressure. I felt like I was watching a rerun of Patrick Roy's performance against our Baltimore team in 1985.

Price eventually was named MVP of the play-offs, but Hamilton's big defensemen were a bigger key to the series. We couldn't get through them. Aside from Game 2, we didn't play tenaciously enough to.

We hit the Bulldogs hard and often to tie the series with a 4-2 win in Game 2. I thought we had to make it a short series. We weren't physically equipped to benefit from a long series because we were smaller than them. That meant Game 3 was critically important.

But we had a major problem: We had to get in a bus the day after Game 2 for an eight-hour ride to Hamilton and play Game 3 the day after that. We didn't have a chance to physically recover from Game 2 and didn't have much energy in a 5-2 Game 3 defeat at Copps Coliseum.

I thought we'd rebound. I had no doubt we'd win Game 4, given our resilience and the fact we had a day off to rest between Games 3 and 4. But we played terribly in a 6-2 loss. That gave Hamilton a chance to close out the series on home ice since the series was a two-three-two format.

We outplayed the Bulldogs in Game 5, which was tied 1-1 after two periods. Hamilton's Ajay Baines, a diabetic like me, scored a short-handed goal at 9:33 of the third and that was it. The Bulldogs won the game 2-1 and claimed the series 4-1. End of story.

Carey Price was sharp, and Hamilton's defense was too big for our small forwards to get enough second shots on him. My concern from the start of the season about center depth surfaced as an Achilles' heel in the Calder Cup finals. Forwards Jakub Klepis and Tomas Fleischmann were by far the best two players we had in Hamilton, but we needed more than that to make up for the losses of Eric Fehr (injury), Kip Brennan (suspension), and Lawrence Nycholat (trade).

Fehr was out with a back-hip problem that first sidelined him when he was up with Washington in February. His size and scoring ability would have helped against Hamilton.

Not having Brennan, a six-foot-four, 230-pound winger who could run guys and fight, was a real blow. Kip got suspended for the rest of the play-offs after a fan altercation with 19.8 seconds left in Game 3 at Manchester. The incident didn't look like a season-ending suspension to me, but that's what the league ruled. The fan came over and grabbed at Kip in the penalty box. Because the box was loose, he could reach through the seam where the penalty box glass met the dasher board glass. The guy pulled away when Kip grabbed him back and got his shirt ripped. Kip's mistake was reaching out of the penalty box after the guy withdrew.

Kip's a lunatic, and I mean that in a paternal fashion. Big, tough, loves the hockey life. In the 1963 movie *Bye Bye Birdie*, amphetamines are given to a turtle and you see its eyes spin in its head. That's Kip. The first couple years I had him in Manchester, he was hard to control. But he's a good kid in his way, and I got to the point where I could control him—for the most part. The biggest mistake he ever made was going after that fan.

We'd probably all react the way Kip did in the heat of the moment. But pro sports leagues are extremely conscientious about protecting fans. The league had to be stern. It cost Kip big-time. Had he had the exposure of playing in the Calder Cup finals, which get a lot of attention in the hockey community, he would have had a chance to showcase himself in order to regain NHL prospect status. Kip ended up signing a two-way contract with the New York Islanders after the season, but I think he'd have had a stronger negotiating hand if he'd been able to play in the finals.

We lost Lawrence Nycholat to Ottawa in a trade-deadline deal. I think we would have won the Calder Cup again had Nychy stayed, though he would have had to clear waivers to rejoin us from Washington; my guess is some NHL team would have claimed him. Our power play would have been much better. But the minors are about giving guys a chance, and Nychy deserved an opportunity to have an NHL chance with another organization. He didn't get to play a game for Ottawa in the play-offs, but he was around for the run to the Stanley Cup finals.

Injuries also caught up with defenseman Dean Arsene, a heart-and-soul guy who succeeded Nycholat as captain. Deano was on the ice for four games in the finals, but he wasn't 100 percent. Later that summer he underwent double sports hernia surgery. Arsene is a tough competitor. The man gave everything—absolutely everything—during the 2005–6 cup season and the 2006–7 season even though he was never fully healthy. His body simply wore out. He never thought about protecting himself, never considered not playing because it might jeopardize his career. He'd tell the team doctors, "Give me a needle; do something to get me through the game." Deano's the embodiment of what it means to be a Hershey Bear.

The finals' loss devastated Alex Giroux and Pete Vandermeer. They came achingly close to being on their first Calder Cup championship team, and it was snatched away.

Giroux is a pure goal scorer who's going to get thirty-plus every year in the AHL. He kind of faded after representing Hershey in the AHL All-Star Classic. I had the season-ending exit meeting with him and said, "You've got to do something in the summer to add some muscle."

Pete Vandermeer, a tough customer who has passed the 300 mark in penalty minutes many times in the AHL, grew on me like Mark Wotton had the season before. At the start of the season, I thought Pete might be the worst player I'd ever seen. I don't think he does a lot of training in the summer. He's naturally strong, and he uses camp to get in shape. He's not a good skater, but he's very responsible and knows how to play. Vandy's going to be a coach and be a good one.

I had a lot of respect for the way Pete took it when we told him he'd sit out a lot early because of veteran roster limit rules. He said, "No problem, I'd rather sit out early than late." Pete had that trigger, though. If you crossed the wires wrong, he was snarly.

The first time Pete played for me, in an exhibition game at Wilkes-Barre/Scranton, he got beat up in fights against Grant McNeill and Dennis Bonvie and was ejected. I thought, What's the point of having this guy on the club? Well, what you discover is that he's a tremendous team guy. Pete's quite a character, and there's a reason he's lasted for more than a decade in pro hockey.

Pete led our Black Aces, the practice squad of players who aren't in the play-off lineup. He did a bang-up job like Doug Doull had done in 2005–6. Vandy kept the Black Aces together and kept the locker room alive. People talk about how I've paid my dues. Pete's a guy who's paid his dues and fought everybody.

I should have learned my lesson the time I let my Muskegon team drink on that ill-fated trip when we bused to Thunder Bay in my first year as a head coach. But I did it again for the ride back to Hershey after we lost to Hamilton. I thought this team was at a more mature age level than the guys were in Muskegon, so I didn't anticipate any trouble. But there was trouble.

We stopped at the U.S.-Canada border, and I let four guys get off to grab beer at the duty-free shop. I thought they'd each bring only a case back. That's ninety-six beers for twenty-two guys, so it's not going to get too out of hand. However, each guy brought back three or four cases. I didn't like it, but I let it go.

When a season ends, players lose a bit of their team loyalty since they can be on different clubs the following season. If you know Louis Robitaille, you know he can be an antagonistic guy, especially when he drinks. He has a habit of saying stupid stuff at the wrong time. The beer flowed, and Robitaille's lips flapped.

Robitaille's digs aren't subtle. It would be like fighting with your wife, and all of a sudden calling her a cow. He told guys they couldn't play or their girlfriends were ugly. Eventually, five or six teammates wanted to beat him up. It got nasty.

I broke up a couple potential brawls between Louis and Deryk Engelland and Louis and Matt Hendricks. Hendy wanted to pound him. The next day they went to a bar in Hershey called Shakey's and Louis started up again. The guys took it outside to the parking lot. I think Louis got hit hard a couple times by Eggo and Hendy, good friends who trained together in the off-season.

Now I swear I'll never let it happen again. We don't drink on the Caps plane, which is great, because George McPhee has instituted that rule.

●

It's heartening to see that my Washington success is maybe helping to open the door for other AHL coaches. You have to know the right people, and you have to be in the right situation to get an NHL head-coaching job. Trust me, I know.

Add it up. Ninety-five regular-season wins over two years, one Calder Cup, a second trip to the Calder Cup finals. An average of 48.7 wins a season the previous three seasons, including two 51-win campaigns. A career regular-season coaching record of 525-361-76.

So how many calls did I get about NHL head-coaching openings during the summer of 2007?

Not one. Not even a sniff.

John Anderson and I would complain to each other about not getting opportunities. I was getting resigned to the fact that I'd never get an NHL chance. I'd dream about it and want it and think I could do it. But I didn't think I'd ever get the call.

I still was happy and excited because I got a new four-year contract to stay in Hershey. I had the best job outside of the NHL for four more years, which would take me to age fifty-six. I was a fortunate guy getting a continuing opportunity to coach a game I love in a town I love. Hershey is so rooted in tradition that the club's equipment manager, Justin Kullman, is the grandson of Bears great Arnie Kullman. No. 9, co-retired in honor of Arnie and Tim Tookey, is one of the numbers that hangs from the rafters at Giant Center. Justin Kullman is an up-and-coming hard worker who can climb to the NHL if he wants.

Sure, I was aware of the whole image thing and frustrated about being ignored by the NHL. At the same time, I was getting defiant: I wanted to make it on who I was, not on what everybody wanted me to be. I'm the working man's guy, and that's why people identify with me.

Thankfully, I had George McPhee, Doug Yingst, and Bruce Landon pushing for me every chance they got. I never would have gotten an NHL coaching opportunity from somebody who didn't know me. Because of the way I look, even if we had won a second Calder Cup in 2007, I don't think I would have gotten an NHL chance outside of the Washington organization.

George McPhee watched us during the 2006 and 2007 Calder Cup play-offs and got to see what I was about. He listened to my speeches and saw the way I ran practices and coached games. I think one of the big turning points for George came one game during the Calder Cup run in 2006. I was at Giant Center doing video at 1:30 p.m. for a 7:00 p.m. game. George asked our trainer, Dan "Beaker" Stuck, why I was there so early. Beaker told him I was always there that early. I think that impressed George.

I know Doug Yingst lobbied hard for me. I think it played a role in me getting a chance in Washington with the interim head-coaching title. If the interim thing didn't work out, the Caps could always pursue a big-name coach, and I could return to Hershey. George McPhee, Ted Leonsis, and Dick Patrick gave their minor-league coach a chance to develop just like they did their players. No matter what happens in the long run, I'll always be grateful for the courage it took for them to take that chance.

At Caps training camp in September 2007, George told me I was capable of being an NHL coach.

"You've got the ability," he said. "I just want you to know that."

I returned to Hershey feeling good about myself because George, with all his experience of being in the NHL for a quarter century, thought I could do the job. It gave me a lot of confidence. It's been fabulous working with George. He is a fierce competitor who hates to lose at anything.

Before that NHL chance finally arrived, I coached the Hershey Bears for the first fifteen games of the 2007–8 season.

The Bears had a thinner roster than the powerhouse lineups of the previous two seasons. That's understandable with the ebbs and flows of AHL personnel. The league is so cyclical that you can't really have a dynasty. I was wary about the season.

The Tomas Fleischmanns and Dave Steckels had graduated to Washington. They were being replaced by young players. We had some veteran guys joining the club who came from teams that hadn't been winning recently, which concerned me. Some of them resisted the way I tried to push them to excel. Joe Motzko, traded during the season after I went up to Washington, should have been better. He should have produced a point and a half a game, but he didn't because he didn't drive himself.

We were 8-7-0-0 when the phone rang on Thanksgiving morning. It was the worst start I'd been involved in since my first season in Manchester. We weren't anywhere near the team we wanted to be.

You can look at it one of two ways. You can complain about your roster, or you can take it as a challenge. I would have welcomed the challenge of coaching the Bears the rest of the season.

# 12

## NO RETREAT

**You never hear about a coach's style** until he gets to the NHL. Nobody talked about my style in the AHL. All of a sudden, when I took over the Caps, the mantra was that Bruce Boudreau had brought his offensive-minded, aggressive-attack style to the NHL.

I guess this was easy to say because my style contrasted with Glen Hanlon's conservative approach. But that's a false analysis—a bad analysis. I've been labeled as an offensive coach because I was an offensive player, but my teams play defense. Our goal as a team is to be proactive. If we're going to make a mistake, we want the mistake on our terms. We want to make the mistake playing our game rather than make the mistake while reacting to the other team's game. Our game is applying pressure in every zone.

Because we attack and don't sit back, critics think we're ignoring defense. Not true. It's really about taking time and space away from everybody anywhere on the ice so they can't make a play and creating a turnover. Pressure defense is what I call it. We apply pressure to create turnovers and then attack when we get the puck.

Once you adapt to the style, you're able to attack and defend. I've always been confused by teams that try to do one or the other. You can do both. When you do both, they feed off each other. Attacking well helps defensively; defending well helps offensively.

If an opposing team has puck possession in their defensive zone, my philosophy is that it's stupid to retreat and let them come to the blue line or red line and gain a head of steam when we can check them in their zone. By checking them in their zone, any potential turnover comes in a spot where we're able to score. We're close to their goal, and they're far from ours. That's simple geography that even I can understand. Letting them clear their zone and dump the puck puts us in our defensive zone; a mistake by us there puts them in a position to score. Why give it up?

How do we do it? We've got to work hard and take short shifts. That means we have to be sharp at recognizing when to come off and when to go on. I don't know if I was a selfish player or not. Usually, offensive players in the minors like me are tagged as selfish players. I hope I wasn't, but I'm sure ten out of ten people will tell you I was.

We preach team, team, team. Out of that players will find individual success. Look at the numbers. I've had league-scoring champions. Guys tend to set personal career highs playing for me. But that individual success evolves from the team concept.

Our style in the offensive zone puts pressure on our defensemen and the forward with high responsibility. I call it a triangle offense. That third forward has to be responsible, and the responsibility rotates among all three forwards depending on where the puck goes. There is freedom for a defenseman to go down deep for a puck too, but somebody else has to make the read and go support the position he vacated so we're not vulnerable to an odd-man rush.

Everything is about support. We can be as aggressive as we want offensively as long as five guys are working together. If you have three guys forechecking and a defenseman goes down low and they chip it by for a two-on-one, that's stupid hockey. That's not being aggressive; that's being stupid. But if a forward cycles to the point when a defenseman goes deep and it gets chipped by for a two-on-two, that's OK.

When players are learning the system, it might look like firewagon hockey. Because the concepts are fairly complicated, they take time to learn. But once the players learn the system and do it right, it's great defensive hockey. The result is you score more goals, but you also allow fewer goals.

Look at the 2007–8 Capitals. Our goals-allowed steadily went down from the first twenty-five or thirty games I was coach, when the guys were learning the system. At the start, we tended to have high-scoring games in goals-for and goals-against. The last twenty games we had one of the lowest goals-allowed in the league (1.85) while our goals-for stayed up (3.3). We allowed two or fewer goals in fourteen of our last twenty games while scoring three or more fourteen times. The concepts were exactly the same the whole time, but the players became proficient at implementing them. So much for that offensive stereotype.

Pressuring defensively creates offensive chances. Apply pressure but be responsible. Responsibility is what you have to teach. The better the players know it, the more responsible they become. Being responsible is recognizing when you have to cover for your teammate. If we have two guys in deep chasing the puck in the offensive zone, we can't have the third forward run in to join. He's got to hit the brakes and stay out and read. Then if the puck moves to a spot where he's got a chance to be the first one on it, he's free to chase, and somebody else has to retreat from being deep and cover his spot. Do that and reduce the number of odd-man rushes you'll face if you don't win the puck battle. Win the puck battle, and you've got a potential scoring chance.

Of course, mistakes will happen and odd-man rushes will result. Yes, it can put extra pressure on the goalie when there's a breakdown. I depend on my goalies to give us that one big breakaway save a game. When we allow an odd-man rush, we apply back pressure and race back claiming position in the middle of the ice. Our wingers are taught to come back to the slot in the defensive zone. We don't chase reflexively. I tell them to speed back, take a deep breath to survey the situation, and then decide where they need to go rather than scramble around and react without thinking.

We never want to surrender the middle of the ice on the backcheck. We want to force the opposing puck carrier to a wall so that it will take two passes instead of one for them to move the puck across ice for a scoring chance. That's why you want to occupy the slot instead of blindly chasing. A body in the slot will more effectively block their opportunity to get it across with one pass. Force them to make two passes instead of one, and there's a higher chance you get the puck back. In all zones, you play close together. You support, and you stay aggressive.

We play positional hockey in the defensive zone. Glen Hanlon used to compliment me on the way my Hershey players played in the defensive zone when the Caps called them up. That's because we taught them what to do without the puck in our zone. I have researched drills and systems my whole life, and I know what works. I demand that we follow systems to the inch. There is no leeway for personal interpretation by the player.

Ever microwave soup? The directions say to do it for ninety seconds. Don't try to do it for eighty seconds or a hundred seconds. The soup company has done the research that says ninety seconds is the optimum time. Same with hockey systems. When I say go underneath the dots, there's a reason for it. Don't deviate. Don't cut through the dots or go above the dots. It takes time to drive it home. I'm not trying to be Colonel Klink. I just know the best way to react to a specific game situation.

●

After we beat the Philadelphia Flyers in my NHL debut, it still felt like I was in a whirlwind. The Flyers were pretty good at that point in the season. They were considered one of the elite teams in the league. They didn't have too many injuries, and it was before they slumped.

I noticed too much of a celebratory aspect in media coverage about the victory. We won. What's the big deal? So what if it was in Philadelphia? We're supposed to win.

My first home game at Verizon Center came November 24 when the Carolina Hurricanes visited. The players were on a high from the Philly game, and the fans were excited. It was a great feeling walking onto the bench and hearing some pretty good cheers. I still didn't know my team very well. We hadn't had a chance to really practice. I was still learning the NHL routine.

Carolina provided my first indication of the increased speed of NHL hockey compared to AHL hockey. The Philadelphia game didn't seem fast. The Hurricanes, boy, they were in transition. They were moving, they were working, and they were flying. We got some great saves from Olie Kolzig, Alexander Ovechkin had two goals, and Michael Nylander had a goal and two assists in a 5-2 victory.

Washington's power play had been slumping before I took over. We scored our first three goals against Carolina on the power play to take a 3-0 lead. In public, we were stealthy about the tweaks we'd made, like they were Pentagon secrets. It wasn't too complicated. We just had to attack the net more, get the right guys to pay the price, and make plays rather than try to be five individuals. Before the game, we showed the highlight of Mike Green's power-play goal against Philadelphia, and I reiterated how the setup worked.

Two wins in a row helped the confidence-building process. I kept hammering away about the lofty aspirations I had for them. A positive mind-set had to be indelibly established.

The first dose of adversity arrived on November 26 when the Buffalo Sabres visited and beat us 3-1. The Sabres were in a groove, and it was their fifth straight win. My big thing was to bounce back and refuse to lose two in a row. A hallmark of my teams, from Manchester to Hershey to Washington, has been consistency. It's rare for my teams to lose two consecutive regulation games. The 2007–8 Caps continued that tradition. We went two straight games without a point just once after I took over. Those two games were in March when Nick Backstrom put the puck into his own net against Pittsburgh and when Boston scored two goals in the last five minutes on dubious penalty calls. Otherwise, we would have gone the whole season without losing two in a row in regulation.

Visiting Florida beat us 2-1 on November 28, but it was in an eleven-round shootout and we earned a standings point. It was more shootout frustration for the Caps and me. In Hershey, we'd struggled in shootouts, which complemented ongoing shootout woes in Washington. During the shootout against the Panthers, my read was that we didn't expect to win it. I tried to build the team up. We went last and had opportunities, but Florida won the shootout 4-3.

Our biggest blow that night was a groin injury suffered by Chris Clark, who scored our lone goal. He'd only play one more game the rest of the season. Down the stretch, we kept talking about how we needed a gritty forward. Well, here was a gritty forward who had scored thirty goals in 2006–7 and was our captain. We really missed him.

A November 30 game at Carolina meant my first NHL plane ride. I didn't need my son Brady's baseball quilt for that trip. It was a short flight, and after we arrived in Raleigh, I went to a movie with Jay Leach.

We should have won, but we lost 4-3. It seemed like all the calls went against us. A Rod Brind'Amour goal was reviewed for a high stick and counted. We had an Alex Ovechkin goal disallowed for kicking after a review, and a Mike Green goal was ruled to have entered the net after time ran out in the second period. We thought we got hosed in the refereeing department. We outplayed them but had lost three in a row, two in regulation. It made me worry about our December 1 visit to Florida.

At Florida, Brent Johnson started his first game in goal for me and had a tremendous twenty-four-save effort. Career minor-leaguer Quintin Laing, who had been called up from Hershey, played his first game for us. He repeatedly blocked shots at the end during a critical penalty kill, and we won 2-1 for a good bounce-back.

I was proud of Quintin Laing. We both started the season in Hershey, where I'd named him team captain. What an average guy. He's your typical rec league player who has worked tremendously hard to climb up from the ECHL. For him to be part of the NHL was a dream come true. He played three games for the Chicago Blackhawks in 2003–4, but he'd mainly been an AHL player in Norfolk and Hershey.

Laing's two-way NHL contract ended after the 2006–7 season, and he settled for an AHL-only deal. It's one of those career-reckoning moments when you realize your NHL window may have closed. But I went to bat to bring him up. We needed a role player, not a guy who was an offensive player for a fourth-line slot. We needed a guy who paid the price and blocked shots.

Though Laing has very average skills, his heart and tenacity are off the charts. He takes direction tremendously well. If I tell him something, he gets it immediately and executes it exactly. He's rarely the one who has something to do with a goal-against. The average fan might look at him, deem him unworthy of the NHL, and consider it a dubious decision to bring him up.

But Laing demonstrated what those of us who'd been around him in Hershey already knew. In Game 5 of the Calder Cup finals against Hamilton the previous season, he had played on one leg for Hershey after suffering a knee injury in Game 4. Took a painkiller shot and gutted it out. That's

Quint. The Washington media eventually nominated him for the prestigious Masterton Trophy for perseverance and dedication. That was so classy.

Laing played a valuable part in our success. He was a perfect thirteenth forward. Although Laing sat out frequently after we acquired Matt Cooke from Vancouver at the trade deadline, he would still do anything for the team. He was a lot like Rudy from Notre Dame, which incidentally is my favorite college football team. Whatever Quintin could do to make us better, even if it was just working hard in practice, he did it.

There were six days between the Florida game and our next game, a December 7 visit to the New Jersey Devils. It was the first time we had a stretch of practices where I could work with the team, and it gave me an opportunity to implement more stuff. We had good practices, and everybody went into New Jersey full of confidence despite the fact the Devils had won eight in a row.

Caps and Devils great Scott Stevens, the hall-of-fame defenseman, was honored before the game. We started sluggish, fell behind 2-0, and lost 3-2. Four losses in five games. I felt the tentacles of mediocrity trying to grip the Caps again, so I ripped into the team because they were accepting the one-goal loss. They thought, OK, we were close. I didn't want them to think close was good enough. They responded with three straight wins.

We returned home to Verizon Center on December 8 and, powered by a two-goal first, beat Atlanta 6-3. Then we won a rematch with New Jersey 3-2 at home on December 10. Laing scored his first career NHL goal in the Jersey game, and Jeff Schultz scored for a second straight game. Schultz was on fire. Schultz is going to be a top-notch defenseman by the age of twenty-five. He keeps gaining in stature and is becoming more physical as he grows into his six-foot-six body. He's got the demeanor to play in any situation because he doesn't get nervous.

Our December 12 game against the visiting New York Rangers was a 5-4 comeback win after we fell behind 2-0 again. Mike Green scored in overtime, and Joe Motzko, whom we'd called up from Hershey, scored twice. That made us 6-3-1 in our first ten under me. They were on a high, and their belief in themselves continued to grow.

However, the three-game streak ended with a 5-3 loss on December 14 to visiting Buffalo. The Sabres, who had our number until the last meeting of the season, outplayed us. Olie Kolzig allowed three questionable goals and was the first one to admit that he didn't play well.

The next night, December 15, we bounced back again with a 3-2 win at Tampa Bay. Brian Pothier, who scored the game-winner, had a good effort after I'd scratched him for two games. That was my second big scratch. The first one came after Alexander Semin said he was ready to play November 24 against Carolina after an injury. I told him he wasn't ready to play. I wanted to skate him harder before he played because I didn't want him to get hurt again. I didn't want Semin to dictate to me when he was going to play; I wanted to establish that the coaching staff dictated when the players were ready to play. I think the players thought that was a good move, and Olie Kolzig reassured me it was a good decision. Semin returned November 26 against Buffalo.

Brian Pothier hadn't been playing well. He was much better than what he was showing. He wasn't getting the systems or something. He responded favorably to being scratched and began playing the way he can play. It was a major blow when we later lost him for the season because of concussion problems.

It's a rare thing when you suffer a defeat and feel good afterward, but that's what happened when we traveled to Joe Louis Arena on December 17 and lost 4-3 in a shootout to a Detroit Red Wings club that would go on to win the Stanley Cup. It was a critical turning point in the season. We outplayed them, outshot them, and fought back to tie it on Semin's goal with 1:34 left in the third period. It showed the Caps they could play with anybody.

I told the team, "You guys just outplayed the best team in the league and deserved to win."

Before that game, the team mind-set was, I think we can. After that game, it was, Yes, we can. It was almost like a lightbulb going off.

Red Wings head coach Mike Babcock approached me after the game. Babcock, Montreal head coach Guy Carbonneau, and I were all 2007–8 Jack Adams Award finalists.

"You guys are good," Babcock said. "You're a very difficult team to play against and I like your team a lot."

Wings assistant coach Todd McLellan echoed that sentiment. Wings goalie coach Jimmy Bedard, a good friend who is goalie coach at my summer hockey school in St. Catharines, Ontario, phoned the next day and said the same thing. I relayed all that praise to the players at the next practice. I told them that if the powerful Red Wings thought they were good, it was another reason to believe in themselves.

Riding that Motown momentum, we looked forward to hosting the Montreal Canadiens on December 20. In a way, that game was a preview of our future. Goalie Cristobal Huet, who we'd acquire at the trade deadline, had thirty-five saves in his first game since December 1, and the Habs beat us 5-2. The Canadiens had only twenty-one shots, but every time they came down the ice they scored. They weren't bad goals. They were opportune goals.

I hadn't seen Huet since he played for me in 2002–3 in the AHL with Manchester. There was a knock on my office door after the game. It was Cris. I didn't think he would remember me. He'd gone on to be a big stud in Montreal. He thanked me for all the stuff I did in Manchester and wished my family well. That was so nice. Little did I know he'd be playing for me again in a couple of months.

We lost 3-2 in overtime on the road against the New York Islanders on December 22. It was one of our two worst games of the season. We had only sixteen shots on goal. We tied it on an Alex Ovechkin goal with fifty-five seconds left with Olie Kolzig pulled, but Richard Park scored in overtime. Park was left open when Mike Green got clipped in the ear by Jeff Schultz's stick.

Turns out Christmas was my last day as interim head coach of the Washington Capitals. The big present came on December 26 when the interim tag was removed from my title. I knew I'd have the job—and get paid NHL money—for at least the rest of the season. Crystal and I had kept saying, "Well, we're here another day. NHL money for another day." It was encouraging that after fifteen games my bosses were starting to think that I could do the job.

George McPhee had a quiet meeting with me. He said he had talked to his bosses, and they wanted to remove the interim designation. I said, "Great, George, good by me. Thank you." Yes, I enjoyed that. But final resolution on the job remained a question.

Fittingly, Dave Steckel and Tomas Fleischmann, two of my Hershey mainstays, had big games that night in a 3-2 home win over Tampa Bay. We always played close games against the Lightning but won the season series. Stecks and Flash played awesome against Tampa Bay all season. Everybody has a team they play well against, and that was their team.

Steckel's been my little project since I had him as a pro rookie in Manchester. With more NHL acclimation, he's going to get even better defensively and be capable of scoring at least fifteen goals every season. Look out once Flash breaks loose. He's a potential thirty-goal guy.

On December 27 we visited the Pittsburgh Penguins. It was a marquee matchup of two talented young teams that I expect will be battling for Eastern Conference supremacy for many years. Alexander Ovechkin and Sidney Crosby are two of the NHL's brightest young stars. Unfortunately, Alex took an ugly skate cut on his thigh worth about twenty-five stitches.

After Brent Johnson exited the net with a sprained knee in the first, we fought back and fought back before losing 4-3 in overtime. It was the first time I'd seen Crosby play in person, and I was impressed. They tied it late in the third on a Darryl Sydor power-play goal set up by a dubious roughing call on Shaone Morrisonn, and they won it on Sergei Gonchar's overtime score. There was a here-we-go-again feeling of defeat since Pittsburgh had dominated recent meetings with Washington.

I launched an angry postgame tirade in the locker room, and I think it had a profound effect. It was early in my NHL coaching career, and I had to make the players understand that I wasn't just an AHL guy, that I was willing to be tough on an NHL team. I had to show I wasn't intimidated. I asked my assistant coaches if I should blast the team and they said no. I decided to do it anyway.

It made everybody realize they could be criticized and appraised on their performance. I wasn't going to allow anybody to take shortcuts. I did it after a loss to the best team in the conference, when I could have made it into a moral victory. At another time, the Caps might have accepted it as a moral victory. I wanted to drive home that we did not accept losing to anybody and we did not accept anything less than a best effort from everybody on every shift. Obviously, it had been an ongoing point, but this was an exclamation point to the theme.

I prefer to do that kind of thing in private. Good coaches don't often publicly rip their players. Once you start doing that, you're just trying to show the ownership you're working hard when what you're really showing is that you're failing. Even inside the locker room, I try not to criticize anybody individually in front of the team, though there are situations where I'll make an exception. I believe that they know in their hearts who I'm specifically talking about when I talk about a particular problem in general. If I rail about the need to keep shifts shorter and not be selfish, the two or three guys who've been taking over-long shifts know who I'm talking about without me mentioning their names. I might also pull them aside and talk privately. Sometimes, after a general talk, one of the players might approach me and tell me he knew I was referring to him and that he got the message.

We closed out the 2007 calendar year on December 29 at Ottawa. The Senators had the best record in the league, but the Caps had beaten them 4-1 on November 8 in Glen Hanlon's final victory as head coach. Joe Corvo, who played for me in Manchester, came up and said hello. Randy Robitaille said hello, and I was so embarrassed because I didn't recognize him. I coached him for only six games in Manchester, and it should have been the opposite: I should have recognized him, and he shouldn't have recognized me. I felt like an idiot.

The game was a showcase of former Hershey Bears head coaches. Ottawa head coach John Paddock preceded me in Hershey and won the Calder Cup in 1988 with an unprecedented 12-0 run through the play-offs. Ottawa general manager Bryan Murray was a former Hershey and Washington head coach. Alexander Semin scored on the first shift, the start of an impressive game for him. It made me think my Pittsburgh outburst had a positive effect on the team.

But the main highlight of the game was Ovie. We didn't know until game time whether he was going to play because of that cut he suffered in Pittsburgh. His leg looked awful. I pictured how the stretching and moving required in playing would stress the stitches. Alex insisted on playing, which was my first indication of how truly tough this kid is.

Alex scored four goals and added an assist in our 8-6 triumph. Five points. Unbelievable. I wish you could bottle Ovie's toughness. His competitive fires are remarkable. That performance came on Canadian soil during a Saturday night national CBC telecast. This showed Canadian hockey fans that, hey, this Caps team was exciting. Whether they're good or bad, we don't know, but they're exciting.

# 13

## MATCH GAME

**The idea of forced line matching drives me nuts.** You might get credit from pundits and observers for allegedly being a tactical wizard by matching all the time. But it isn't necessarily all that smart.

When I played for the Toronto Maple Leafs, my friend Jack Valiquette got traded to the Colorado Rockies. The Rockies were a weak team. Jack, a fourth-line guy who played six minutes a game in Toronto, became a first-line centerman in Colorado. When we played the Rockies, Roger Neilson pulled the Darryl Sittler–Lanny McDonald line every time Jack's line came on the ice because he wanted to match our checking line against Jack's "No. 1" line. It made no sense. Why worry about matching Valiquette's line? It reduced ice time for the Sittler-McDonald line. Jack's line played twenty-two or twenty-three minutes, and Darryl's line played fifteen or sixteen minutes. Don't we get more value if Darryl's line is out twenty-two or twenty-three minutes?

Fast-forward to today and we're playing, say, the Pittsburgh Penguins. If the Penguins send out Sidney Crosby's line, why would I take Alex Ovechkin's line off and put out Dave Steckel's checking line instead? If I do that I reduce Alex's ice time to fifteen minutes. That's stupid. That puts Pittsburgh in a better position to win because odds are that Crosby's line is going to outscore Steckel's line over the course of twenty-three minutes.

You've got to be savvy about this stuff. I don't mind the occasional situation where our fourth line might be caught out against a foe's No. 1 line. I don't panic and pull them. Obviously, you're not aiming for that matchup twenty minutes a game. But if they're caught out there, I want them to keep playing instead of looking for a line change.

If our fourth line dumps it in for a change, we've given away one possession for no good reason. It gives the opposition a chance to bring up the puck and force us to play defense again. Even if our best defensive line comes out to replace the fourth line, they're likely to face a situation where the puck is back in our zone. Having our fourth line out with a chance to move the puck into the offensive zone is a better transaction for us than having our third line facing a defensive situation in our defensive zone.

●

We opened calendar year 2008 on January 1 when Ottawa visited Verizon Center. The Senators had Ray Emery in net, and we won 6-3 to improve to 3-0 against them and 16-19-5 overall as we started to nose into the play-off picture. It was an easy win despite the fact Ottawa took a 2-0 first-period lead. Olie Kolzig got his 289th victory and moved into twenty-fifth place on the NHL's all-time victory list. Mike Green had two goals and an assist and was starting to realize how good he could be. Someday Green's going to win the Norris Trophy as the NHL's top defenseman.

Confidence was important in Mike Green's situation. I told Jay Leach, responsible for the defensive pairs, "Play him, just play him. I don't care about mistakes." You can't play your best when you feel handcuffed and think you'll be benched if you make a mistake. I let them know when they make a mistake; I don't allow it to go unnoticed. But they're still going to play.

That night after the game, I took Crystal to the Capital Grille in Washington for her birthday. I don't know how Caps majority owner Ted Leonsis knew we were going to the Capital Grille for dinner, but he knew. We were eating our meal and a bottle of champagne arrived. The manager told us it was from Ted Leonsis. I said, "Wow, that's awesome." So, like the American Hockey League people we are, we looked up the price on the menu and found out it was $399. We were flabbergasted by the nice gesture. Ted, for the record, it tasted great.

Then they came over with a big dessert tray and said it also was compliments of Ted. Shaone Morrisonn and Mike Green were there with dates, so we shared the champagne and dessert tray with them. When Shaone's on his game, he's as good a defensive defenseman as there is in the NHL—and I keep wanting to call him "Shoney" because of the way his name is spelled. It's pronounced "Shawn."

When we went to pay, we found out Ted Leonsis was taking care of the whole bill, tip included. I was floored. He didn't have to do it, but he did. I'll never forget it.

On January 3 we had a stinker at Boston and lost 2-0. The Bruins played a boring game, and we accomplished nothing. Zdeno Chara was all over Alexander Ovechkin. They sat back and took advantage of our game.

On January 5 we played at Montreal in another situation where we got national exposure in Canada. Green had the game-winning goal and another three-point game in a 5-4, come-from-behind win in overtime. Montreal played Carey Price in goal. Price had been named AHL play-off MVP in 2007 after he backstopped the Hamilton Bulldogs to the Calder Cup, culminating with a five-game defeat of my Hershey Bears in the Calder Cup finals. I was worried when I saw Price in net, but he didn't play well. We thought Montreal was the best team in the Eastern Conference at that point, so we were pleased with the triumph.

The Colorado Avalanche visited on January 9, my fifty-third birthday, and we won 2-1. Donald Brashear and Dave Steckel scored, and Olie Kolzig, who had a shutout until Marek Svatos scored late in the game, was strong against the beat-up. Avs. defenseman Milan Jurcina assisted on Steckel's goal, accounting for one of his nine points all season. Milan's got size (he's six foot four, 235 pounds), tools, and untapped potential. Consistency will come with maturity. Jay Leach says it takes a defenseman three hundred NHL games to finally know the game.

That was the first game of a Colorado road trip against Southeast Division teams, and the Avs helped us by beating all our division rivals. My old New Brunswick teammate, Joel Quenneville, was Colorado's head coach at the time, and we got to visit the next day. Joel apologized for playing a trap style, but he had to do it because of all their injuries. It was a lesson to me about how you have to gear your game to the personnel that you have at hand.

Alexander Ovechkin's thirteen-year $124 million contract extension was announced on January 10. I wasn't privy to any of the negotiations. Ted

Leonsis and George McPhee did an unbelievable job keeping that under wraps. George played the announcement to me to deadpan perfection.

"We couldn't get a seven-year deal done," George lamented. "We wanted to. We tried."

George apologized. Ovie's long-term Washington future, I figured, remained an open question. And then George coyly said they got a thirteen-year deal done. Rim shot. The hair on my arms stood up. What a goose bump moment.

Alex is the best hockey player on the planet, and he's treated me well. He wants to win. I'm blessed by being his coach; it's not the other way around. He's listened to me and respected me. People have a concept that superstars are prima donnas, and he's not that way at all. Ovie's a hardworking guy. If he has requests, they're always quiet ones, and he always asks respectfully.

We followed the big announcement with a January 13 clunker against visiting Philadelphia, which beat us 6-4. Our young guns—Ovie, Alexander Semin, and Mike Green—all scored. But we were too sloppy in the defensive zone. In the second period Matt Bradley fought Flyers captain Jason Smith to try to give us some spark.

Bradley isn't the best fighter, but he'll fight anybody. He's not the greatest scorer, but he works his butt off. He keeps everybody loose in the dressing room. It's necessary to have a guy like Bradley on your team.

After the Flyers loss, we got back on track and won four in a row. It was a season high we'd match two other times.

We beat visiting Ottawa 4-2 on January 15. It was our fourth and final game against the Senators. My pregame speech was all about the fact we had to beat them to set a tone. We couldn't let them know they beat us because we might have to play them in the second round of the play-offs. I voiced the assumption that we were going to make the play-offs and win the first round. I wanted everybody to subconsciously understand that. Players told me later that was a terrific motivating point. In fact, if Pittsburgh had beaten Philadelphia in the final game of the regular season to place first in the Eastern Conference, we would have played Ottawa in the first round.

Earlier that day we learned centerman Michael Nylander would miss the rest of the season with a torn left rotator cuff. I know how painful that is.

The previous season in Hershey, I suffered a torn left rotator cuff when Jonas Johansson ran over me during practice. I refused to get surgery because it would have taken me away from the team. I've lived with it, and it's gotten better. I'm limited in my ability to raise my arm, but my golf swing is OK.

Nylander's loss left us needing a forward. But the NHL is different from the minors. You might identify a need, but you might not be able to fill it immediately. In the AHL and the ECHL, it's easier to add a player to fill a gap. There's much more involved in the NHL owing to the intricate contracts and the salary cap. I sympathize with the complexities George McPhee faces as a general manager. But, as we would discover at the trade deadline in February, George was working on things.

Wins against Edmonton (5-4 on January 17), Florida (5-3 on January 19), and Pittsburgh (6-5 on January 21) followed the Ottawa game. We won a shootout against Edmonton on a Matt Bradley tally. I wasn't planning to use Bradley in the shootout, but he put himself in for the twelfth round.

"I'm going out and I'm going to score," Brad said.

"Wait, wait, wait," I protested, but he was moving toward the ice. "Well, go score then."

We all laughed when Bradley scored—and made it look easy—to give us our first shootout win.

The Florida victory made us .500 for the season at 21-21-4. I noted we'd officially reached mediocrity. A .500 record couldn't be credited as a milestone. We're supposed to be scoring. We're supposed to be winning. In the mind-set of a winning team, .500 is no achievement. We had to keep pushing and keep climbing.

I'm considered media-friendly. A lot of it is just my personality. I usually say the first thing that comes into my mind, and I usually have to face the ramifications later. It has hurt me occasionally. There have been many times I've said things and then thought, Oh, no. I think people like to hear an honest person speaking from the heart. That's pretty well what you get from me.

But I also use my head. You can use the media as a tool. That's why I said in my postgame comments we'd only reached mediocrity when we reached .500. You can use the media to reinforce points you want to stress with your team. You also can use it to plant ideas in the minds of your opposition.

For example, before Hershey played Wilkes-Barre/Scranton in the 2006–7 Calder Cup play-offs, I trotted out Eric Fehr and had him "practice" with us. Eric was still battling his back-hip problem, and we knew he wasn't going to play. By putting him on the ice, it made for a natural newspaper story and planted the seed that he might play. If they spent even five minutes thinking about it in the Wilkes-Barre camp, that was five minutes they didn't use preparing for us.

We won the Pittsburgh game in a shootout at home to go above .500. Alex Ovechkin and Evgeni Malkin, both destined to be Hart Trophy Award finalists, each scored twice and were fabulous. It was Nicklas Backstrom's second straight four-point game that vaulted him into the league rookie scoring race.

There was so much hype about Nicky as the fourth overall pick in the 2006 NHL entry draft. But it would have been unfair to expect the kind of production from Backstrom that Ovechkin had when he won the Calder Trophy as Rookie of the Year in 2005–6. There was a growing period for Nicky. I put him on the fourth line when I took over the team to take off some pressure. I kept giving him his power-play minutes and gradually increased his responsibilities. You won't find a quieter, more respectful kid. Nicky is going to be a stud in the NHL for a long time.

January 23 was a natural date for me to circle on the calendar. The Caps visited the Toronto Maple Leafs. The hometown kid got to return as an NHL head coach. There was an amazing amount of media attention. I don't know why. I'm one of so many Toronto natives who are in the NHL.

I met Air Canada Centre ushers I knew from twenty-five years before at Maple Leaf Gardens. Many members of the Leafs alumni visited me. John Iaboni, who was a major newspaper figure for the *Toronto Sun* before he retired, paid me a wonderful compliment by saying I was his all-time favorite player to interview in a journalism career that spanned more than thirty years. Then-Leafs general manager Cliff Fletcher congratulated me for becoming an NHL head coach.

The game itself, which prevented us from getting two games above .500, didn't provide a storybook ending for the visit. Mats Sundin scored with

29.2 seconds left to give the Maple Leafs a 3-2 victory. The Pittsburgh win was emotional, and it often happens that you're not as good the next game. We weren't. I was quite downhearted because I wanted to come into Toronto and win.

However, we rebounded the next night, January 24, and beat the Leafs at home. Brent Johnson had a thirty-one-save performance that sent us into the All-Star break just a point behind first-place Carolina in the Southeast Division.

Coming out of the All-Star break, Montreal and Cristobal Huet got us again on January 29. Huet had thirty-five saves in a 4-0 shutout. I love the atmosphere in Montreal. As a coach, as a player, you want to go to Montreal. It's hallowed hockey ground. But you can see how people don't like playing in Montreal. Even when they were up by four goals, the crowd wanted more. They sang that nah-nah-nah good-bye song. You love to win in Montreal when you get the opportunity.

Two days later we got another shot at the Habs when they visited Verizon Center. We talked about how we had to bounce back because they had beaten us so badly. Ovie, who had represented Washington at the All-Star Game, delivered another showcase of his toughness in a 5-4 overtime victory. He scored four goals again, including the overtime game-winner, and added an assist. One goal he scored on Cris Huet was the hardest wrist shot I've ever seen.

This was after he broke his nose and took stitches for a cut lip. Montreal defenseman Francois Bouillon, who is a short guy, clipped Alex with his helmet. It happened right at the bench. You could hear the mask hit his face—crack!—and Alex fell. I went, "Oh, no." I didn't want to look. When Alex, already sporting a gash under his left eye from a prior game, got up, his nose spewed blood. He sat on the bench, didn't go to the trainer's room, and didn't miss a shift. Unbelievable grit again. Montreal defenseman Mike Komisarik was on top of him all night long, and he still scored four goals. Here's a kid who had just signed this huge contract and he still played with total dedication and abandon. Alex is made different than everybody else.

# 14

# TRADE WINDS

**Put on a Washington Capitals uniform** and come to practice and these are the things you'll hear from me every day: work hard, put passes on tape, drive the net, make stops and starts. I harp on those things, starting with working hard. This is a tough game, a tough league, and you'll become road kill fast if you're lazy. There's no substitute for passion and effort.

I preach work because I don't want to be at practice a long time, especially after Christmas, when you want to limit the physical toll on players as the long season progresses. If players work hard, we can do a high-tempo practice and be off the ice in fifty minutes or less; if they don't, well, they'll be out longer. That's the way it is.

Look at the Montreal Canadiens and Detroit Red Wings. Why did they have success in 2007–8? They were by far the best passing teams in the NHL. Sloppy passing makes me mad. I stop practice and correct it immediately. When passes are on, it shows you're having a good practice.

Players don't drive to the net enough. That's where most goals are scored. I don't care if you're five foot six or six foot five: drive to the net. You have to make that a habit and not play a perimeter game.

Stops and starts get you in shape in hockey. Off-ice conditioning is important, but the only thing that truly gets you in hockey shape is skating. And stops and starts get you in good condition the quickest on the ice. It's so easy to turn instead of making a hard stop, but when you swing you can go past a play. It looks like you're lazy and makes a play easier for the opposition player. When you stop and start, it intimidates the other team because they see you're a workhorse team ready to play. When you stop and start and get in the other player's face, he's got a tougher play because you're in position quicker.

Hockey players are smart people. At the same time, when they're playing the game, they don't want to think. They want to instinctively know what they're supposed to be doing. So simplicity is a philosophy. Play to win, and play for each other.

When I was younger, sometimes I was a selfish player, but I learned to be a good teammate. Doing things right is part of being a good teammate. Amid the systems, I want the players to use their instincts. Hockey is not like football with set plays. You've got to adjust to a situation at full speed.

You give players concepts and ideas and stress playing within those concepts and ideas. But you also give them the freedom to be creative. For me to tell Alexander Ovechkin to dump it in all the time would be stupid. If you can beat a player, beat him. If you have to dump it in, dump it in. If you have to chip it by, chip it by. Just make the decision that doesn't create a turnover.

●

We badly outplayed Atlanta on February 2, had a 36-13 shot advantage, but Kari Lehtonen was a wall in net and we lost 2-0. It was a 0-0 game until Todd White scored midway through the third period. Marian Hossa, who'd be traded to Pittsburgh later in the month, scored an empty-netter.

Alex Ovechkin scored twice, including the game-winner in overtime, in a 4-3 victory at Columbus on February 5. Defenseman Tom Poti tied it 3-3 for us with 6:53 left in the third. It was one of the two goals Tom scored all season, but he's a tremendous defensive defenseman.

The most heartening thing about the game was the return of right winger Eric Fehr. Fehrsie missed ten months with mysterious back-hip trouble. He finally got back on the ice and played eleven games for Hershey in the AHL before we brought him up. Maybe it was a little too quick, maybe not, I don't know. There are not too many six-foot-four, 220-pound guys who can shoot the puck and compete like Fehr. We knew he could be a good role player for us all year.

The Blue Jackets led 2-0 after the first period. Claude Noel, one of their assistant coaches, was quoted in a newspaper that a 2-0 lead should be good enough to win. I disagree. Hockey is evolving, particularly in the wake of the post-lockout rule changes, and you've got to push all the time. The days of being able to play conservatively and sit on a lead are gone.

We moved into first place in the Southeast Division when we beat Philadelphia 4-3 on February 6 at Wachovia Center. Not bad for a team that had been written off in November. Brooks Laich got us going with the first goal in a game we led 4-1 before Philly scored a couple late goals. This is where Brooksie started to come into his own. He's got a strong built-in confidence. When I put him on the fourth line for one game, he came into my office and told me he could do more for the team. He proved it the last thirty games of the season.

I've never seen a guy who loves hockey more than Brooks Laich. He would never miss an optional practice. I had to physically prevent Brooks and Mike Green from going on the ice for some optionals so they wouldn't wear themselves out. If we had played three games in four nights, they'd go on before the fourth game and want to practice for an hour and a half.

Our first-place stay was brief. Carolina visited on February 8 and beat us 2-1 to retake the top spot. We outplayed the Hurricanes the last forty minutes, but Cam Ward frustrated us with a thirty-three-save effort and kept us from getting three games above .500. We knew Carolina wanted to get back to first, and they dominated in the first period while taking a 2-0 lead. It was a terrific learning experience. This was the kind of big game I savor.

My attitude is I want to face the best and beat the best. Pro wrestler Ric Flair always said, "To be the man you have to beat the man—and I'm the man." What better way to test yourself than to play a strong team in a critical situation? It provides a measuring stick that tells you what you've really got. The players learned a little more about the price you have to pay to win.

Afterward we went over video that showed how the Hurricanes finished checks and how they came out storming. I told the guys that this could be a cheap lesson if we realized how we have to match intensity. Sometimes when you give away two points, it's beneficial down the road. During the late-season stretch, in all those games we had to win, this was a game that showed us how to do it. We learned you have to be ready every day. Success doesn't come to those who want it periodically. You have to want success all the time.

The New York Rangers provided another measuring stick when they visited on February 10. They were a strong team that was playing well. Olie Kolzig played his 700th career game, and Mike Green gave us a 3-2 victory with an overtime game-winner.

Washington fans were still angry at Jaromir Jagr. He signed for big money to play for the Caps and didn't deliver big-money production. Fans booed him every time he touched the puck. Personally, I was impressed with his strength. Another thing that caught my eye was Scott Gomez's speed. Never seen a player skate that fast before. I said, "Wow, no wonder New Jersey won those Stanley Cups when he was a Devil."

It was another giveth and taketh exhibition by Sean Avery. He scored a goal for New York but also took a stupid unsportsmanlike conduct penalty for his mouth in the second period. Avery sat on the bench and yelled at guys. I told myself, "He hasn't changed from the time I had him in Manchester. He's still an idiot." He shut up after taking the penalty, though.

Avery's jawing reminded me of Dave Schultz when I coached Mississippi in the ECHL. One night we played in Baton Rouge, Louisiana, where Schultz was head coach, and a five-on-five brawl erupted. I was watching the players go at it. Next thing you know, Schultz crashed into the glass between the benches and started swearing at me. Huh? His team started the brawl. Schultz climbed the glass, and I went, "Uh-oh, what's going on here?" He pulled his chin over like he was doing a pull-up and barked, "How many goals did you score in the NHL? I got so many more points than you." I go, "Wow, this guy's lost it."

We wasted another chance to go three games above .500 when we visited Atlanta on February 13. Kari Lehtonen, who finished with thirty-nine saves, was strong against us again. I knew we were in trouble when we outshot them 18-3 in the first period and were still stuck in a scoreless tie. Lehtonen was in a groove, and you realized he would be tough to beat. The other team is usually going to come back because it's so hard to sustain that kind of pressure. The Thrashers won 3-2 in a shootout to move into a three-way tie for first with us and Carolina.

We had a 2-1 lead after Tomas Fleischmann scored early in the third on February 15 at Florida and collapsed, allowing the Panthers to rally for a 4-2 win. We worried because we played at Tampa Bay the next night and a loss would drop us back to .500.

The Lightning, playing well after getting healthy, were making a play-off push. We controlled the game and blew a 2-0 lead when they scored two goals in thirty-three seconds in the third. Alexander Semin scored with three minutes left to give us a 3-2 win. There were a lot of smiles because we showed resilience. Tom Poti was out with a lower body injury. Sami Lepisto, called up from Hershey, made his NHL debut and did a solid job. George McPhee said of Tampa Bay, "That's one good team over there right now."

We blew a 2-0 lead again in the next game, and it didn't end as well. The visiting New York Islanders recorded a 3-2 shootout win on February 20. The Islanders played a boring game. We played up-tempo, but they dumped it in and dumped it out. It was a frustrating game. They put everybody to sleep and earned two points. One positive was that it was the sixth straight game we didn't allow a power-play goal.

I learned from Bill O'Flaherty when I was with the Los Angeles Kings organization that it's important to at least be equal five-on-five and win the special teams battles on the power play and penalty kill. Do that and you're going to win a lot of games. Penalty killing correlates more strongly to success than the power play, especially in the play-offs. We demand that we be the best at penalty killing. It's not what you get, it's what you give.

I work on the power play a lot. Most coaches designate assistant coaches to be in charge of the power play and penalty kill. As head coach, though, I always want to do the power play. I lived off the power play as a player. One thing I did for twenty years was play the power play. Who's going to be better at that than me unless it's, say, Wayne Gretzky? OK, Gretzky was better at it than I was, but it doesn't mean he's got more knowledge about it. So I took over the power play from Jay Leach when I came in, and Dean Evason stayed in charge of the penalty kill.

Our penalty-kill streak came to an emphatic end when Carolina scored four power-play goals in a 6-3 win on February 23 in Raleigh, North Carolina. It was the Hurricanes' third straight victory over us and strengthened their hold on first place. Our penalty killing was often tremendous. This was one time it was horrible.

I told Dean Evason, "I don't want you to go in and technically talk to the players about penalty killing. I want you to rip them for not doing the job." I knew the players respected Dean and would respond to him. We had a good penalty-killing run after that.

Martin Brodeur got help from the goal pipes, and New Jersey beat us 2-1 in overtime on a John Madden goal when we visited on February 24. That was the last game before the February 26 NHL trade deadline. Our roster was about to get some dramatic additions.

●

General manager George McPhee let me sit in the Caps war room on trade deadline day. I'm fascinated by this stuff. Like any hockey fan, I do fantasy trades in my head. It was exciting to watch it unfold in reality. George is right on top of things. There are so many variables and timing is so important. George is really analytical and fast-thinking in an environment where speed is of the essence.

"Well, we've got Cristobal Huet," George said.

I was a bit shocked but pleasantly surprised. I knew Cris was a quality goaltender and person. The Caps sent a 2009 second-round draft pick to Montreal to get Huet, who was destined to become a free agent following the 2007–8 season. Nothing much happened after that for about two hours. We wondered if the phones would ever ring. Things hopped once they started ringing.

We got the great Sergei Fedorov from Columbus in exchange for prospect Theo Ruth. We acquired winger Matt Cooke from Vancouver in exchange for winger Matt Pettinger. George really bolstered the roster.

Adding Fedorov, who had turned thirty-eight in December, filled the hole left when Michael Nylander was lost for the season. About three weeks before the trade deadline, George came up and said out of the blue, "I watched Columbus last night. Jeez, that Fedorov still has some game left. He was the best player on the ice."

I'll never forget the day Fedorov arrived. I was sitting in my office when George came through the door with him. Sergei looked like a classic Jean

Beliveau. He wore a nice winter coat, scarf, and one of those Russian fur hats.

I told him, "Sergei, are you ready to play twenty minutes a game? I'm going to use you on the power play, the penalty kill, and a regular shift. You think your body can handle it?"

"Oh, for sure," Sergei said, exuding a quiet confidence.

His eyes lit up like he hadn't been counted on like that by a team in a while. Weeks later Sergei told me that Columbus head coach Ken Hitchcock limited him to a maximum of fourteen minutes a game. He played more for us and was a wonderful addition.

It looked like Sergei really enjoyed mentoring the two young Russians, Alexander Ovechkin and Alexander Semin. Ovie and Semin took to him so well. Sergei liked being one of the top guys, one of the accountable guys, again on a team that was in a play-off hunt. He felt the vibe in the room that he was considered an important part of the team, and it lifted him. He mentioned numerous times how much he enjoyed playing our brand of hockey.

Fedorov is my son Brady's favorite player. After we beat Boston in early March, Sergei spent some time with Brady. Real genuine time where he asked questions and interacted with him. Brady was so excited.

When I coached in Manchester, we started a kid reporter bit with Brady. He'd get a microphone and a video crew and interview players. He asks straight questions or off-the-wall questions that get played on the video screen during games. He might ask a player about his love life. He might ask him why he takes so many dumb penalties. Fans seem to get a kick out of it—as does Brady—and we continued it in Hershey and Washington.

About a week after his meeting with Fedorov, Brady did a kid reporter session with Mike Green. Green, who'd already known Brady from Hershey and had a rapport with him, asked Brady who his favorite player was and obviously expected to hear his own name.

"It's not you, Mike," Brady stated. "It's Sergei Fedorov."

The main immediate fallout from the trade deadline was that we suddenly had three goalies: Cris Huet, Olie Kolzig, and Brent Johnson. Three-goalie situations are difficult. As a coach, it's something that's thrust upon you, and it's your job to do the best you can.

Nobody likes doing things that are unpleasant. General managers don't like firing coaches. Coaches don't like cutting players. But it's part of the job description. If you can't do it, you have to get out of the game. You have to make hard decisions. As George McPhee says, "The right thing to do isn't always the easiest thing to do, but we've got to do what's right for the team at all times."

I wrestled with how to handle it. I talked to Brent Johnson first.

"It's going to be tough, but it looks like you're going to be the odd man out," I told Brent. "I'm going to try to get you into a game or two down the road."

Initially, I thought we'd manage to somehow play all three goalies. But we eventually decided it was going to be Olie Kolzig and Cris Huet, and Brent wouldn't play. That's because it's not good to have three goalies on the ice for a practice. Three goalies, two nets. It doesn't add up. So I had to tell Johnny he wasn't even going to practice. That was hard because I really like Brent.

Brent had to be irked about the situation because he and Olie are close friends, but he didn't show it. He stayed a very good team guy. He worked out hard on his own, faithfully coming out every day after the team concluded practice. Johnny could have made it difficult, but he made it easy for us because he was such a good teammate. That's what you call being a classy pro. All the good things that people in the game have said about Brent Johnson are true.

In January we had sent Brent to Hershey for a one-game injury rehabilitation assignment. Like most NHL veterans, he didn't want to go. George McPhee and I sat him down and said, "Brent, this is not a negative thing. We want you to start against Ottawa on January 15, but you've been out for a month and we think you need a rehab game. This is not purgatory. It's nothing more than one game."

Sometimes players think one game could turn into forever and balk at going down. Believe me, I understand. I'm a guy who's been in that situation too many times to count. But my Caps players are finding out I'm honest with them. If I say we're bringing you back, we're bringing you back.

Johnny played extremely well for the Bears on January 11 at Wilkes-Barre/Scranton. He made thirty-seven saves and was the No. 2 star of the game despite a 3-1 Hershey loss. Brent didn't go down sulking, and he was fabulous in the locker room with our AHL kids. And when he came back, he thanked us and said, "That might have been the best thing for me that ever happened."

Back in the immediate trade deadline aftermath, I talked to Olie Kolzig and Cristobal Huet after I talked to Brent Johnson.

I told Olie, "This doesn't mean you're in purgatory. You're going to play. In the end, we'll probably run with one goalie, but it doesn't mean anybody in particular."

I told Cris, "We brought you in here to play. We would like to see if you could be the guy. You're going to have to play great because Olie is a professional and he's a good player. He's been around Washington for a long time and he's an icon, so you're going to have to be outstanding to gain the ice time or fans will balk."

At first, I alternated them. Sometimes I'd play them back-to-back if they won, but then I'd return to the rotation. After we suffered a March 19 loss at Chicago, which turned out to be Olie's last start, we ended up riding Cris. After we won at Carolina on March 25 and had five regular-season games left, I told goalie coach Dave Prior it would be tough to continue the rotation and that Cris would play until he lost. And he didn't lose. I like to be fair to players. But at crunch time, you have to play your best players. When Cris got on a roll, Olie wasn't going to get in.

Olie was pretty quiet. He understood and never caused a wave. I made a point of talking to him every day to make sure he was OK. It bothered me that he wasn't playing. I really like him and wanted to make sure he was all right, almost like a parental thing. I avoided him for a couple of days or so after deciding to go with Cris because I didn't know what to say to him. Then, I decided, the heck with this. Olie's the same person. He's just not the one playing. Making tough decisions doesn't mean you have to treat guys like crap.

It wouldn't have worked if Olie Kolzig and Brent Johnson weren't the kind of people they are. Yes, Cris Huet was the one who played and was in the spotlight. Though they were in the background, Olie and Johnny were absolutely critical to the success we enjoyed.

The night of the trade deadline, Olie responded with thirty-four saves in a 4-1 home victory over Minnesota. Eric Fehr scored his first goal since

February 2, 2007, and it was a big relief for him. None of the new guys we had acquired played against Minnesota; they didn't have enough time to join the team.

The trade might have disrupted team chemistry a little at first. But Matt Pettinger was the only player who left. The trade to Vancouver was a good thing for him. He was the one player who seemed to be unhappy. I don't know what it was. I had a hundred talks with him. I don't know if he believed what I was saying. Petti was close to Glen Hanlon, and maybe he resented me. Understandable. Sometimes players need a breath of fresh air. Matt Cooke was stale in Vancouver and gave us energy when he arrived in Washington.

In the big picture, the moves George McPhee made at the trade deadline were immensely beneficial. Now, in addition to my telling the team I believed in them, Capitals management showed they believed in them by making moves to get better. This was the first time in five years the Caps didn't sell off assets to gain prospects. We added assets to make the club better. It's no coincidence we took off and went 15-4 the rest of the regular season.

Cristobal Huet and Sergei Fedorov made a sensational Washington debut in a 4-0 win over visiting New Jersey on February 29. Cris had an eighteen-save shutout; it was nice to see him get a shutout for us instead of against us. Sergei made a sweet no-look pass to set up a Mike Green goal. Those opening acts made us eager to see what we could do down the home stretch.

The Devils puzzled me by continuing to trap in the third period when they trailed by four goals. It didn't seem like a way of wanting to win. We don't play like that in a similar situation. It might finish 6-0, but we attack and try to rally.

We finally got three games above .500 with the triumph over the Devils: 30-27-8. We'd made a leap during a leap year February.

To make the play-offs, though, the task for March was clear: come in like a lion and go out like a lion.

# 15

## IFFY WAGON

**Being a head coach in the NHL means** being the lead dog in a room of people who have spent their lives as the lead dog in their respective packs. You have to be tactically and technically proficient, but the ability to be lead dog is the X-factor that makes the difference between being successful or not. It's at the heart of the mystery of why some coaches make it and some fail. I don't know if it's even definable or explainable.

You have it. Or you don't.

You have to have command of the locker room. It involves the way you present yourself, the tone of your voice, the respect you have before you get in there, and whether the players believe what you're saying is true. On the one hand, I've had coaches who've had a fabulous message, but they deliver it in a monotone without passion and the message doesn't get across. On the other hand, I've had coaches who screamed all the time. That's too much the other way. If the jackhammer is constantly pounding, it turns into white noise and loses impact.

You need a feel for the moment. I've been around hockey my whole life. Everybody is good at one thing, has a special talent. I guess my thing is hockey coaching, so I think I've got a good command of the room. But I'm like anybody else, with good days and bad days. Sometimes I'll reflect and think what I said, say, at a pregame skate didn't sound right, that it was plastic. On days like that, I know I've got to be better between periods during the game to make up for it.

I know I can get a team going every night. Every game there's a different reason to be at the top of your game. It's my job to figure out that reason and sell it. There's got to be variety. It can't be the same reason all the time.

During pregame speeches, I go into a zone and sometimes don't even know what comes out. It's just passion. One time in Mississippi, I paced back and forth and told the guys to take the cow by the horns. Not the bull, the cow. OK, sometimes my words run together and I sound like an idiot. But the guys understand that I speak from the heart.

I know what I want to say and have a plan. When I got to Washington, I'd run my plans past assistant coach Dean Evason. I didn't know if my style would work at the NHL level or whether the players would think it was hokey. I like to show movie clips or team videos that I hope will inspire the players. Dean told me, "Listen, I don't know what you do, but your instincts are fabulous." By saying that, he gave me the confidence to keep doing what I'd always done.

Sometimes it's the look you give rather than what you say. At the end of a morning skate, when I pull them in for a thirty-second talk, I'm trying to hit an emotional nerve that gets them thinking about that night's task. They've got all afternoon to think about it and get prepared and excited. I'm an average guy. I figure what affects me emotionally will affect everybody else emotionally. That's how I seek my cues on what to tell them. If I find a vein that gets me pumped, I trust it's going to do the same for the players.

I've got five keys for every game. The first four are technical and strategic keys tied into the team we're playing against. The fifth key is always an emotional key. It's the last thing the players hear me say before they step onto the ice. For any of that to work, though, the players have to believe you know what you're doing. It's like any leader in any setting. If they believe in you, they will follow you. If they don't believe in you, they will question you.

When I arrived in Washington, I was helped by built-in credibility with the guys who played for me in Hershey in the AHL. I'm sure Mike Green told his teammates, "Believe in this guy and we'll win." I'm sure Dave Steckel and Brooks Laich said the same thing. You have to put in more effort than you're demanding of the team. I don't skate the miles they skate and take the physical punishment they take, but I make sure to pay a price as coach.

If I mention at practice that I've been at the rink since 6:00 a.m., it's not because I want the players to think I'm Mr. Wonderful. It's because I want them to know that I'm willing to work as hard as they are to get the job done. The leader has to be like Russell Crowe in *Gladiator*. He has to take his men into battle from the front. I've got to do everything they're willing to do and beyond. I've got to be ready to take fire first.

●

So much for entering March like a lion. The Toronto Maple Leafs beat us 3-2 at home on March 1. Don't even talk to me about it. We had a huge crowd of 18,277 at the Verizon Center. We were generating excitement, fans were getting turned on to the team, and we laid an egg on them.

Mats Sundin had three points, one a lousy goal on a slap shot. I lost it a little bit after the game and challenged the team the next day at practice. The Maple Leafs, who played the night before in Florida, shouldn't have come in and outworked us when they had nothing to fight for and we desperately needed to win.

We gave the home crowd a much better performance on March 3 when we scored six first-period goals and beat the Boston Bruins 10-2. Alexander Ovechkin had a hat trick in the first period and passed the fifty-goal mark to reach fifty-two. Alex had scored one goal in the previous eight games, and you knew that lull wouldn't last.

Matt Cooke scored the game's first goal thirty-two seconds into the first. Matt didn't play well in his debut two days earlier against Toronto. We were wondering what we got in the trade that sent Matt Pettinger to Vancouver. I initially thought, Well, we've still got Quintin Laing to use in that fourth-line, energy role. Then I decided I didn't want to be the kind of coach who wouldn't give a guy a chance. If Matt had played poorly against Boston, he probably would have been in and out of the lineup the rest of the year. But he played well and was subsequently used as a regular.

Though we led 6-0 at first intermission, we didn't let down at the beginning of the second. In Manchester in the AHL, we led a game 6-1 going into the third against Worcester and lost 7-6 in overtime. No wonder a lot of the hair I have left is gray. Boston scored in the first minute to make it 6-1, but we answered with two more goals to make it 8-1. There was a feeling of jubilation after bouncing back so strong after the Toronto loss. Fifteen players got points. Those things don't happen often.

I don't like running up a score. I played Ovie three shifts in the third period. And Don Cherry, who once coached the Bruins, admonished me on television for running up the score. Don has been a tremendous advocate for me. I wanted to talk through the TV screen and say, "Don, no-no. I didn't want to run up the score." Plus, we were scheduled to play the Bruins again on March 8 and didn't want to give them any added motivation.

On March 5 we beat Buffalo 3-1 on the road to move into tenth place in the Eastern Conference, a point behind ninth-place Buffalo and two points behind eighth-place Philadelphia. Ovie had two goals to raise his total to a league-leading fifty-four. Olie Kolzig was terrific in net. This was a quietly critical game because the Sabres had handled us in our previous meetings. They were the one team that had sort of dominated us. Whether they were close games or not, they were in control the whole time. We had to win for psychological reasons as well as the hard math of the conference standings.

Buffalo is close to St. Catharines, Ontario, and I had more friends at this game than the game in Toronto. We were ecstatic about winning because this also was a big game for Buffalo in the play-off race. We were in control the whole game and played as solid as we could play. The Sabres were in reverse mode from us. At the trade deadline, they got rid of defenseman Brian Campbell instead of adding players. I think this was the game that really knocked Buffalo out of the play-off running. Not officially, but mentally. That was important because we also were fighting for a conference play-off spot as well as trying to chase down Carolina for the Southeast Division championship.

The Bruins, in the wake of their 10-2 loss to us, beat us 2-1 on March 8 at Boston. We were hit with dubious late penalties, and they scored two five-on-three goals to rally from a 1-0 deficit. We scored a goal early in the first and controlled the game before the late controversy.

Pierre Maguire and other people criticized me on TV for putting Donald Brashear on the ice in a one-goal game with seven minutes left. People didn't understand that sometimes Brash was our most responsible player. Donald is a lot better player than people give him credit for. He can play the game, and he's got that trigger. You don't want to mess with him. He's a massive man who is very tough. Brash knows what to do and how to do it, so I had no qualms about playing him the last five minutes, the last seven minutes.

Brashear took a double-minor at 13:19 of the third for high-sticking, which was accidental. However, he snapped and punched Shane Hnidy in the face and got an extra two for roughing for a total of six minutes. That made me an easy target for analyst barbs. But we still thought we'd be OK because our penalty kill had shut them down.

Then referee Chris Rooney made a chintzy call in an important game on John Erskine for hooking in the neutral zone where he didn't touch the guy. Rooney, a young ref, was on the other side of the ice and put his hand up. That put us down five-on-three for a full two minutes. We killed off most of it before Zdeno Chara scored to tie it 1-1.

And then they called Tom Poti for slashing to put us down five-on-three again. Quintin Laing and Dave Steckel blocked shots like crazy, but Marco Sturm scored the game-winner at 17:44. I was livid at Rooney. I'd had issues with him in the AHL. We were in full control of the game and were going to win, and Rooney took us right out of it.

As a rookie NHL head coach, I felt I didn't get some calls, especially with the refs I didn't know. George McPhee would say, "Look, you're the new guy on the block. You're not going to get the calls." I think we also didn't get calls because we were the Caps, who had struggled for many seasons and weren't expected to get calls against good teams. It changed by the end of the season, and we started to be treated more evenhandedly—though not in the last play-off game against Philadelphia.

The refs don't do it intentionally. It's just the way it is. If you're playing Detroit with all those great players, well, if one of the great players falls, there's an assumption that he had to have been tripped because that's the only way Washington could be keeping up.

I try to treat referees with respect. With refs, you have to take the approach that every day is different. You must let go of the past. If a ref was lousy one game and you have him again the next game, you can't bring animosity from the previous game because you won't get a break.

I don't think any ref goes out there and wants to favor a team at the start of a game. But you certainly will catch more flies with sugar than vinegar. If I'm constantly in a ref's face, he's human and he's not going to give me a break. If you get stopped by a cop, you may or may not get the ticket. If you're nice to him, you might get let off; if you're a jerk, you're definitely getting the ticket. And the refs are the cops on the ice.

We all get caught up in the heat of the moment, and refs have good games and bad games, just like coaches and players. I want them to talk to me. I want them to understand where I'm coming from. It might not get me anything at that moment, but it might help me down the road when I feel I have justified reason to scream at them. I won't get ahead if I scream at every call.

I've learned my lessons because I've had battles with refs I wouldn't let go. All it did was hurt me and my team. There was a ref named Richard Trottier when I played in the AHL. I counted about fifteen or twenty games either our team lost or I got no points with him officiating. The reason was because my focus was on being mad at Trottier instead of playing the game.

I got hit from behind one time, and Trottier laughed at me instead of calling a penalty. It made me boil. I wanted to shoot the puck at him. But what did it accomplish for me and my team? Nothing. You gain wisdom and realize you can't hold grudges. As a player, by and large, I got along well with refs—except for Richard Trottier.

Referees can be characters. Paul Stewart was a goon hockey player who became a ref. He talked to the benches during play. He wanted to be a comedian offering funny running commentary.

In an AHL game in Nova Scotia in the mid-1980s, Stewart refused to make a call on a new rule that was supposed to result in a delay of game penalty if a goalie shot the puck over the glass. An opposition goalie shot the puck over the glass and no penalty resulted.

I said, "Stewie, this is a new rule you've got to call."

"I'm not calling it," he said. "Face-off over there."

Our head coach, Larry Kish, called me over.

"You tell that bleep," Kish said, "that this is a brand new rule in the book and he's got to call it."

I went back to Stewart and relayed Kish's blunt message. Stewie said, "I know it's supposed to be a penalty. But I don't like this rule and I'm not going to call it."

What do you do? You throw up your hands. At least he explained himself. I've got a picture of myself looking dumbfounded while reacting to that call. Stewie was the kind of guy you'd see after a game wearing plaid pants and a striped shirt. He looked like one of the Festrunk brothers—"wild and crazy guys" Dan Aykroyd and Steve Martin—from *Saturday Night Live*.

Mick McGeough was the only NHL ref who yelled at me in 2007–8. He was hyper. Donald Brashear has a tendency to say things from the bench. Brash said something one game. McGeough's face turned red, and he yelled at Brash to shut up or he'd kick him out of the bleepin' game. It seemed like an overreaction to what was said. I went, "Whoa, lighten up."

Mick came to the bench about three minutes later, and I told him to relax. He went off again, saying he was going to run Brash. Well, then do it. Don't yap about it. Now Mick's retired. Maybe that's why he's retired.

I've had a lot of AHL run-ins with Dean Morton. I've chased him down the hall and called him names. But I trust we both forget our past encounters when we run across each other. We've got to start off fresh each game because we're in trouble if we don't. There are rules and interpretations. Calls can sit in what I term the Iffy Wagon. A call in the Iffy Wagon can go either way. You don't want a ref in an angry mind-set where he won't give you a call sitting in the Iffy Wagon.

●

After the Boston game, we stewed on the plane. But we had the Pittsburgh Penguins the next afternoon at home. You've got to snap out of it. You can't feel sorry for yourselves.

I don't think there was a lingering effect from the Boston game, but we lost 4-2 to the Penguins on March 9. That's when poor Nicky Backstrom put the puck in his own net with twenty-eight seconds left in a 2-2 game. I felt so bad for Nicky.

Boston and Pittsburgh were the only consecutive regulation losses we suffered the whole regular season after I took over. We went forty-eight games—the longest streak in 2007–8 by any NHL team—before it happened. That's consistent hockey, and I pride my teams on consistent hockey.

I talk a lot about what I call ruts and grooves. It's something I picked up when Gene Ubriaco was my coach in Baltimore in the AHL, and it makes so much sense. Being in a rut and being in a groove are the exact same things, except one is negative and one is positive. There's a fine line between being in a rut or a groove. If we've won one, lost one in overtime, and lost one in regulation, we're poised to be in either a rut or a groove heading into the fourth game. Win and you're sliding into a groove; lose and you're slipping into a rut. The key is to make it a groove where you keep feeling good about yourself.

Two straight regulation losses put us in a situation where we faced the prospect of falling into a rut. And we couldn't afford a rut, since we'd dropped seven points behind first-place Carolina. A lot of people wrote us off at this point. Well, they're done. Nice try. Good effort, Caps, maybe next year. They didn't understand our resiliency.

We rebounded at home to beat a good, physical Calgary team 3-2 on March 12. Alex Ovechkin scored two goals, including the game-winner with 1:54 left. Olie Kolzig earned his 300th win. I was delighted for Olie. That's a major milestone. That's the result of a lot of years playing at a consistently high level.

We knew the Flames were going on a Southeast Division swing that started against us. If we beat them, that would make them more motivated to beat the other Southeast teams they'd play and help our cause. Calgary, like Minnesota and Colorado earlier, went on to do just that.

We beat Atlanta 4-1 at home on March 14. Brooks Laich scored twice. We outshot the Thrashers 37-12, one off the Washington record for fewest shots allowed in a game, and thoroughly deserved to win.

Cristobal Huet came up huge in a 2-1 March 16 shootout victory over visiting Boston. Cris had thirty-nine saves and held the Bruins zero-for-two in the shootout. This was one of the few games all season we won that we didn't deserve to win. Goaltending stole it for us.

The victory moved us within two points of eighth place in the Eastern Conference. It also was our last home game of the month. We had to close March with a season-high stretch of six straight road games. A brutal challenge in a situation where we had little margin for error.

The road trip started with a 4-2 win at Nashville on March 18. Ovie assisted on goals by Alexander Semin and Nicklas Backstrom as we took a 3-0 lead in the first period, and he scored in the third for a three-point game. The Predators had climbed into eighth place in the Western Conference. I thought they would be tough and dynamic at home, but they were flat.

I tell the goalies the day before a game who's going to start. I told Cris Huet he would start in Nashville and Olie Kolzig he would start the next day in Chicago.

That March 19 game at Chicago was so unfortunate for Olie. It turned out to be his last game for Washington. We were riding a season-high, four-game winning streak and looking for a fifth consecutive win. For the first time in my Caps tenure, we maybe took a team lightly because we thought we were better than them. Chicago had a presentation for Tony Esposito before the game, which delayed the start. It was an emotional ceremony in front of a full house of nearly 21,000. There also was a stirring national anthem; Chicago's national anthem is the best in the NHL.

They had us down 4-0 in the first period before we could blink, and we lost 5-0. Nikolai Khabibulin, in his own personal tribute to Esposito, pitched a twenty-five-save shutout. Chicago played well and made us look bad. That's what their young talent—Patrick Kane, Jonathan Toews—can do.

Remember, I played briefly for the Blackhawks, but the only Chicago nostalgia I felt was that Rick Paterson was there for Tony Esposito. Rick was pumped up. He said, "You were the best man at my first wedding and Tony was the best man at my second. And I'm here watching both of you. What a cool thing." I hired John Weidman, Chicago's radio broadcaster, to his first job when I was head coach in Muskegon. And my ruts and grooves guru, Gene Ubriaco, who'd gone on to work for the AHL's Chicago Wolves alongside my buddy John Anderson, was there too.

In addition to the play-off position damage it caused, the Chicago loss concerned me. There are trends in team dynamics that aren't necessarily reflected on the scoreboard. Losing streaks follow winning streaks, and we'd been on a winning streak. I sometimes show a chart to players of how teams go, their ebbs and flows, their ascending or descending performance curve.

Losing streaks follow winning streaks because you're not playing well by the time you reach the end of a winning streak. You're hanging on and ultimately you lose. You're going up the arc while you're playing well. But you can't sustain that level and eventually start descending. We were in the descending part of the curve and had to snap out of it.

That didn't happen the first two periods on March 21 at Atlanta. We were awful. We trailed 3-1, and I ripped the team at second intermission, pointing out that there were only six games left after this one. It was a major rant. This was a game we had to win to make the play-offs. I asked them if they were scared to win.

"If you guys are afraid to win," I barked, "how are you ever going to win?"

They responded—and how. We outshot the Thrashers 23-2 in the third, scored four goals in the final ten minutes, and rallied for a 5-3 triumph. Nicklas Backstrom scored twice. Alex Ovechkin, who also scored in the first, scored twice to become the first NHL player in twelve years to reach sixty goals.

The guys were ecstatic after a third-period effort that snapped us out of that descending slide down the flow chart to a high that put us back on an ascending performance track. We couldn't afford to lose, and we sensed that we weren't going to lose again the rest of the regular season. We felt confident we weren't going to be denied.

We visited first-place Carolina on March 25 in our latest biggest game of the season. If we lost, there was pretty much no way we could catch the Hurricanes. If we won, we'd have a light at the end of the tunnel. We were jubilant after a 3-2 shootout win. Cris Huet was huge in goal, and Alex Ovechkin scored No. 61 to pass Dennis Maruk, my old Junior B teammate, for Washington's single-season goal-scoring record.

It was a tough game, but we deserved to win. Viktor Kozlov scored in the shootout as the last shooter, resulting in another two-inch vertical victory leap by me on the bench. That's when Sergei Fedorov nicknamed Kozlov the "Terminator" for his shootout prowess.

Yes, we had a shot at it with five games left.

Tomas Fleischmann, continuing his Lightning success, lifted us to a 4-3 overtime victory at Tampa Bay on March 27. Cris Huet followed with a thirty-two-save shutout in a 3-0 win at Florida on March 29, and we reached the forty-win mark, the first time the Caps had done that since 2000–2001.

Viktor Kozlov, a former Panther, had a goal and an assist, and I felt good because that's where his family lives and they got a chance to see him play well. The Panthers put up a terrific fight early, but we kept pushing and mathematically eliminated them from the play-off race.

We finished the road trip 5-1-0. We went 10-4-0 in March. We won in different ways. Coming from behind. Leading start to finish. Winning in overtime or a shootout. There were different heroes. It wasn't always Alex Ovechkin.

It was an impressive roll to launch us into April. We trailed Carolina by two points for the division title and Philadelphia by three points for the eighth and final play-off berth in the Eastern Conference. We had to win all three remaining games to stay in the play-off picture. To win the division, we had to win them all and get some help.

All three games would be played at Verizon Center. Home sweet home. We'd discover our road success had generated a surge in fan excitement. Their rock-the-red storm of support would propel us across the finish line.

# 16

## BANNER EFFORT

**We had started drawing bigger crowds** at Verizon Center, where the attendance figure for a sellout is 18,277. In April our fan support reached a frenzy, and we played every game before capacity crowds that produced sonic booms of excitement. The Capitals, often relegated to the background in the Washington sports scene, suddenly bathed in media attention. We were a hot team and a hot ticket.

Caps fans had been through a lot of tough seasons. A huge sense of anticipation built because we had a chance to reward all that loyalty by earning a play-off berth. Our April 1 game against first-place Carolina was no April Fool's joke. The Hurricanes would clinch the Southeast Division title with a regulation win. In the final analysis, this was truly the biggest game of the regular season.

The Verizon Center crowd, dressed in red for a redout to support the team, was crazy. They produced, well, a hurricane of noise. I didn't know about the redout plans, but I coincidentally wore a red dress shirt. My poor fashion sense again. When I got dressed, I thought I looked sharp in a red shirt. When I arrived at the rink, Caps majority owner Ted Leonsis jokingly zinged me for the red shirt. At least I inadvertently blended with the crowd.

Gosh, it was so loud, and the crowd didn't stop. They chanted "MVP! MVP!" for Alexander Ovechkin. I called guys for line changes and they couldn't hear me, even though I stood right behind them. I started pounding on their shoulders and yelling to get through. It was a championship atmosphere. We fed off the crowd. I was so charged up I wanted to play. When there's a crowd like that, you don't feel tired, you don't feel fatigued. They're lifting you all the time.

The fans wanted it. We wanted it. And we dominated. We pushed and pushed and weren't going to be denied. Washington Capitals 4, Carolina Hurricanes 1. It was an overwhelming win and an emotional rush.

We took a 2-0 lead on first-period goals by Matt Cooke and Brooks Laich, who'd finish the season with a career-high twenty-one goals. Alexander Semin played a terrific game. He scored a second-period, power-play goal that put us up 3-1, and he hit people all night. Semin's amazing potential is like tapping into an oil well. There could be a billion dollars down there. He can be a sixty-goal scorer. His shot wasn't accurate for about twenty-eight games because of injuries, and he still scored twenty-eight goals. He's a superstar in the making.

Ovie scored the capper late in the third, sparking another crescendo of "MVP!" chants. After the game, though, I toned it down. There are times to have celebrations. This wasn't one of them.

"You've got ten minutes to enjoy yourselves," I told the team. "Then it's back to business. We've done nothing. We're in position, but it's up to you guys."

We were tied for first with Carolina with ninety points, but we were still a point out of eighth place in the Eastern Conference. Carolina held the head-to-head tiebreaker advantage and controlled its destiny. We had to win our final two games against Tampa Bay and Florida.

The Lightning didn't have much fight left in them and didn't have a real good lineup for our final matchup, which we won 4-1 on April 3. Ovechkin scored twice to make history. Ovie reached sixty-five goals to pass Luc Robitaille and set the record for the most NHL goals scored in a single season by a left winger.

Alex was so deserving. Every team we play targets their game plan to stop No. 8. Against Pittsburgh, teams have to check Sidney Crosby and Evgeni Malkin. The focus isn't all on stopping one guy. Thus, it's an incredible feat to score sixty-five goals when every game is geared to check you. Alex is a freak of nature. My hope for him is that his body holds up because he plays with such abandon and desire.

Our power play was only 14.6 percent when I took over. So Ovie played twenty-one games in 2007–8 where the power play wasn't working. If he stays healthy, I don't see why seventy goals or more isn't within reach. He scored 163 goals his first three years. Only Mike Bossy and Wayne Gretzky scored more goals than Ovie in their first three seasons. After five years, he might be in the three hundred club. How ridiculous is that?

I love Alex and his approach to the game, the whole game on and off the ice. You never see Sidney Crosby vulnerable when he does an interview. He always gives the perfect, safe answer. On the other hand, Alex can say off-the-wall stuff and laugh about it. It humanizes him. I'm the same way. That's a refreshing thing to people. That's why he's going to be the face of hockey.

There was no euphoria after the Tampa Bay win. It was strictly a business atmosphere. When you start thinking about what you're going to do when you win a championship, where the parties are going to be, you never win. You have to take care of business and let the aftermath just happen.

Florida helped on April 4 by beating Carolina in the Hurricanes' regular-season finale. A lot of coaches claim they don't watch the scoreboard. I always watch the scoreboard, and I kept an eye on the Florida-Carolina game. In the third game of the regular season, I'll be watching the scoreboard. Carolina's loss meant we'd win the division if we won our regular-season finale against Florida on April 5. The Hurricanes were in the clubhouse and couldn't do anything to stop us.

The pregame mood for the Florida game was tense. Sometimes I feel I have to say something emotional and passionate. I knew I didn't have to say anything like that. Sergei Fedorov broke a 1-1 tie with a second-period goal, and Alexander Semin scored a power-play goal early in the third. Cris Huet made twenty-five saves. We won 3-1 to complete our improbable climb to the Southeast Division championship.

What a feeling of satisfaction on the bench in the final minute. The crowd was insane the last twenty seconds. I slapped the players on their backs and yelled, "You're champions, you're bleepin' champions! Now we're going for the cup!"

Quite an accomplishment. Rising from the depths in late November to claim Washington's first play-off berth in five years. Closing by winning eleven out of twelve, including a seven-game winning streak that was the team's longest in fifteen years. We became the first NHL club in history to come back from fourteenth or fifteenth place in a conference at midseason and make the postseason.

What a treat to see a group of players who had given everything they had get rewarded. Especially Alexander Ovechkin, who led the NHL in goals and points and joined the likes of Wayne Gretzky, Mario Lemieux, Phil Esposito, Guy Lafleur, and Jarome Iginla in the elite group that has accomplished that feat. It was wonderful to see Alex enjoy team success along with his individual success. It also was wonderful to see George McPhee and Ted Leonsis enjoy success after all the faith they placed in me.

We went 37-17-7 after I took over on Thanksgiving to finish at 43-31-8 with ninety-four points, a twenty-four-point improvement from 2006–7. That pace projects to 109 points over a full eighty-two-game season. Only Detroit, Pittsburgh, and San Jose had better records after Thanksgiving.

In addition to Ovie, Mike Green led all NHL defensemen with eighteen goals, Nicklas Backstrom set a franchise rookie record with fifty-five assists, and Cristobal Huet won his last nine starts for the longest winning streak for a Caps goalie since Pete Peeters won nine in a row in 1986–87. That's what I mean when I say individual success flows out of the team concept.

Next thing I knew, we were discussing postseason dates. The club written off in November owned the No. 3 Eastern Conference seed in the Stanley Cup play-offs. Against all odds, a season that seemed like a dream was continuing.

●

We went into the play-offs feeling a sense of destiny. We honestly thought we were going to win the Eastern Conference, where I guessed Pittsburgh would be the biggest hurdle, and advance to the Stanley Cup finals. Maybe I was out to lunch, but that's what I thought.

It was crazy that Pittsburgh went into Philadelphia and didn't really try to win its last game in the regular season. The Penguins would never admit it, but in the back of their minds I think they preferred playing Ottawa instead of Philadelphia in the first round. And that's what they got by losing that game. The Flyers had played well against them in the regular season. Owing to injuries and play-off attrition, Philadelphia wasn't the same team they had been against us when they eventually lost to Pittsburgh in the conference finals. The Flyers played with the same emotion and intensity and bigger beards, but they were banged up after two rounds.

We felt we could play with the Flyers. We worried about their depth at forward. The unknown factor was goalie Martin Biron. We didn't know how good he would be in the play-offs. He'd never carried the play-off load when he played for the Buffalo Sabres.

We trailed 4-2 after two periods at home in Game 1 on April 11. We stormed back in the third to tie it 4-4 on two goals by Mike Green. I'd already seen in two years of Calder Cup play-off action with Hershey in the AHL how Green elevates his game in the postseason. He was doing it again.

After the season, Green was in Halifax, Nova Scotia, playing for Canada at the International Ice Hockey Federation (IIHF) World Championships. I had just made an appearance on Canadian TV. He phoned and left a message, saying, "Bruce, I'm just at the Worlds and I watched you on *Hockey Night in Canada*. Very good. And, by the way, you looked very handsome." That's so Mike Green. He's got a dry wit. What did he do after the season? He took his brother to Disneyland.

I've coached an awful lot of players. I love Mike Cammalleri as a player and a person. And Jeff Giuliano and Chris Schmidt and Dave Steckel. Mike Green has a special place in my heart. I think he's the greatest kid. I'd love to be his dad. At times when things aren't going well for him, he seeks my advice and takes every word I say to heart. I'd love to coach him for a long time.

After Green tied Game 1, Alex Ovechkin, who had been held without a shot, took advantage of a defensive gaffe by Lasse Kukkonen and scored the game-winner with 4:32 left.

Ovie was in perfect position. He attacked, stole the puck, and fired a shot past Biron. It showed our system worked, because we knew how the Flyers would try to play in their defensive zone. It seemed like the same-old, same-old, sort of an echo of my debut against Philly when that power-play scheme worked.

Maybe that was the problem. That 5-4 victory might have been a bad thing for us. Even though it was a fantastic ending and gave us a 1-0 series lead, it might have been better to lose. We might have woken up faster.

The Flyers did a good defensive job on Ovie for the first four games of the series. Alex put a lot of pressure on himself. He had talked about wanting to make the play-offs for so long, and now it was here. He was super conscientious about positioning instead of just playing. It took him three games to figure out it's still just hockey. The last four games of the series, he was extremely good.

Martin Biron started to prove his play-off mettle in Game 2 on April 13. He had twenty-four saves in a 2-0 shutout that tied the series 1-1. Aside from the third period of Game 1, Philly had controlled play in five of six periods and the trend continued in Game 3 on April 15 at Wachovia Center.

The Flyers took a 3-1 lead in the first period. We were outplayed but somehow were in position to steal the game late in the third after Brooks Laich scored to draw us within 4-3. But Mike Richards scored on a penalty shot and Mike Knuble added an empty-netter for a 6-3 Philly victory.

As general manager, my old Johnstown roommate Paul Holmgren had done a masterful job of rebuilding the Flyers from a non-play-off team in 2006–7 into one of the Eastern Conference's best teams in 2007–8. After we lost Game 3, George McPhee and I ran across Paul and his wife as we exited Wachovia Center. There had been newspaper stories about our days together in Johnstown, and I told Paul he was right when he told reporters that I was the sloppy one. Holmgren chuckled. He was probably a lot happier than we were.

Game 4 on April 17 was a heartbreaker that we lost 4-3 in double overtime. We were ahead 3-2 when we got hit with a too-many-men penalty midway through the third, and Danny Briere scored on the ensuing power play to tie it. We got hosed when Viktor Kozlov was pushed into Martin Biron late in the third period and got whistled for a ludicrous goalie interference penalty. Shouldn't have been called. That effectively took away any chance we had to win in regulation. We had our chances initially in overtime, but we didn't score. Knuble scored at 6:40 of the second overtime to give Philly a 3-1 series lead.

Defenseman Steve Eminger scored the second-period goal that gave us a

3-2 lead. I felt terrible about the fact that Steve played in only twenty regular-season games for us. All the power to this kid. He went through a lot of garbage, came back, and played hard for us when we needed him late in the regular season and the play-offs, where he played five games against Philly. It takes a tough guy to do all of that. His performance impressed the Flyers enough that they traded for him after the season.

The Wachovia Center crowd was extremely loud, and we were a little nervous. But we were starting to understand what play-off hockey was all about. Even though we were in a big hole, I knew we still had a chance. I recounted my ECHL experience from Mississippi, when we rallied from a 3-1 deficit against Richmond to win the Kelly Cup. I sort of stare blankly when I talk, so I don't know if any eyes rolled when I mentioned the ECHL. The players might have thought, Oh, you idiot, why don't you also talk about your midget year in 1971?

But I firmly believe hockey is hockey and situations are situations. NHL or ECHL, it was the same thing. Three-one is 3-1. My task was to not let them look at it as an unclimbable mountain. It's daunting if you say you've got to win three in a row. I told them nothing had changed in the series since we'd lost Game 2.

"All we have to do is win our home games and win one in Philly," I said.

I also told them the Flyers probably were thinking celebration, that they might be mulling the idea it would be more fun to clinch at home in Game 6 than on the road in Game 5. And they didn't clinch in Game 5 on April 19 at Verizon Center.

Though it finished as a 3-2 game, we initially led 2-0, and it was a convincing performance. I took some pundit criticism for changing line combinations and the power play four games into the series, but it was nothing new to me. After we lost Game 1 of the Calder Cup finals the year before in Hershey, I made major changes before Game 2 and we won our lone game of that series against Hamilton. The changes during the Philly series worked too. We had tons of confidence heading into Game 6. We expected to force Game 7.

After the Flyers took a 2-0 lead, we dominated Game 6 at Philly on April 21. I guess it was symbolic of our season as a whole. Rally in the face of long odds and play well. Trailing by two goals and facing elimination, we apparently had the Flyers right where we wanted them. We tied it 2-2 in the second period, and Alex Ovechkin scored twice in the third, the first on a breakaway set up by a sweet Viktor Kozlov feed. The game ended in a 4-2 win that sent us back home for the deciding game in the series.

Momentum was rolling our way, and Game 7 was scheduled for the next day, April 22. But I knew the Flyers were as resilient as we were, and it wouldn't be easy. Down the stretch, everybody counted out the Flyers the same way we'd been counted out. The Flyers faced a tough schedule and won the games they had to win to make the play-offs. You knew they weren't going to give up. I tried to make our team understand that Philly wouldn't roll over.

The thought that stays with me about Game 7 is it was 2-2 when Alex Ovechkin intercepted a puck with about three minutes to go in regulation. He faked a shot and tried to pass to Sergei Fedorov. Once Fedorov saw Alex wind up, he looked at Martin Biron and waited for a rebound off the expected shot. That was the way to play it. So when the puck came to him—instead of shooting, Alex made a great pass to Fedorov—Sergei wasn't watching. If he had been looking for a pass, it would have been a goal. We outshot them 16-5 in the third, and the Flyers didn't have a sniff. They seemed done. But once it got to overtime, the advantage switched to Philly.

There were two controversial calls by my neighbor, referee Paul Devorski. Devo and I owned homes in the same subdivision in Harrisburg, Pennsylvania. He lived two doors away. Yes, it's a small world.

On the first call in the second period, Philly's Patrick Thoresen checked Shaone Morrisonn into Cris Huet, knocking Cris down and leaving an open net for Sami Kapanen to score. The goal should have been disallowed, but it stood to give the Flyers a 2-1 lead at 9:47.

In a game against Tampa Bay in April, Brooks Laich scored a goal and they didn't count it because they said Tomas Fleischmann pushed a defenseman into the goalie. They called it incidental contact. No penalty but no goal. Well, that should have been the call when Thoresen did it. But you've got refs calling the same situation differently. I don't care what the rule is, but it's got to be a black and white rule. Make the same call every time.

At least there was time to recover from that call, and Ovie tied it 2-2 at

15:29 of the second. If Kapanen's score had been the overtime goal, there would have been a huge furor. Poor Devorski's house would have been toilet papered every night for about a month. Just joking.

In overtime Devo made a neutral-zone hooking call on Tom Poti that set up Joffrey Lupul's power-play series winner. I understand the standard is to not let everything go. The problem is that a no-whistle tone had been set. They didn't call any penalties in the third period and didn't call John Erskine earlier in overtime for a trip that stopped a potential Kapanen breakaway. A call on Erskine, a defenseman who competes his butt off and provides a needed physical element, would have been a more valid penalty to decide the series on.

I give Paul credit for having the guts, whether he's right or wrong, to make the call on Poti. Devo had an explanation for everything. However, he was the back referee. Why did he make that call? Why didn't ref Don Koharski, who had the play right in front of him, make that call? I don't understand that.

I had a bad gut feeling when we got the penalty. Poti was our best penalty killer, and he was in the box. We almost killed all of it, but Lupul scored at 6:06 with nine seconds left on the power play for a 3-2 Philly win. I tried not to look at the Flyers' celebration. You hate it when you lose. I wanted to hug all my players. I'd believed they were going to go deep into the play-offs. I was so proud of their effort. It would have been easy for them to quit on many occasions.

We did our best, and it was just one of those things that went the other way. A great hockey game, a great series. I didn't have a lot to say in the locker room.

I told them, "I'm so proud of the way you guys worked for me as a guy who just showed up. You could have said you're waiting until you get a big-name coach. But you worked your hearts out for me, and I'm so proud of you. You did something great, and we're on the verge of being really great."

They weren't ready to hear it. They were crushed. But they needed to keep their heads up.

I was numb. I didn't have any emotion left, either sadness or happiness. You're going a hundred miles per hour, all your senses are operating at their peak, and everything comes to a sudden halt.

The bottom line is it was time to say good-bye. To the 2007–8 season. To a special group of players.

We had the traditional end-of-season exit meetings with the players. After meeting with Brooks Laich, he left the room and then poked his head back in.

"Bruce, I wanted to tell you," Brooks said. "Sergei Fedorov said the best two coaches he ever had were you and Scotty Bowman, for instincts behind the bench and stuff."

I don't know if it's true. But, boy, it hit me. Being in the same breath with Scotty Bowman in the eyes of Sergei Fedorov. What a moment. For a minor-league guy who had been shot down most of his life, that was pretty incredible.

It was announced in public on April 23, but I knew on the final Sunday of the regular season that I was getting a multiyear contract to remain as head coach of the Washington Capitals. George McPhee had a brief meeting with me to tell me I was staying. I told him I was really happy. I'd finally managed to stick in the NHL.

"Bruce, a lot of people come into my office demanding a lot or saying they deserve this and they deserve that," George told me. "You deserve it, and you did a great job."

That made me feel better than the money. It hasn't sunk in that I'm an NHL head coach. It will take me a while to get over the minor-league thought process—that I'm not an interim, that I'm not a temporary. I'm a bona fide NHL head coach. Privately, I'm a confident person. But I'm insecure about projecting that outwardly because I've been in the minors so long. I've got to get over that.

When I got home to Harrisburg after we'd wrapped up the season, I took my son Brady to Paul Devorski's house.

I knocked on the door and said, "Paul?"

"Yes?" he warily answered.

"No hard feelings." I shook his hand, and Paul seemed relieved

"Good," Devo said. "Now will you phone my son? He hasn't talked to me in three days."

"I'm over here to say there's no hard feelings," I added, "because you're the only one in the neighborhood who has a pool. And we're going to have to use it this summer."

In the final analysis, was it better to lose out the way we did, in an exciting seventh game with controversy, than to advance and maybe lose in the second round in less stirring fashion? What result would have left the better can't-wait-till-next-season feeling?

It's an interesting question. You imagine that you would have kept winning. But who knows?

# 17

## FANTASY BONE

**As the 2007–8 season progressed,** our dramatic improvement raised speculation that I might be a contender for the Jack Adams Award. The Adams is given annually to the NHL Coach of the Year. Talk like that tickles your fantasy bone and makes you wonder if you're going to get it. The three finalists were scheduled to be announced on May 1. I approached our public relations guys, Paul Rovnak and Nate Ewell, and asked if they'd heard anything. They hadn't. You don't want to sound vain, but you sort of want to know.

I found out that night. I was in Washington watching a game on TV, and my son Andy was watching another game in Canada. Don Cherry announced the nominees on the Canadian broadcast, and Andy phoned me.

"Dad, you're nominated," Andy said. "Did you know?"

"Holy cow," I said. "I didn't know."

I had no idea about the magnitude of the thing. Detroit Red Wings head coach Mike Babcock and Montreal Canadiens head coach Guy Carbonneau were announced as the other two finalists.

The *NHL Awards Show* was held on June 12, 2008, at the Elgin Theatre in my hometown of Toronto. A year earlier—to the month—I had bused out of Ontario after the Hershey Bears lost to the Hamilton Bulldogs in the Calder Cup finals. Now I'd return to Ontario to be recognized as one of the NHL's top coaches. Sitting on that bus, I never could have imagined the dramatic turn my life would take in the coming twelve months.

My initial desire was to have my whole family at the *NHL Awards Show*. Then we found out tickets cost $450 apiece.

"You guys are all watching on TV," I said.

My wife, Crystal, and I arrived in Toronto the day before the *NHL Awards Show*. I wanted to stay incognito. I still felt like, Wow, I'm this minor-league guy among all these big-name NHL guys and maybe I don't really belong. We went to the launch of Alexander Ovechkin's new fashion line of designer street wear for men. It was a neat event. It reminded me of what New York is like with the fashion shoots.

That night we went to Yorkville, a section of Toronto known for its shopping. Playing big shot, I ordered a round of drinks. It gave me another case of sticker shock and reminded me of the forty-dollar hamburger in Philadelphia. I had forty dollars ready. Four drafts, a glass of white wine, and a Diet Coke came to $61.50. I had to dig out more cash and give the waitress seventy dollars just to make a good tip. Some big shot.

Awards show day was a whirlwind. Crystal and I didn't know what to do with ourselves. We went for walks and idled around. At 2:00 p.m. we had a show rehearsal. They originally didn't have my tuxedo ready. They lost all the fitting information, so they had to remeasure me. I worried they wouldn't have a tux for me and people would point and the whole suit thing would flare up again. But my tux was ready in time for the rehearsal, which elicited a major sigh of relief from the Boudreau family. It fit well and felt comfortable.

It was a blur from 2:00 p.m. to 7:00 p.m. There was a media session. We did a walk on a red carpet, which was neat for a guy who never expected to experience something fancy like that. I was excited for Crystal to be able to walk down a red carpet after she'd walked beside me through so many tough times.

We got seated in the theater. The show came on. I soaked it all in. I was in awe when Gordie Howe walked past. When you're a guy who's watched the show on TV and seen the class of everybody, it's surreal when you're there yourself.

It was a proud evening for the Washington Capitals. Ovie was up for the Hart Memorial Trophy as NHL Most Valuable Player and the Lester B. Pearson Award, the MVP honor voted on by members of the NHL Players'

Association. Alex already had garnered the Art Ross Trophy and Maurice "Rocket" Richard Trophy as the league's leading point scorer and goal scorer. Nicklas Backstrom was a finalist for the Calder Memorial Trophy, given to the NHL Rookie of the Year.

I wanted Nicklas Backstrom to win so badly. I was extremely disappointed when Nicky didn't win, not that Chicago's Patrick Kane didn't deserve it. I just thought our guy had a good shot. I've never been at an award ceremony where I wanted a guy to win as bad as I wanted Nicky to win that.

When it came time for the Jack Adams Award announcement, I didn't expect to win. I watched an in-house TV screen where they had youth players introduce the finalists and their credentials. When they talked about Mike Babcock, I thought, He's a shoo-in; look what he did. Then they talked about Guy Carbonneau. He's more of a shoo-in than Babcock, I thought. When they did me, I thought, Oh, it was a nice little story that he got here, but that's as far as it goes.

Scotty Bowman announced the award. In my mind, I had come full circle. When I started my coaching career in Muskegon, I had sought his help. Scotty was so generous about giving advice. I'd get off the phone and think, Wow, Scotty Bowman is giving advice to me and who am I to even ask? In Toronto, I told Scotty I remembered all the help he provided and thanked him.

All I remember was Scotty Bowman saying "Bru-." I went blank. I didn't hear the full announcement that Bruce Boudreau won the Jack Adams Award. I was robotic. I knew I had to go on stage. I know I didn't turn to Crystal or give her a hug and a kiss. Sorry, dear, but I was in a daze.

I walked up on stage, high-fiving kids along the way. Now what was I supposed to do? I didn't know whether to accept the trophy or put it down or hold it or whatever. You can say until the cows come home that you have a speech planned and you know whom you want to thank. I thought I had a speech prepared in my head. But when you get up there, you develop an immediate sense of sympathy for people who have screwed up at the Academy Awards. They get befuddled and sound ridiculous. Sally Field, I know how you felt.

Stand in that spotlight and you don't know what you're saying. I knew I wanted to thank George McPhee, Ted Leonsis, Crystal, and my children—and, fortunately, I did. I wanted to say stuff about my mother and father, but I forgot. I wanted to congratulate Mike Babcock and Guy Carbonneau, and I forgot. I did remember to say thanks to Bruce Landon and Doug Yingst for their years of backing me.

Then I exited the stage and took pictures with the trophy. There were rows and rows of press guys tossing questions while cameras flashed. I kept thinking about what an amazing year it had been.

When I returned to my seat, George McPhee, Ted Leonsis, and Zach Leonsis, Ted's son, exuded delight. I didn't realize it would affect them that much. They were so genuinely happy for me that I was taken aback.

Our smiles continued when Alex Ovechkin, who'd earlier claimed the Lester Pearson, won the Hart. He turned around and gave me a hug as his coach, and my heart swelled. Alex became the first player in NHL history to win all four major individual awards: Hart, Pearson, Richard, Ross. Up on stage, he seemed charmingly overwhelmed, but underneath he's so smart.

It was a big night for Russian players. In addition to Ovie, Detroit's Pavel Datsyuk won the Lady Byng Memorial Trophy as the NHL's most gentlemanly player and also the Frank J. Selke Trophy as the top defensive forward. Pittsburgh's Evgeni Malkin was a Hart finalist. I'm no deep political thinker, but it's amazing how far we've come since my playing days. The Cold War was going on back then.

Every now and again, I watch the 1972 Summit Series between Canada and the Soviet Union. I was in eleventh grade when it was played. The thing about that wasn't a hatred for the Russians. Our big thing was we thought we were so good as Canadians that nobody was close to us in hockey. And these guys came in and started beating us. Are you kidding me?

We got smoked 7-3 in Game 1 in Montreal when we thought we were going to dominate. I was at Maple Leaf Gardens for Game 2. The Canadian team won 4-1, and I saw Peter Mahovlich score an amazing short-handed goal. It was so loud.

It was like a national holiday in Canada for the eighth game. Everybody got the day off from school. Nobody would have gone to school anyway. We all went to friends' houses and watched the game. Canada won 6-5 in Game

8 on Paul Henderson's famous goal with thirty-four seconds left, and Canada won the series 4-3-1.

The best thing about the Summit Series is that it changed the Canadian way of thinking about conditioning. It used to be that you didn't do formal training during the summer and used training camp to get in shape. The series was played in September, and the Russians were far better conditioned. After that, summer training came into vogue in Canada.

The Russians also innovated the day-of-game skate. Before that, on the day of a game, we'd informally go out without a coach in our sweats and take a few shots. It eventually transformed into full equipment and formal practices. Now we're leaning toward going back the other way, making game-day skates lighter, because there's so much hockey. With a long season, pregame skates aren't as important for preparation, and we need to reduce the physical toll on players.

The teen who saw Game 2 of the Summit Series in person has subsequently had the honor of coaching Alexander Ovechkin, Alexander Semin, Sergei Fedorov, and Viktor Kozlov in Washington. It's amazing what you don't know. And when you don't know, you make assumptions about folks and hold stereotypes. We didn't know the Russians back in the 1970s, so we assumed they were all vodka-drinking, no-emotion people. That narrow thinking is quite embarrassing in retrospect.

The Russians I've known are some of the nicest people I've ever met. Ovie and Semin are still kids. The two older statesmen—Kozlov and Fedorov—are such polite and wonderful men. What a treat for me to be able to say I coached Fedorov. Age meant he wasn't the overwhelming force he was at twenty-four, but what a teacher and what a leader.

I had a Russian named Maxim Kuznetsov in Manchester. He was a six-foot-five defenseman traded from Detroit to Los Angeles along with Sean Avery. Max wasn't a good skater, and the Kings sent him to the AHL. I sat him out in all but two games of the play-offs in 2003–4. I wanted to play him because of his NHL experience, but assistant coach Jim Hughes didn't want him on the ice. I let Jim have the say, something I wouldn't allow today as a head coach. Thus, Kuznetsov sat. After the season, Maxim, who had played for Scotty Bowman, came into my office, gave me a hug, and told me

I was the best coach he'd ever had. I sure didn't expect that.

At the *NHL Awards Show* after-party, I got congratulated out. I wasn't used to being such a focus of attention. I had a long talk with my old New Brunswick teammate Ron Wilson, who had just been named head coach of the Toronto Maple Leafs.

"Me and you were the toilet seats of the Leafs," Ron joked. "You'd get called up and get sent down. Then I'd get called up. We both should have been in the NHL for long periods of time, but we were in the wrong organization at the wrong time."

Guys who wouldn't have given me the time of day if they saw me on the street six months before gushed over me. Loads of people wanted their picture taken with me, and I can't stand to have my picture taken. Attention gives you an odd feeling. It's weird to hear people whisper your name in the background. "Oh, there's Bruce Boudreau." It's fun but crazy. The fame thing is strange. It's not about whom you are as a person. Frankly, it's shallow. It gave me a better understanding of the Hollywood experience.

Crystal and I reflected on things after we left the after-party. It wasn't a jumping up and down excitement. It was a reserved, joyful contemplation of what had happened to us as a couple and a family.

●

The wild ride continued the following week. I returned to Manchester, New Hampshire, for the annual Ace Bailey Golf Classic and went to Ottawa for the NHL entry draft.

It rained all morning the day of the charity tournament, held in honor of my late friend Ace, who had been killed during the September 11, 2001, terrorist attacks. As soon as the tournament was scheduled to start, it stopped raining and became a nice day for five and a half hours. Then it started raining again. It seemed like the weather gods were on our side.

Kathy Bailey, Ace's widow, gave me a big hug, and we reminisced about Ace. She said Ace would be proud of me. Hubie McDonough, my old Manchester Monarchs antagonist, was there. I give Hubie credit for showing up. It took a lot of courage on his part to shake my hand. I appreciated that. I knew it was tough for him. He's probably a good guy. I wish we'd have talked more when I coached the Monarchs. I'd like to know what it really was that he hated about me.

Great news kept coming at the NHL entry draft, where I had one of the best days of my life. My best friend John Anderson was named head coach of the Atlanta Thrashers, joining me in the NHL ranks. It was long overdue for John, who led the Chicago Wolves to a second Calder Cup championship in 2007–8. Dream seasons for both of us.

I knew John was going to hear at the draft whether Atlanta, the Wolves' NHL parent club, was going to promote him. I was like a nervous kid and kept phoning John and asking whether he'd gotten word. I was floored when he told me he indeed got it. I don't know if I've ever been that happy for anybody before.

John and I had tried for so long to get to the NHL. I got there because of George McPhee's and Doug Yingst's zeal in promoting me. John had all the credentials too. I think John got there, in part, because I was successful when given a chance. I guarantee it wouldn't have helped John if I'd fallen flat on my face. I think the success I had, especially dealing with the young players who were in the farm system, helped John. That makes me feel real good. It was a great fit for Atlanta to bring up a coach who had success with their young kids and also brought new ideas.

On top of that, my friend Barry Melrose was named head coach of the Tampa Bay Lightning three days after the draft. It wouldn't work as fiction. It would be dismissed as preposterous. That put all three of us—John, Barry, and me—in the Southeast Division. Temporarily. Barry got fired early in the 2008–9 season.

Congratulations kept coming my way at the draft. I was flummoxed. People approached and I'd say, "Thank you, I appreciate it," before they even opened their mouths. Being on the floor at the draft and going to the podium for the announcement of Washington's first pick, Anton Gustafsson, was fascinating. I didn't want to screw up and say things I wasn't supposed to say, so I mainly rode along like a piece of luggage. A giddy piece of luggage.

●

The tables for the Washington Capitals and Carolina Hurricanes were next to each other at the NHL entry draft. Jim Rutherford, Carolina's part-owner and general manager, called me over for a visit. I scored my first NHL goal against Jimmy when he played for the Detroit Red Wings. My goal was the first one of the game in a 6-0 Toronto win at Maple Leaf Gardens.

I don't know if I was floating or not. I came back near our blue line, and Randy Carlyle collected the puck behind our goal line and fed me a pass that set up a breakaway. I felt like I was going a hundred miles per hour, but it might have been ten miles per hour. I shot over Rutherford's glove hand, top shelf, and the puck went in. I jumped and went nuts. I also got an assist and was first or second star. I thought I'd score a lot more NHL goals, but we know how that turned out.

Rutherford and I later played together briefly for Toronto. We've had a good long-term relationship for two guys who don't know each other that well. Jimmy sent me a signed Hurricanes jersey to give away at the 2008 banquet for my annual summer hockey school in St. Catharines, Ontario. I was golly-gee tickled when it arrived. A real NHL jersey speckled with player autographs.

It's a treat to hand stuff like that to kids. For me, it's a rewarding way to give back. Seeing the thrill on kids' faces makes banquet day my favorite day of the year by far. The banquet has become a huge deal and is now attended by more than five hundred people.

My Golden Horseshoe Hockey School started in 1981. It wasn't my idea. It was Rocky Saganiuk's idea. He was a teammate with the Leafs and in the minors. Sports camps were in their infancy back then. That first year I had Brian Papineau, who was sixteen at the time and grew up to become the Leafs' trainer, round up the counselors. I don't know how we survived our early ineptitude. There have been some shaky times, but the school has survived and grown. Since 1996 it's been considered a premier day camp to go to in the Niagara region of Ontario. We run it for two weeks in August, and 220 to 240 kids attend.

I never thought it would last this long. But I always want to be the best, and I brought that competitiveness to running the camp. It's not about money. It's part of me. This is my summer routine. I wouldn't have a clue what to do in August without it. It keeps me in touch with St. Catharines. Now I've got children of former campers coming. I won't give it up until I can't do it anymore. My goal is to reach at least thirty years. Without donations from sponsors, we'd never be able to run it because of costs. There are too many sponsors to thank by name, but I'm grateful to all of them.

We've had kids attend from Australia, England, and China. One kid from Australia had never skated or even seen hockey, but he wanted to come. He loved it, and all the kids made him a big banner, which they signed and presented to him at the banquet. He cried. His mom cried. It was really touching.

I wish I had a list of all the kids I've had who became pros. I'm sure Owen Nolan attended. I'm sure Bill Berg and Bob Berg both went. I bet virtually anybody who's gone on to play pro hockey from that region has come to my camp. Brendan Brooks came to the camp and later played for me in Lowell and Manchester in the AHL. Brendan attended camp for the first twelve years and then worked at the camp for ten.

A guy named Ross Chater has been with the camp as either a student or a worker since its inception. He started at age four and takes a week off work to serve as a counselor every year. My older kids—Kasey, Ben, and Andy—all have been counselors. And Brady will do it when he's old enough. It gives me a chance to be around my children for a week or two.

We all want to make our kids better at hockey, but the premise of the school is to provide a good experience. Honestly, how much better is a kid going to get from a week at hockey camp? When we first started, our strongest group in attendance was the thirteen-to-fifteen age range. By the early 1990s there were hardly any kids that age coming. That told me everybody was putting too much pressure on young kids to be good, and they quit once they realized they weren't going to make the NHL. It bothers me to see kids walk away from the game at that age.

I don't want them to view my camp as purely a preparatory step to the NHL. I want them to come away loving hockey so that when they're twenty-one or twenty-two, they're still playing recreational hockey like they would play softball.

I'm hands-on twelve hours a day, on and off the ice. Crystal organizes everything; she's much better organized than I am. We have a policeman do a drug talk. We hand out nutrition information. We go bowling.

The school is run as a tournament, with points awarded for hockey performance and off-ice behavior, like keeping the cafeteria clean. The winning team gets tickets to a Buffalo Sabres exhibition game. The kids are competitive about it. We play the national anthem before games, announce three stars of the game, and have NHL referees officiate. The winning team earns the Swiss Chalet Trophy, and it gets lugged around like the Stanley Cup.

The banquet is the grand finale. I get gifts from all over the NHL, AHL, and ECHL. Some of the stuff we give out is small potatoes, like posters and key chains. We also give out skates, sticks, jerseys, and goalie pads. Dan "Beaker" Stuck, my trainer in Hershey, has been terrific at using his connections to get stuff. So has Brian Papineau of the Leafs. Brian came up with a day with the Leafs where a kid gets to be stick boy on the bench for a pregame skate and gets tickets to a game. That one made me cry. As a Toronto boy, I imagined what that kind of gift would have meant to me as a kid.

I brought the Calder Cup to camp when we won it in Hershey. If I'm ever fortunate enough to win the Stanley Cup, I'll bring it. That's what I'd do with my day with the cup.

I get deep satisfaction out of giving gifts because I've received so many gifts from the game of hockey.

A special one came from Ted Leonsis. Ted called me into his office after the 2007–8 season ended. I initially thought, Uh-oh, am I in trouble with the owner? I shouldn't be that way, but I'm always on guard. Maybe that's why I push so hard to succeed; I never again want to get that sick feeling that my job could be in jeopardy.

Ted presented a Rolex watch to me. It's a ten-thousand-dollar piece. I'd never worn a watch that cost more than fifty bucks.

The Rolex is worth more than the Kelly Blue Book value on the Chevy Impala I drove to Arlington, Virginia, when I was summoned from Hershey, Pennsylvania, on Thanksgiving morning in 2007. Well, I didn't get lost when I became head coach of the Washington Capitals. My direction was true.

When I looked at the Rolex, gleaming on my wrist, it told me more than a.m. and p.m. The watch reminded me of all the hours and years it took to get here. It showed me I met my personal test of time.

# AFTERWORD: ELIMINATION GAMES

**This is an autobiography,** but you look at all the foreshadowing from my past that came into play during the 2008–9 season and you start to wonder if it isn't a novel. Barry Melrose. John Anderson. Sean Avery. The AHL. Pennsylvania.

Hey, if anybody reads anything between the lines that foreshadows a Stanley Cup, please let me know.

We accomplished a lot in my first full season as head coach of the Washington Capitals—a second straight Southeast Division championship and a first-round play-off victory over the New York Rangers—but we are still pursuing the Stanley Cup.

I received my call to the NHL while living in Pennsylvania. For the second straight year, though, our season ended against a Pennsylvania team. I have a weird love-hate relationship with Pennsylvania. I love going a couple hours up the road from Washington to Hershey and Harrisburg. If I go basically due north and get to Hershey, I'm quite happy. But if I go left or right, I'm angry the whole time because I'm going toward Pittsburgh or Philadelphia.

The Philadelphia Flyers beat us in 2007–8. The Pittsburgh Penguins eliminated us in 2008–9. The NHL got a dream series when the Capitals and Penguins met in the second round of the Stanley Cup play-offs. We didn't get our dream ending. Before I get into the details of that seven-game series, there is a lot of good stuff to address about a season that ended nine wins short of our ideal.

●

I have been blessed to have many nice things happen to me recently. I'm kind of wary about it. At some point, you figure the guy upstairs is bound to say, "OK, Bruce, that's enough good stuff for you."

My son Ben made me proud by playing in four minor leagues and scoring a goal in each one in 2008–9. I told him he's the only guy in history who has ever done that. This is a kid who played senior and pickup hockey and, at age twenty-three, just decided to dedicate himself in the summer to working out and becoming a player. Doug Yingst and Bob Woods with the Hershey Bears were fabulous; they let him come to their training camp, and he scored a goal for the Bears in an exhibition game. I got to see it live at Giant Center in Hershey, and I was pretty pumped for Ben.

Ben also played in the IHL for Flint, the ECHL for South Carolina, and the CHL for Wichita. He did a really credible job for his first year of pro hockey. He definitely wants to try to continue it. Maybe he still can make a little career out of this. All he has to do is get stronger. I don't see why he can't become a good AHL player.

The AHL named me to their Hall of Fame. I would be lying if I said from the year they started the AHL Hall of Fame in 2006 that I wasn't looking to see who was elected. It was an overwhelming honor. When you are playing hockey in your driveway as a kid, you think of two things: scoring the winning goal in the Stanley Cup finals and being elected to the hall of fame—any hall of fame.

The induction ceremony was held during the AHL All-Star Classic in Worcester, Massachusetts, in late January. The way things worked out, the Caps were scheduled to visit the Boston Bruins the next day, so I was able to attend in person. I would have traveled from Alaska to get there. Before the induction ceremony, I was pretty calm about the whole thing; how big it was hadn't hit me. But it started to overwhelm me when I arrived at the luncheon, saw all the people there, and watched highlights of my AHL playing and coaching career recounted during a video presentation.

I got goose bumps. I brought my son Brady to the stage with me for my speech. I had two thoughts. The first one was, Wow! The second one was that I needed to be short with my remarks so that the AHL players could get back to their rooms and rest for the game. I also needed to get to my team's practice. Always a coach. I had a lot I wanted to say, but I was brief because of that.

When you get a Hall of Fame ring, people come up to congratulate you. I took their comments with deep pride. The AHL has existed since 1936–37. It has featured a tremendous number of great hockey people. When I played, Mike Emrick, who has won the Lester Patrick Award for contributions to hockey in the United States and the Foster Hewitt Award for broadcasting excellence from the Hockey Hall of Fame, was the play-by-play guy in Portland, Maine. And John Forslund, now with the Carolina Hurricanes, was the play-by-play guy in Springfield, Massachusetts.

The AHL is doing great due diligence on all the player selections. They are not forgetting the older players. It's not like they said, "Take Bruce Boudreau because he's a big name now." They have made well-considered selections. That makes me feel even prouder that I was one of the choices.

Thanks to the AHL, I got to be around one all-star event during the season. I also came really close to getting to serve as an assistant coach to Boston Bruins head coach Claude Julien at the NHL All-Star Game. But we lost 5-4 at Montreal on January 10, and Canadiens head coach Guy Carbonneau got the gig because his team had a better winning percentage based on that victory.

Claude Julien texted me before the Montreal game. He wished me good luck and said he'd like to see me as his partner. That was so cool. If we had gotten one point out of the game, just reached overtime, that would have made me an assistant. I didn't say a word about it, but I know the team was cognizant of the whole idea.

The score was 4-4 with a minute left. I said, "Let's get this thing to overtime and we'll win in overtime." The Canadiens flipped the puck into our zone. They weren't even trying to score. There were fewer than twenty-five seconds left when rookie defenseman Karl Alzner tried to push the puck over the blue line, but it went through his glove and landed in defenseman Milan Jurcina's feet. Jurcina looked around like he couldn't find the puck.

It was like I was watching this thing in slow motion. The puck went between Jurcina's legs and Montreal's Sergei Kostitsyn took a shot. It went in the net with 21.2 seconds left. I fell right against the glass. Then I said, "Oh, well," and laughed it off. It would have meant a busy All-Star break weekend, but it is certainly one I would have given up to be in Montreal, which hosted the All-Star Game during its hundredth anniversary season.

Anybody who says they don't want the slot is a liar. It is an honor. It would have been cool to see Alex Ovechkin do his stuff and see the fun they have, and to be with all the those unbelievable players. I would have asked for their autographs. I would have grabbed some sticks for my hockey school. It didn't work out, so maybe some other time.

By no stretch of the imagination do I take myself seriously or think I'm an important guy. Thus, two other things that happened made me laugh. In its annual ranking of the one hundred most powerful people in hockey, the *Hockey News* listed me as fifty-six. And the Capitals had a Bruce Boudreau bobblehead doll made.

I don't think I will be on *The Hockey News* list again. A lot of people phoned me and got a good chuckle out of that. It was pretty wild. I guarantee I'm not the fifty-sixth most powerful person in hockey. I'm just happy to have a job in the NHL.

You don't have to rewind too far back to find a time I was nothing. They could have had the five hundred most powerful people in hockey a year earlier and I would have maybe ranked ahead of some guy coaching Midget Hockey in Toronto. Something is wrong when Caps general manager George McPhee is not on the list and I'm on the list. Not many NHL general managers have held the job for more than a decade like George.

I was shocked by the bobblehead doll. Come on. And they made the body look thin. Other than the four chins on it, I thought it was a pretty good thing. It looked pretty neat. Who would have thought? The Caps had bobblehead dolls made for both Alex Ovechkin and me. I was in pretty good company.

The bobblehead did its job. Verizon Center sold out the night they gave them out. I think I signed the bald head of every one of them over the course of the season. With a little practice, you get used to writing on a miniature head. Of all the great people they could have done—Mike Green or Nicklas Backstrom or Sergei Fedorov—they chose me. Holy smokes. It was an honor that, well, left me shaking my head.

●

On the ice in the regular season we finished with 108 points, second in the Eastern Conference and fourth in the league. I was an in-season replacement in 2007–8, so 2008–9 was my first shot at running the summer prospects camp and training camp. They went off without a hitch. That is important to the players. They want it to look like we know what we're doing.

I was taken aback when we lost the season opener 7-4 at Atlanta. That was a big game not only because it was the opener. It marked the first time Thrashers head coach John Anderson and I went head-to-head in an NHL game.

John and I talked about the first game at my daughter Kasey's wedding in July. You have the tension and a couple libations and the jaws start flapping. We both genially vowed to beat each other. We didn't talk on the day of the game. The meeting of best friends who labored for a long time in the minors was a natural media story, but we had separate interview sessions and didn't even look at each other.

When you play a club that didn't make the play-offs the previous season, the players are excited about having a chance to get back on the right track. I knew Atlanta would overachieve. The Thrashers did that, and we didn't play as well as we could have.

I didn't talk to John Anderson for a couple days. Then I said, "Oh, heck," and called and congratulated him. He did the humble thing and said they had gotten a couple of breaks. It was like he was talking to a reporter, and I got mad at him.

We eventually won the season series 4-2. When his team lost to us, John would phone me and say, "Well, you took it to us tonight." We won the next three in the series, and he phoned me immediately after the game each time. Then they beat us in Washington, and I wouldn't phone him. He got on the phone the next day and left a message: "I phoned you after every loss, and you could have had the class to phone me after we won." When he called, I was sitting on a bus next to George McPhee. I sure wasn't going to answer it in that situation.

John and I are close to the vest in what we talk to each other about regarding our teams. We talk about generic stuff. We don't get into the tactical secrets of why we won or lost. It's more ribbing each other.

John and I started a charity golf tournament together in Brampton, Ontario, to raise funds to help underprivileged kids get started in hockey. We did a commercial for it. At the end of it, John says, "Bruce, how come your name is first in the Bruce Boudreau–John Anderson Celebrity Golf Classic? How come you're always first?" I say, "Well, John, we made the play-offs and you didn't."

After the loss at Atlanta, we won five of eight the rest of October. A major turning point in our season was a 5-0 loss at Buffalo on November 1. The game was played Saturday, and the team was supposed to have the day off Sunday. We canceled the off-day and practiced instead. It was a punishing skate. The message: Hovering a little above .500 isn't good enough. We won six of our next eight after that practice. That gave us some breathing room because the other teams in the Southeast Division weren't winning.

One of those six wins was against my friend Barry Melrose and the Tampa Bay Lightning. It was the only game I would coach against him. The Caps won 4-2. Tampa Bay fired Barry just sixteen games into the season later that week.

I know what kind of team Barry wanted. Hard-nosed and hardworking. They weren't there yet when we played them. They were sort of in transition. The next day, I think, Barry didn't show up for practice because he was so mad. He had assistant coach Rick Tocchet run it. I think that is when it started blowing up and led to him being replaced by Tocchet.

I was surprised when Tampa Bay let Barry go. I don't really know the inner workings of other teams. Everything can look great on the surface, but you never know. Evidently, there were some issues. It wasn't all peaceful in Tampa Bay.

I subsequently talked to Barry several times. He attended Game 7 of the Pittsburgh series. We had a good long talk and laughed together. I still think he is an excellent coach. People can talk about him being away from the game, but he is not away from the game. Maybe he is not coaching the game, but he is watching every game every night while working in television. I think he eventually will surface as a general manager.

Other coaching changes led to the in-season promotion of two more coaches from the AHL. Cory Clouston moved up from Binghamton to the parent Ottawa Senators. Dan Bylsma moved up from Wilkes-Barre/Scranton to the parent Pittsburgh Penguins.

There was talk about the "Boudreau Effect." I just think the whole thing is that they are really good coaches. I sure can't take any credit. It was all them. They did it on their own merits. With Danny Bylsma, Pittsburgh was definitely a different team than when Michel Therrien was head coach. I don't know if it had anything to do with Danny or the players playing for him.

You take a little pride that NHL general managers are looking at things a bit differently, that they deem AHL coaches as being capable of moving up and doing the job. It is so important to be able to communicate. When you have coached your farm club, you communicate a little differently than you do in the NHL. It is more homey and friendly in the AHL. A coach has got to be more of a mentor in the AHL than he is in the NHL, and you get to know the players better. If you have to make a change in midseason, it makes perfect sense to have your affiliated guy move up rather than having a guy who doesn't know anybody come in and take over. I thought those teams made smart decisions promoting from the AHL.

Down in the AHL, there was a major scare in February. The Albany River Rats' team bus crashed in Massachusetts. Nobody was killed, but four players and a team broadcaster were hospitalized. It certainly brought back memories. Albany is a scary travel city. There is snow everywhere they go. It is a tough ride sometimes in the middle of winter.

For all the bus miles I traveled as a player and coach in the minors, I remember only one close call in Worcester when I coached in Manchester. That wasn't a crash, just a jolt from the brakes when we had to stop fast. Maybe there were other close calls I don't know about because I was asleep. Sometimes you roll through the night so long; I wonder how the drivers can stay up. It can be an eerie thing, especially when the weather is bad. I always tried to stay awake as much as I could, but you can't avoid falling asleep and you just hope that everyone stays safe. As coach, I was always in the front seat; you are going over first if it crashes.

My most memorable bus odyssey didn't involve a crash. I was playing for Dallas in the CHL. It was either 1976 or 1977. We were returning home from Oklahoma City, and there was an ice storm with freezing rain.

They are not used to freezing rain in Texas. We were going about two miles per hour when we started moving on a slant and began to slide down an embankment a little bit. The tires just spun as we perched at the edge of the road.

Cops came to help, but they didn't know what to do. They couldn't push us, so they got out their guns and started shooting in front of the tires to try to melt the ice. Boom! Boom! Boom! Boom! Bullets flew all over the place. We had a bunch of Canadians on the bus. We thought, What is going on here? As it turned out, it didn't work. But we eventually made it back OK.

The biggest regular-season struggle the Caps had in 2008–9 had nothing to do with travel. We had a February–March stretch where we played nine of ten at home and lost five of the games at Verizon Center. If we had performed up to our capability during that period, we would have finished with 114 or 115 points.

●

We had regular-season stretches without Alex Ovechkin, who briefly went home to Russia to visit his terminally ill grandfather, and Mike Green, who suffered a shoulder injury. Both of them experienced memorable nights at Tampa Bay.

Alex doesn't let you know that something is bothering him, but early in the season you could tell how concerned he was about his grandfather, Nikolay Kabayev. He was extremely worried about leaving his teammates. "This is family first," we told him. "You've got something wrong. You've got to take care of your family." Alex came back from an October visit with his grandfather, who passed away in November. He was more relaxed and at peace and ended up scoring fifty-six goals to lead the league again.

Goal fifty turned into quite a controversy. Alex scored it on March 19 at Tampa Bay. He celebrated by placing his stick on the ice and pretending it was on fire and too hot to touch. At first, I was like everybody else with the conservative reaction. This is hockey; we're not supposed to show our emotions like that. I apologized to Lightning head coach Rick Tocchet the next morning and told him Alex didn't mean anything by it.

I didn't see the goal celebration live because my view from the bench was blocked. The more I saw it on replays, the more I thought the controversy was overblown. All Alex did was make the game fun. It was not like it was an 8-0 game and he scored in the last five minutes. He had been sitting on forty-nine for two games, so he had time to think. He scored in a 0-0 game on a beautiful goal. The entire stick's-on-fire thing lasted five seconds. The constant chastising really started to bother me.

One of the vocal critics was Don Cherry, who already had kindly written the foreword for this book. Don went off on Alex, and suddenly I was in a tough spot. I had to respond. I didn't want to make it sound bad on Don, but I wanted to stand up for my players.

Don is Don, and he is an icon in all of Canada. He protects and promotes his Canadians all over the place, and I have often been one of the people he has promoted. Sometimes he thinks it is still a conservative hockey world. Ironically, Don was probably one of the most colorful coaches. He let his emotions come out. All Alex did was let his emotions come out.

I had to respond by saying that, as much as I respect Don, I thought he was wrong in this case. We're fine. Don understands that I have to protect my players. In addition to the book foreword, Don did commercials for the charity golf tournament John Anderson and I organized.

We played in Toronto, hockey central, five days after Alex Ovechkin scored his fiftieth goal. We got nothing but questions about it. I wanted to put it to rest, but people kept asking about the celebration and wanted to know if there would be ramifications when we played Tampa Bay again. For what? For showing that you were happy to score fifty goals? I would feel worse if a guy scored his fiftieth and said, "Eh, it's only fifty, I plan on getting more." To me, that shows up somebody more. Here is a guy who took great pride in scoring his fiftieth.

This went on every day for more than a week. I got fed up with it. When we played Tampa Bay at home on March 27, the Sports Network (TSN) made a special trip from Canada because of the rematch. It was ridiculous that TSN wasted money sending a crew to Washington. It was almost like they were trying to promote the Lightning to jump Alex and make a bigger story.

I finally erupted at a press conference. I had been warned that another question was coming about the celebration. I planned to explode on whomever asked it. I was wishing it would be somebody from TSN, but unfortunately it was Katie Carrera from the *Washington Post*. I blew up about the stupidity of keeping this thing going and again pleaded to put it to rest. I felt bad that Katie was the one in the blast zone. I apologized profusely to her the next three or four times I saw her.

Mike Green's historic moment in Tampa Bay on February 14 wasn't controversial. Just wonderful. Mike became the first defenseman in NHL history to score goals in eight straight games. I felt almost parental about it. There was such a sense of pride since I had coached him in Hershey as a wide-eyed nineteen-year-old just oozing talent. You are watching him mature before your eyes into the next Paul Coffey or Scott Niedermayer. His thirty-one goals ranked first in the NHL for a defenseman in 2008–9.

Mike scored the record-breaking goal on a power play with his father, Dave, in attendance. We made that part of our our pump-up videotape for the season. You look at Mike and he is so proud when all his teammates leave the bench to congratulate him. Then the shot goes to his dad. If you wanted to look at a proud parent, that was it right there.

We had a difficult stretch after he was injured on a Chris Pronger hit at Anaheim in November, and he also was slowed by shoulder problems in the play-offs. One player doesn't make a team, but it gave us some understanding of how important Mike is to the Caps. We were an average team without him. Boy, that and his production made a pretty good argument for saying Mike merited the Norris Trophy as the NHL's top defenseman.

Is Mike Green the best defenseman in the NHL? I don't know if that is the case just yet. But did he have the best regular season? He had the most goals among defensemen. Yet he played ten or twelve fewer games than most of these guys. He was plus-twenty-four. His ice time was twenty-five or twenty-six minutes a game. He played in all situations. No other Washington defenseman had more than three goals. Where would we have been without Mike Green?

For the second straight year, the *NHL Awards Show*, which was held in Las Vegas in June, was a special night for me. Mike Green was a finalist for the Norris Trophy, but it was awarded to Boston's Zdeno Chara. Alex Ovechkin won the Hart Memorial Trophy as NHL MVP again, becoming the first player since Dominik Hasek in 1996–97 and 1997–98 to win it two straight years. Alex also won the Lester B. Pearson Award for a second straight year as the NHL's top player as voted by members of the NHL Players' Association.

I also was delighted to see St. Louis Blues head coach Andy Murray be a finalist for the Jack Adams Award as NHL Coach of the Year, which was won by Boston's Claude Julien. Andy meant so much to me when he was head coach of the Los Angeles Kings and I coached their AHL affiliates in Lowell, Massachusetts, and Manchester, New Hampshire. Andy would never say this, but if it weren't for him teaching me so many things that prepared me to be an NHL head coach, there is no chance I would have been able to get the job done when I got the NHL shot.

Everything we did in the AHL was based on what Los Angeles did, and that was all Andy Murray. From getting into work at 7:30 in the morning, to video study, to the way practices were organized. I have kept all the sheets for every Andy Murray practice I ever attended. When I run out of ideas, I go back to the sheets. He has been a big part of my success. Watching him and talking on the phone with him for six years gave me the ability to coach in the NHL. Andy is fine with telling you every one of his trade secrets. He is all about hockey and wants everybody to learn.

I am more aware of how to deal with the public because of Andy. I remember one postgame situation in Los Angeles in particular. Andy Murray, Bill O'Flaherty, Dave Taylor, and I were driving in a car. Fans were standing and cheering at the parking exit ramp. Andy stopped and shook hands with them. Bill noted that Andy was really good with the fans. I think it is something I do pretty well myself. That vision always comes to me when I see people on the street and I decide to talk to them. I think it is so important to connect with fans.

Andy Murray is a solid man. He did a terrific job with the Blues. They became the best team in the Western Conference the last thirty games of the season, and they are young. They are going to be a team to be reckoned with.

●

The Capitals played the New York Rangers in the first round of the Stanley Cup play-offs. That meant I would have to deal with Sean Avery again. Remember, Avery was a handful for me when I coached him briefly in Manchester in the AHL. Avery began the season with the Dallas Stars, but his mouth started a remarkable turn of events that delivered him back to the Rangers.

I am not going to repeat the insult Avery directed at actress Elisha Cuthbert. She was dating Calgary Flames defenseman Dion Phaneuf, and Avery's jab involved the fact that he dated her first. I was stunned that anybody would say something that trashy on camera, but I understand what happened. When Dallas visited Calgary, Avery was trying to goad Phaneuf into doing something stupid against him in the game. In Avery's warped mind, he did it for his team. It was just an over-the-top comment. It made hockey look stupid, got Avery suspended, and effectively ended his tenure in Dallas.

I always thought Avery could help a team if he just matured and got along with his teammates. Avery fits the bill if you are looking for a winger who can get you fifteen goals, get maybe a hundred penalty minutes, and get under the skin of everybody else. If only he did it without all the extra baggage.

Yes, the six-game suspension the league assessed was warranted. That wasn't his first time in trouble. I didn't see too many people go to bat for Avery to appeal it in Dallas, which didn't let him return to the team. Hockey is a classy sport and we try to keep up our image. It is wrong when people have to explain to their kids what the garbage Avery said means. In a politically correct world, it was a horrible statement.

Dallas eventually put Avery on waivers, and he got claimed by the New York Rangers, his 2007–8 club. I kept thinking Steve Howe. Major League Baseball player Howe kept coming back despite all those cocaine violations because certain teams thought, Well, if you can pitch, you can play. I don't know if I would have taken a chance on Avery. Not because he can't play, but just because of the teammate he might be.

I didn't say one word to Avery during the Caps-Rangers series. I wouldn't look at him the whole series, whether he took a bad penalty or played well. You could see in Game 7 that it was like Rangers head coach John Tortorella said, "Sean, be you. It's Game 7. Do whatever you have to do." Avery may have been the best player on the ice in Game 7.

At one point in Game 7, there was a delay because the glass was broken. Avery looked at me and tried to get under my skin. He told me I was the biggest, fattest bleeping pig he had ever seen. He told me I was fatter than bleeping Ken Hitchcock. He told me I was going to die because I was such a fat bleep. Avery just leaned near our bench and said this stuff casually, like he was a neighbor chatting over a picket fence or a doctor giving me a medical diagnosis.

Obviously, I fight my weight. After the game, his jabs bothered me. I ignored it during the game. I just turned my head and went to the other side of the bench. Alex Ovechkin wanted to go out on the ice and kill Avery. The guys wanted to jump up and get him. That would have been exactly what Avery wanted. You have to say, "Hey, it doesn't matter what he said. Focus on the game."

His conduct was way over the line. It went far beyond trying to get under somebody's skin. But that's Avery. He has absolutely no class. That kind of antagonism is ridiculous. There is a little bit of sportsmanship involved in sports, and I don't think he has any. Avery says things with a cut in mind. He doesn't say stuff like "you stink" or "you can't skate" or "your mother wears army boots." He says stuff truly intended to hurt you.

At least there was the solace of the scoreboard. We won 2-1 in Game 7 to capture the series after we had lost the first two games at home. We lost 4-3 in Game 1 and were a bit perplexed because we played much better than the Rangers. New York goalie Henrik Lundqvist was terrific. Meanwhile, we were left to ponder our goaltending situation. Do we stay with Jose Theodore or switch to rookie Semyon Varlamov, a first-round draft pick who had spent most of the season in the AHL with Hershey and had appeared in just six NHL games? We had a couple days off, which gave us time to think. Goalie coach Dave Prior, our assistant coaches, George McPhee, and I discussed the situation.

Theo's numbers hadn't been very good down the stretch of the regular season. He won games, but his save percentage was .874 his last ten games. But Theo had bounced back in the past. Do we just run with him? Or do we make a daring move by switching to Varlamov and throwing him into a high-pressure play-off situation?

My theory became that if we waited to do it and Theo didn't bounce back and had a bad second game, we would then be forced to make the move to Varlamov. It was unknown whether or not Varlamov could do the job. If he debuted in Game 3 and didn't do it, we could be down 0-3. Thus, we decided to go with Varlamov for Game 2. If he wasn't up to the task, we would be able to come back with Theo and his bounce-back ability in Game 3 and still have a chance in the series.

Jose Theodore was very professional. I think he totally disagreed with us, which is great because it shows he is a competitor. I brought him in the next day and explained my thinking. He didn't believe it or didn't agree with it, but outwardly to the media he was excellent. He was a good teammate, and he supported everybody.

Varlamov was tremendous and gave us a big lift. We lost 1-0 in Game 2, but "Varly" was outstanding. Only Henrik Lundqvist's goaltending prevented us from winning. Since Varly played so well, we decided to stick with him. Even though we were down 0-2, we still thought we could beat New York. In Game 3 at Madison Square Garden, Varly shut out New York 4-0. Now we had to ride the wave.

We lost 2-1 in Game 4, but Varly was terrific again. We were down 3-1 in the series, but we had a lot of confidence that we were the better team in all four games. That was our mind-set. It was a lot like the mind-set Pittsburgh would have against us in the second round. Really, it was the same situation we had against Philadelphia in the play-offs in 2007–8, when we forced Game 7 after being down 3-1.

In the first four games, Lundqvist made the difference. If you really study their system, the Rangers block a lot of shots. Not enough shots were getting through, and Lundqvist saw what was getting through. We had to find a different way to get at him. Dave Prior did a great job breaking down his strengths and weaknesses. We started trying to move the puck out from behind the net to reduce the Rangers' ability to block shots.

When we won 4-0 in Game 5 back at home, we knew Game 6 would be tough. Rangers coach John Tortorella got suspended for Game 6 after a water bottle altercation with fans at Verizon Center in Game 5. It was wacky, just wacky. I don't know what the deal was. I don't know if we ever will know the whole truth about who squirted whom. It worked to our benefit. It took New York's focus off playing great because everybody was getting asked questions about Tortorella. We went back to Madison Square Garden and dominated the game to win 5-3 and force Game 7 back at Verizon Center.

We tried to forewarn our players how good the Rangers would be in Game 7. They played their best hockey by far in the series. I thought we had been outplayed and maybe shouldn't have won 2-1, but Semyon Varlamov was terrific.

Our fans played a huge role in Game 7. When Sergei Fedorov scored to break a 1-1 tie in the third period, they stood and roared for the last five minutes of the game. What a situation. We needed a goal, and Feds got it. The building exploded. It was unbelievable. What a feeling.

●

We want to avoid seventh games in the future. Not a lot of teams come back from being down 3-1. I am big on having the guys create history. We did it by coming back against the Rangers, but it caught up to us in Game 7 of the Pittsburgh series because that was our fifth elimination game and it was only the Penguins' first.

We faced a lot of elimination games in 2007–8—down the stretch of the regular season and in the play-offs—and in 2008–9. We have great character. It is a testament to our guys that they have done so well in elimination games. But you've got to have a series where you win in four or five games so you still have enough in the tank to go the distance and win a Stanley Cup. Our problem is that every series we've played has gone seven games. That is an awful lot of hockey. We had fourteen play-off games in twenty-nine days. Usually you play thirteen games a month in the regular season, which is not as rigorous as the postseason. Physical and mental fatigue catch up to you. I hope that is the explanation for our Game 7 performance against Pittsburgh because that is as flat as I have ever seen us play.

Our win in the Rangers series meant the NHL got a marquee matchup: Washington Capitals versus Pittsburgh Penguins. Alex Ovechkin, Mike Green, Sidney Crosby, Evgeni Malkin. Welcome to the circus. That is what I said during my press conference after Game 7 against the Rangers.

I immediately understood the Washington-Philadelphia rivalry when I arrived in Washington. It took a while for me to get up to speed on the Pittsburgh-Washington rivalry, even though I was involved in the intense Hershey Bears–Wilkes-Barre/Scranton Penguins rivalry in the AHL. Initially, the Washington-Pittsburgh rivalry was kind of foreign to me, but it is not anymore. Now I understand what Capitals fans have understood for years.

After we lost to the Penguins in the play-offs, I couldn't stand watching them on TV. Pittsburgh head coach Danny Bylsma is a really great guy, and I was happy for him when his team won the Stanley Cup. It is more the name Pittsburgh. You see that and you want to beat them if you are from Washington.

All the attention generated by the Washington-Pittsburgh series, which featured two ascendant teams with a lot of the NHL's brightest young stars, was exciting. Sometimes when you are in the middle of it, you don't realize how much attention it is getting. That may sound silly, but you are focused on the game. You are focused on the media interviews while they are happening, but after that you are just focused on the game. You have to have blinders on, and that is how we stayed focused. It wasn't until the season was over, when all anybody wanted to talk to me about was the Pittsburgh series, that I realized the full extent of the interest in the rivalry.

Since we had done well against the Penguins during the regular season, we had reason to believe that we could beat them in the play-offs. Pittsburgh had a tough six-game series against Philadelphia in the first round. We had the seven-game series against the Rangers and were riding the emotion of that victory. We won the first two games at Verizon Center by a goal and had a realistic chance to put away the Penguins with a Game 3 victory.

Game 3 in Pittsburgh was one of those contests where we knew from the start we were going to win the series if we won the game. But Pittsburgh did exactly to us in Game 3 what we did to New York. The Penguins showed great resiliency in a 3-2 overtime triumph. We should have learned from watching them against Philadelphia. Or maybe we did, and we just couldn't do anything about it.

Alex Ovechkin had a shot to win Game 3 in overtime but didn't score. They came back the other way, and Kris Letang scored the game-winner on a deflection off Shaone Morrisonn's butt. I don't care how good the Penguins were playing. If they go down 0-3, they are not coming back. It is amazing how you get bounces one way or the other. Alex was so mad after that.

Pittsburgh came right back with a little bit of energy from Game 3 and beat us 5-3 in Game 4. Now it was a 2-2 series. We still thought we were going to win because we have rarely lost three games in a row. But we lost

Game 5 the next day at home 4-3 in overtime as Pittsburgh took a 3-2 series lead. Once again, we faced elimination and had to travel to Pittsburgh for Game 6.

We played our best game in Game 6. We matched them. It was off the charts in excitement. It didn't get the attention of Game 2, where both Alex Ovechkin and Sidney Crosby had hat tricks, which was what the whole world wanted to see. But Game 6 was a tremendous 5-4 overtime victory for us.

Dave Steckel, whom I have seen raise his level of play so often in the play-offs, both in Hershey and Washington, scored the game-winner to tie the series 3-3. When Dave scored, I jumped up and down on the bench like an idiot, like we had won the Stanley Cup. Assistant coach Jay Leach rubbed my head; I thought a genie was going to pop out of there or something. We had a good laugh in the dressing room. They're my emotions. I wear my heart on my sleeve. If we ever win the Stanley Cup, I will jump on the celebration pile on the ice. I wonder how I will be able get away with something like that in the NHL, but I am who I am. Fifty years of your life for one goal. Holy smokes, surely you are allotted a little breathing room to make an idiot of yourself.

Goalie Semyon Varlamov, playing his first season in North America, had done so well since we turned to him in Game 2 of the New York series and had become a fast fan favorite. This wasn't your normal twenty-year-old. Varly has an exciting, acrobatic style and expends a lot of energy every time he plays. Varly has amazing potential. We also are high on goalie prospects Michal Neuvirth and Braden Holtby. I think the Caps' future in goaltending is as strong as any team in the NHL.

Rookie Neuvirth, who appeared in five regular-season games with the Caps, was named MVP of the Calder Cup play-offs for backstopping my old team, the Hershey Bears, to the 2008–9 AHL championship. Remember, Bob Woods, my Hershey assistant, took over the head-coaching job there when I was promoted to Washington. I was proud to see Woody lead the Bears to the Calder Cup.

The Bears, touted as a preseason Calder Cup contender, had a lot of talented players. That can be a tough situation for a coach. It is a difficult thing to keep everybody happy, make sure they play their best, and win a championship. Woody handled it really well. After the season, he was hired to join the Caps' staff as an assistant coach.

For Game 7 against Pittsburgh at Verizon Center, we might have relaxed a bit and thought we were going to win because we had such a strong track record in elimination games. I really don't know what happened. We fell behind 5-0 and lost 6-2 to end our season.

Maybe fatigue took a little bit out of us, but that is an excuse. It is not difficult to get fired up; we were all ready for the game. But it is difficult to maintain that high standard of playing when you are on the brink. That is why it doesn't happen a lot. It is tough to keep playing as well as you can over a long period of time.

The Penguins were really determined and played great in Game 7. Pittsburgh goalie Marc-Andre Fleury made a big save on Alex Ovechkin in the first period to prevent us from taking a 1-0 lead. I truly believe that if Alex had scored on the breakaway early in the game, it would have been a totally different game. He scores, and it is 1-0 for us. Even if they still get two first-period goals, they are up by only one at first intermission. We have come from behind so many times, I think we would have been fine. Alex was so dynamic in the play-offs, scoring eleven goals in fourteen games despite playing through injuries.

Give Pittsburgh credit. The Penguins got it done against us and followed by beating Carolina and Detroit to win the Stanley Cup. In the Stanley Cup finals against Detroit, the Penguins won a second Game 7 on the road at Joe Louis Arena.

The coach in me says, "OK, it makes it look like you were closer to winning the Stanley Cup because Pittsburgh went on to win it." But it is a strong rivalry between Washington and Pittsburgh. The fan and rivalry guy in me didn't want Pittsburgh to win it. I would have preferred to see Detroit win.

We lost to the Penguins by one game and, with a break, could have been up 3-0 in the series. Usually a break or two decides who is going to win and who is going to lose. In the end, we are judged by results. Not by effort. Not by being close. We didn't achieve the goal we sought. That goal remains winning the Stanley Cup.

Sure, there will be growing pressure to do just that. I welcome it; we welcome it. We think we are an excellent team. We want to win the Stanley Cup. That is what we talk about. We will put more pressure on ourselves because we think we can win the Stanley Cup. Good teams do that.

I can't really say I have a formal philosophy of life. I want to be the best every time I step on the ice. I want to win all the time. I want to win at everything I do. If that is a philosophy, then that is my philosophy. Everything has to be competition. Chasing the Stanley Cup is the ultimate competition.

If we win the Stanley Cup, we will get a trip to the White House to visit President Barack Obama. It would be absolutely cool if the president attended a Capitals game. But I want to meet him during a January when the Stanley Cup champions visit the White House.

We would be delighted to make that trek on foot from Verizon Center should we get the opportunity. What are a few more blocks compared to the distance I have traveled?

# INDEX

# ABOUT THE AUTHORS

**Bruce Boudreau** is head coach of the Washington Capitals and won the Jack Adams Award as NHL Coach of the Year in 2007–8. Boudreau also has served as head coach of the AHL's Hershey Bears (2005–6 Calder Cup champions), the AHL's Manchester Monarchs, the AHL's Lowell Lock Monsters, the ECHL's Mississippi Sea Wolves (1998–99 Kelly Cup champions), the IHL's Fort Wayne Komets, and the CoHL's Muskegon Fury. As a player, he ranks eleventh in all-time scoring in the AHL and is a member of the league's Hall of Fame. Boudreau played parts of eight seasons for the Toronto Maple Leafs and Chicago Blackhawks, recording seventy points in 141 career NHL games. He won two Memorial Cups with the Toronto Marlboros and set a Canadian Hockey League single-season scoring record that stood until it was broken by Wayne Gretzky.

**Tim Leone** is an award-winning sports columnist and reporter for the *Patriot-News* in Harrisburg, Pennsylvania. He also has worked for the *Sarasota Herald-Tribune* and *Los Angeles Daily News*. Leone, a graduate of the George Washington University and the University of Southern California, is the author of *The Hershey Bears: Sweet Seasons*.